Jesus in the Biblical Holidays

Illuminating God's Appointed Times in the Old Testament Feasts

Robin Sampson

Heart of Wisdom Publishing

Jesus in the Biblical Holidays: Illuminating God's Appointed Times in the Old Testament Feasts

Copyright © 2024 by Robin Sampson

Ebook ISBN: 978-0-9819407-4-8

Paperback ISBN: 978-0-9819407-2-4

Heart of Wisdom Publishing Inc, All rights reserved. jesusinthebiblicalholidays.com

Scripture quotations are from The ESV® Bible (The Holy Bible, English Standard Version®), copyright© 2001 by Crossway. Used by permission. All rights reserved.

No portion of this book may be reproduced in any form without written permission from the publisher or author, except as permitted by U.S. copyright law.

Contents

Preface	1
Reviews for Jesus in the Biblical Holidays	3
Part 1: The Treasure Hunt	
1. Unearthing Spiritual Treasures	7
2. God's Timeless Treasures	11
3. Who Buried the Treasure?	17
4. Your Treasure Hunt	21
5. Agricultural Parallels	26
Part 2: Sabbath	
6. Sabbath	31
7. Jewish Traditions of Sabbath	35
8. How Sabbath Reveals Messiah	39
9. Celebrating Sabbath	43
10. Sabbath Recipes	46
11. Sabbath Questions	50
Part 3: The Spring Holidays	
12. The Spring Holidays	53
Part 4: Passover	

13.	Passsover	57
14.	The First Passover	61
15.	Jewish Traditions of Passover	64
16.	How Passover Reveals Messiah	70
17.	Celebrating Passover	75
18.	The Role of Communion	79
19.	Passover Recipes	83
20.	Passover Questions	87

Part 5: Unleavened Bread

21.	Unleavened Bread	89
22.	Jewish Traditions of Unleavened Bread	93
23.	How Unleavened Bread Reveals Messiah	96
24.	Celebrating Unleavened Bread	99
25.	Unleavened Bread Recipes	101
26.	Unleavened Bread Questions	103

Part 6: Firstfruits

27.	Feast of Firstfruits	105
28.	Jewish Traditions of Firstfruits	108
29.	How Firstfruits Reveals Messiah	111
30.	Celebrating Firstfruits	115
31.	Firstfruits Recipes	118
32.	Firstfruits Questions	122

Part 7: Feast of Weeks

33.	Feast of Weeks	125
34.	Jewish Traditions of Feast of Weeks	128

35.	How Feast of Weeks Reveals Messiah	132
36.	Celebrating the Feast of Weeks	137
37.	Counting the Omer	143
38.	Feast of Weeks Recipes	149
39.	Feast of Weeks Questions	152

Part 8: Fall Holidays

40.	Fall Holidays	155
41.	The Rapture and Second Coming	159

Part 9: Feast of Trumpets

42.	Feast of Trumpets	163
43.	Jewish Traditions of Feast of Trumpets	166
44.	How the Feast of Trumpets Reveals Messiah	169
45.	Celebrating the Feast of Trumpets	172
46.	Feast of Trumpets Recipes	175
47.	Feast of Trumpets Questions	179

Part 10: Day of Atonement

48.	Day of Atonement	181
49.	Jewish Traditions of Day of Atonement	184
50.	How the Day of Atonement Reveals Messiah	189
51.	Observing the Day of Atonement	193
52.	Day of Atonement Questions	196

Part 11: Feast of Tabernacles

53.	Feast of Tabernacles	199
54.	Jewish Traditions of Feast of Tabernacles	203
55.	How the Feast of Tabernacles Reveals Messiah	207

56. Was Jesus Born During Tabernacles?	212
57. Celebrating the Feast of Tabernacles	215
58. Feast of Tabernacles Recipes	218
59. Feast of Tabernacles Questions	221
60. EXTRA HOLIDAYS	223

Part 12. Hanukkah

61. Hanukkah	225
62. Jewish Traditions of Hanukkah	229
63. How Hanukkah Reveals Messiah	232
64. Celebrating Hanukkah	235
65. Hanukkah Recipes	238
66. Hanukkah Questions	241

Part 13. Purim

67. Purim	243
68. Jewish Traditions of Purim	247
69. How Purim Reveals Messiah	249
70. Celebrating Purim	252
71. Purim Recipes	255
72. Purim Questions	258

Part 14. Final Thoughts

73. Treasure Unveiled	261
74. Jesus int he Holidays	262
75. 12 Bible Eras Class	264
76. A Hebraic Prespective Bible Women	267
77. Bibography	269

Preface

A TIMELESS, TRANSFORMATIVE EXPLORATION

Welcome to *Jesus in the Biblical Holidays: Illuminating God's Appointed Times in the Old Testament Feasts*. This book marks a new chapter in my exploration of the biblical holidays, distinct from my earlier work, *A Family Guide to the Biblical Holidays*, written in 1999 for homeschool families (known as the big purple book). With twenty-five years of additional wisdom and insight, I delve deeper into these ancient celebrations, offering fresh perspectives.

This book is not a revision. This journey is not about revisiting well-trodden paths with a fresh coat of paint. It's about venturing into uncharted territories, guided by the lamp of scripture, to reveal insights previously concealed. By connecting the Old Testament feasts with the life and mission of Jesus, we uncover a tapestry of prophecy and fulfillment, a continuous thread that weaves through the fabric of biblical history, illuminating the role of Jesus as the cornerstone of our faith.

A Journey of Renewed Understanding

Embark on a journey of transformation. This book invites you to see the Old Testament festivals anew as they highlight the path to a deeper understanding of Jesus. Each page is designed to enrich your faith and bring the sacred stories to life. It's an enlightening experience that bridges ancient traditions with modern faith, revealing Christ's continuous presence through history.

The practice of observing biblical holidays serves as a potent tool for spiritual education and personal growth. These holidays were bestowed upon us by God with the intention of imparting important information. Consider, for instance, the significance of Thanksgiving in understanding the Pilgrims' story. If we were to neglect the annual observance of Thanksgiving, our knowledge of this historical event and its cultural importance would be greatly diminished.

In much the same way, the biblical holidays are designed to enhance our comprehension and strengthen our connection to the principles and narratives of our faith. God granted us these holidays as a means of instructing us through active, tangible ceremonies. These celebrations transcend mere acts of remembrance or rituals; they immerse us in profound experiences that actively engage us with the core values of our faith.

Whether you're a seasoned believer, new to the faith, or intrigued by ancient traditions, this book is a gateway to the biblical feasts and their relevance to Jesus. Each chapter is thoughtfully structured around a distinct theme, unraveling the spiritual symbolism of these holidays and their connection to the journey of Jesus.

Practical Insights

Every chapter concludes with practical insights, transforming complex theological ideas into memorable and actionable takeaways. These are not just to be read but lived, offering new ways to integrate these biblical holidays into your spiritual life today. The book adds to your experience with holiday readings and traditional recipes, helping you dive into the heart of each celebration.

This approach is straightforward yet rich, engaging and accessible, guiding you through the Christ-centered meanings of the Old Testament holidays. More than an academic read, it's a relatable and enlightening journey for those eager to discover Christ's narrative hidden in these ancient celebrations.

Free Charts

The print version of this book features charts that may not display optimally on Kindle devices. To access these charts in a printable PDF format, please visit jesusinthebiblicalholidays.com or join our Facebook group at facebook.com/groups/bibleholidays

Join Our Enlightening Journey

We invite you to uncover the dazzling beauty of the biblical holidays. This exploration promises to enrich your faith and family life in ways you've never imagined.

Reviews for Jesus in the Biblical Holidays

Blown Away

I was blown away by Robin Sampson's new book, Jesus in the Biblical Holidays. What I assumed would be an update of her 2001 "Big Purple Book" (as many of us called it), is actually a complete overhaul. The result is the most comprehensive, historical, practical resource about the biblical holidays ever written.

God focused, Christ centered and honoring the biblical, historical and traditional Jewish context of these holidays, this book approaches each holiday from a variety of angles, including practical tips for celebration and recipes.

If you are looking for information about the biblical holidays—whether you are just starting out or have been on the journey for a while—you will not be disappointed!—Hope Egan, Author of *What the Bible Says about Healthy Living Cookbook* and *Holy Cow! Does God Really Care About What We Eat?*

Outstanding

I just want you to know, Robin, that *Jesus in the Biblical Holidays* is outstanding! I have been following you for many years now, and your prolific writing and artistic expression are amazing. I have learned so much from you, and thank God for putting you in my path! God bless you!—Vanessa joy

Beautifully Written

Jesus in the Biblical Holidays is a very informative. I learned so much I didn't know or understand. And the recipes were a wonderful bonus, knowing how the food was made added to it. Robin did a beautifully written and well thought out. Definitely a great read.—Michele Clark

A Fuller Revelation of Jesus

I was delighted to receive a pre-release copy of this book to read and give an unbiased review. I jumped at the chance as I am very familiar with Robin Sampson's previous work, some of which I used when homeschooling my boys, and it was a huge help.

I was not disappointed. With her usual style, she has produced an inspiring and informative guide to the Biblical Holidays, which would be equally useful to those who know much about these feasts and how they came about and those who know nothing. It is both easy to read and full of insight.

There are several ways that the book can be used. It can simply be read through and will give the reader a better understanding and appreciation of the biblical holidays. It could be read in sections as each biblical holiday arises. The book can also be used as a starting point for a deeper study because of the information Robin gives on each holiday. She also provides questions to reflect on and a list of resources on the subject.

I would recommend this book for anyone who wants to grasp a fuller revelation of Jesus, not just on an academic level, but in a much more holistic way, which can be made even more decadent by taking part in some or all of the activities provided in this charming book. I know it's a book I will come back to again and again.—Angela Marchington

Remarkable Journey

Jesus in the Biblical Holidays: Illuminating God's Appointed Times in the Old Testament Feasts is a remarkable journey through the Old Testament feasts and holidays while relating them to Jesus in the New Testament. This book covers it all, from the origins of the names of these celebrations to the details and even recipes that can be used for current celebrations. There are tips for deeper study and thought-provoking questions that are excellent for further reflection or group study.

Robin Sampson shares her wealth of knowledge in an easy-to-follow outline and then expounds the details in a highly understandable, easy-to-read format, including scripture references.

This book has strongly heightened my understanding of the importance and relatability of the Old Testament holidays to my life with Jesus. I have a much deeper appreciation as I read these accounts now. I strongly encourage every Bible lover to read *Jesus in the Biblical Holidays: Illuminating God's Appointed Times in the Old Testament Feasts.*—*Trish Clark*

Honors Jesus

This book thoroughly explains Hebrew and English terminology, symbols, themes, and the Biblical significance of God's Appointed Times. The author describes how the holiday is observed in the traditional Jewish community but also enriches the faith walk of New Testament believers as they are invited to join in the celebrations in ways that honor Jesus. This book features:

- Appealing graphics that effectively illustrate themes.

- Following each holiday section are study questions called "Illuminating Reflections," which encourage readers to consider further how elements of God's Feast Days relate to us personally.

- Additional devotional readings which are appropriate for each holiday. I especially appreciate the numbered Bible references in the section about Counting the Omer, in which it is traditional to count the 50 days leading up to Shavuot (also called the Feast of Weeks or Pentecost).

- Engaging activities that would be fun for families or faith communities and provide a more immersive experience for learning about God's calendar are suggested.

- Many appealing recipes are provided for each Feast day. I will sample some of these because they look tasty.

- An extensive bibliography of trusted and interesting authors is given to guide your additional research.

I was familiar with the Biblical Feast Days before reading Mrs. Sampson's book, but I was curious about any new insights she might share. I learned something interesting about the Ten Commandments there was a reference that the Commandments might have been inscribed on blue sapphire stone tablets. I will have to research that further.

Mrs. Sampson's book is a well-organized lifestyle guide to the Biblical holidays you would want to add to your home or congregational library for future reference as these special days approach during each year of God's holy calendar.
—Fran Kuik

Share Your Thoughts with Us!

If this book has enriched your spiritual journey or offered new insights, please consider sharing your experience with a review on Amazon. Your feedback supports our mission to share God's word and helps others discover this resource. Whether it's a personal reflection or how the book influenced your faith, your review is greatly appreciated. Thank you for contributing to our community and making a difference with your voice.

Unearthing Spiritual Treasures

My Biblical Holidays Journey

Four decades ago, I embarked on a remarkable journey into the heart of the biblical holidays. What began as a fascination with ancient practices soon became a profound adventure, revealing spiritual and historical narratives far richer than I had ever imagined.

This book chronicles that journey, tracing the path from familiar traditions to enlightening discoveries. I invite you to join me in uncovering the beauty and significance of these time-honored celebrations, transforming them from mere dates on the calendar into profound moments of connection with God.

Challenges: Resistance and Skepticism

Initially, I was surprised by the hostility that my journey elicited from others. As I delved deeper into these sacred matters, skepticism and resistance emerged. My passion for God's Word seemed to spark defensiveness and anger in some, leading me to navigate their doubts and my own confusion.

In conversations with critics, I consistently emphasized that salvation is through Christ alone and not through any religious practice. This belief aligns with the understanding that exploring the Old Testament enhances our grasp of the New Testament, which was written in a Jewish context. In my pursuit of open and respectful dialogue, I aimed for mutual comprehension rather than engaging in debate. As I faced personal hurdles and skepticism, my journey gained a significance that extended beyond my own experiences. It illuminated the deep and intricate connection between the faith traditions and their Jewish origins, enriching my spiritual understanding and revealing the rich tapestry of history and tradition that underpins these beliefs.

Embracing Our Roots

Understanding the Jewish context of the Bible's holidays highlighted how Jesus' teachings and actions were deeply embedded in these traditions. This realization opens the door to a broader understanding of Christianity, inviting us to appreciate the deep historical and spiritual bonds that link it to its Jewish origins (Romans 9–11).

As Paul affirms, the story of the Messiah grafts Gentiles as wild olive shoots onto the cultivated olive tree of Israeli heritage. The spiritual destiny of Christians is thus intertwined with that of Jews. Appreciating these common roots fosters fellowship across faith lines. Through deepening our understanding of this shared wellspring, we gain a more profound grasp of God's grand narrative of redemption coming to fruition in the Messiah. The rich fabric of history, tradition and theology that binds our faiths together is illuminated.

I discovered how the early church's distancing from its Jewish roots led to a disconnect between the New Testament and its foundational Hebraic context in the Old Testament. There is an unbroken continuity in the historical narrative from Genesis to Revelation, presenting a compelling case that views Christianity not as a separate entity but as a branch grafted onto the rich Jewish olive tree.

God put in me a passion to share how the Bible is one unified story that reveals the continuous thread of redemption intricately woven within its original Jewish context. The realization that the roots of Christianity extend deeply into Jewish soil has profoundly impacted my approach to biblical study and sharing. It has allowed me to appreciate the seamless continuity between the covenants, seeing them not as disjointed elements but as integral parts of a divine tapestry that God has been weaving since the beginning of time. The holidays, with their messages of hope, and restoration, set the stage for the coming Messiah—a promise intricately linked to the Jewish expectation of a Redeemer.

In the teachings of Jesus and the writings of the apostles, this expectation is fulfilled, and the redemption narrative reaches its climax. However, this fulfillment is not the replacement of the old with the new but rather the blossoming of the ancient promises into their full glory. Understanding this, the Christian gospel can be seen as the continuation and fulfillment of the Jewish scriptures, a realization that brings a richer, more nuanced understanding of faith.

This Jewish context provides a robust framework for interpreting the New Testament's teachings, parables, and the very life of Jesus Himself. It sheds light on the cultural, religious, and historical backdrop against which Jesus ministered and the early church grew. Recognizing Christianity's Judaic roots enriches our understanding of Jesus' teachings, allowing us to see them in the light of Jewish tradition and thought.

This realization is especially relevant in an era marked by the alarming persistence of anti-Semitism and a global tendency to overlook Israel and the Jewish people's historical and spiritual significance. As the world risks distancing itself from its Judeo-Christian heritage, I aim to be a voice calling for balanced reawakening of these roots.

A Love-Driven Exploration

Inspired by Edith Schaeffer's statement, "Christianity Is Jewish," and guided by St. Augustine's insight, "The New Testament lies hidden in the Old and the Old Testament is unveiled in the New " my journey became more than an academic pursuit. It evolved into a love-driven exploration to align more closely with God's will, recognizing that Christianity is a continuation, not a replacement, of Jewish traditions.

Embracing this view has not only deepened my faith but also expanded my approach to teaching and sharing the Bible. It compels me to approach Scripture with a reverence for its Jewish heritage, encouraging others to explore the Bible's depth through this lens. This approach fosters a greater appreciation for the complexity and beauty of God's redemptive plan, inviting believers to explore the rich tapestry of history, prophecy, and fulfillment that binds the Old and New Testaments into one unified story of divine love and salvation.

Embarking on a Path to Illumination

Join me in *Jesus in the Biblical Holidays: Illuminating God's Appointed Times in the Old Testament Feasts*, an adventure that unveils the hidden treasures of God's Word. This book is an invitation to revitalize your understanding and appreciation of God's grand narrative. Let this journey of spiritual discovery guide you to a richer, more profound connection with our Father.

HOLIDAY	PURPOSE	MESSIANIC SIGNIFICANCE
Passover (Pesach) Nisan 14	During the first Passover, the Israelites marked their doorposts with lamb's blood as a sign for the angel of death to pass over their homes, sparing their firstborn in Egypt. This lamb was brought home four days prior to its sacrifice for a period of inspection.	Jesus, the sacrificial lamb, was crucified for our transgressions. Precisely when the Passover lamb was to be sacrificed on Nisan 15, Jesus met the same fate. Similarly, during the four days before death, He was scrutinized by religious authorities and deemed faultless.
Unleavened Bread (Chag HaMatzot) Nisan 15	God commanded Jews to eat unleavened bread, matzah, for seven days, removing leaven, which symbolizes sin, to commemorate purity and recall deliverance from Egyptian bondage.	Jesus, the sinless "Bread of Life," was born in Bethlehem—Hebrew for "house of bread." Like matzah, which is striped and pierced, so was Christ. His burial coincided with this Feast, linking His sacrifice to the symbolism of matzah.
Feast of Firstfruits (Bikkurim) Nisan 17	The first of the barley harvest was offered to God by the priest, who waved it to acknowledge that the land and its yield were divine gifts to the Hebrews. This act served as a sacred reminder that the bounty of their fields was a blessing from the God.	Jesus is the Firstfruits of resurrection, heralding a harvest of souls (1 Cor 15:20-23). Just as a wheat grain must die to yield a rich crop (Jn 12:23-24, 32), so did Jesus' rising on Firstfruits symbolize the promise of new life for believers.
Feasts of Weeks (Shavuot or Pentecost) 50 Days after Firstfruits	Fifty days post-Firstfruits, Shavuot commemorates the Torah's revelation to Moses at Sinai, featuring two leavened bread offerings to God and recalling Jewish enslavement in Egypt (Dt 16:9-17). On this day, three thousand were killed.	Fifty days after Jesus' resurrection, the Holy Spirit descending on Jesus' followers, birthing the Christian Church. It marks the empowerment to speak various languages, symbolizing Christianity's spread and the Spirit's gifts to believers.
Feast of Trumpets (Rosh Hashannah) Tishri 1	Rosh Hashanah, the Jewish New Year in Tishri, ushers in the High Holy Days, celebrating the world's Creation. It features trumpet blasts, symbolizing the coronation of God as King.	The trumpet's sound may symbolize the church's rapture, gathering believers (1 Thes 4:16-18; Rev 19), and judging the wicked. Alternatively, it could represent Jesus' second coming, heralding His reign as Earth's King.
Day of Atonement (Yom Kippur) Tishri 10	The holiest Jewish day, involves fasting, prayer, and confession for divine forgiveness. Annually, the high priest would enter the holy of holies, offering sacrifices, including two goats, to atone for the nation's sins.	This day mirrors Christ's role as our High Priest, who entered heaven's Holy of Holies, offering His blood for our atonement. His ultimate sacrifice ensures our full forgiveness and redemption, symbolizing a time for personal repentance and recommitment to God.
Feast of Tabernacles Tishri 15	God told the people they should live in booths for seven days so that the generations would know that His people lived in booths when He brought them out of Egypt. Each Sukkoth, the Jews build and dwell or eat in booths or temporary dwellings for seven days. A joyful celebration!	Christ is our tabernacle or dwelling place (Jn 14:14). May represent the 1000-year reign of Christ on earth. Many believe Jesus was born during this Feast because He was born in the late fall in a "booth." Or this is possibly when we tabernacle (dwell) with God in heaven.

God's Timeless Treasures

Appointed Times

In Leviticus 23, God sets apart specific feast days as sacred, holy convocations for the Israelites to meet with Him. He commands they cease work and gather to worship at these designated times. These festivals, ordained by God for spiritual renewal, involve consecrated observances like sacrifices, offerings, and celebrations to commemorate His past deliverance while also foreshadowing the ultimate redemption through the coming Messiah.

The Hebrew Word Moed

The Hebrew word "moed" is significant in biblical and Jewish contexts, carrying the meaning of appointed times, festivals, or meetings. Derived from the root "yad," which means "to appoint," the term is often used in the Torah to refer to specific times that God has designated for worship, celebration, and remembrance.

Meaning and Implications

- **Divine Appointment:** "Moed" signifies a time that God has specifically set aside for meeting with His people. These times are sacred, distinct from ordinary days, and are meant for worship, reflection, and community.

- **Cyclical Nature:** The moedim underscore the cyclical nature of the Jewish year, with each festival recurring annually. This cyclical aspect highlights the enduring relationship between God and His people, commemorating historical events and the agricultural calendar of the Land of Israel.

- **Remembrance and Anticipation:** While many of the moedim commemorate historical events (such as the Exodus from Egypt during

Passover), they also have a forward-looking aspect. For example, the Feast of Weeks (Shavuot) celebrates the giving of the Torah at Mount Sinai and anticipates future harvests.

- **Community and Identity:** Observing the moedim is a communal activity that strengthens the bonds among the Jewish people. It also serves as a key component of Jewish identity, linking individuals and communities to their history and the land.

- **Usage in the Bible:** It appears over 200 times in the Old Testament in relation to the appointed times and festivals of Israel.

- **Moedim:** The Moedim (plural of moed) usually refers to the 7 major biblical feasts/festivals revealed to Israel in Leviticus 23.

Holy Set Apart Days

The Hebrew word *qadosh* that Moses used in Leviticus for "holy" conveys the meaning of being "set apart and distinguished, that which is unlike the ordinary." When God declared something holy, it marked it as unique and designated it for divine purpose. For example, God sanctified the Sabbath day by setting apart that time exclusively for the Israelites to rest and commune with Him (Exodus 16:23). He ordained the priests as holy by consecrating them to perform sacred duties, ministering in His presence (Lev. 21:7-8), including wearing unique holy garments forbidden for everyday wear (Exodus 28:2). Offerings brought as tithes were made holy, rendered sacred for the service of the Lord (Lev. 27:30).

The Leviticus Holidays are Not Jewish

The Scripture from Leviticus 23:2,4 emphasizes that the feasts mentioned are not merely Jewish feasts but are described as *"The feasts of the Lord."*

> *Speak to the children of Israel and say,*
> *"The feasts of the LORD,*
> *which you shall proclaim to be holy convocations,*
> *these are My feasts....*
> *These are the feasts of the LORD, holy convocations*
> *which you shall proclaim at their appointed times."*
> Leviticus 23:2,4

This distinction is crucial. The passage begins with the directive, Speak to the children of Israel and say to them, which indicates that while the immediate audience is the Israelites, the ownership and initiation of these feasts belong to the LORD. They are His feasts.

This framing suggests that these holy convocations are Divine in origin and purpose. God established them for the Israelites to observe, but their significance transcends a specific ethnic or cultural identity. Instead, they are meant to be a time for all believers to acknowledge and celebrate the works and character of

God.

These feasts serve as a reminder of His sovereignty, a celebration of His provision and deliverance, and an opportunity for believers to come together in worship and remembrance. By calling them "My feasts," God asserts His lordship over these times and invites His people, irrespective of their ethnic background, to participate in these moments of holy assembly, reflection, and celebration.

Jesus, the Disciples, and Paul Observed the Holidays

Jesus was a Jew; He could trace his ancestry in the Davidic line, extending from Abraham (Matthew 1:1–16). He lived during the era of the Second Temple, diligently followed the Law of Moses, observed the holy days, contributed to the Temple, and instructed His disciples to uphold every aspect of the Torah meticulously.

The Gospels tell us about His worship on the Sabbath (Luke 4:16), His teaching at the Feast of Tabernacles (John 7:37–39), and His powerful sermon at the Temple during Hanukkah (John 10:22–30). This shows the continuity of these holy days in Messiah's life and ministry.

The apostle Paul and his disciples continued to observe these biblical holidays, including the Sabbath, after Jesus's resurrection. Though an apostle to the Gentiles, Paul kept a solid connection to his Jewish roots. He regularly spoke in the synagogue every Sabbath (Acts 18:4) and maintained Jewish customs, as seen in Acts 21. He even encouraged the Corinthians to celebrate Passover (1 Corinthians 5:7–8), showing the ongoing relevance of these holidays for believers in Christ. These festivals are meaningful shadows of God's truth, something to be explored positively, not dismissed as mere legalism.

Paul uses the metaphor of a shadow to describe these religious practices. A shadow is an image or outline of something lacking substance or reality. In this context, he is saying that the Old Testament rituals and observances, such as festivals, new moons, and Sabbaths were like shadows or previews of something greater that was to come.

Paul emphasizes that these practices' true essence or reality is found in Christ. In other words, these Old Testament practices pointed forward to Jesus Christ and the spiritual realities that He fulfilled. Christ is the fulfillment of the Law and the Prophets (Matthew 5:17), and believers find the fullness of their faith in Him.

The Early Church

The early church was called derekh, meaning "the way." Jesus' declaration, "I am the Derekh (Way)," as noted in Acts 24:14, defined the identity of his early followers, including Jews and Gentiles, as the people of the Derekh—people of the Way.

The early Christian church was initially comprised mainly of Jewish believers due to historical, theological, and cultural factors. Jesus and His earliest disciples were Jewish, and Christianity emerged as a movement within Judaism.

The early church focused on Jews who saw Jesus as the messianic fulfillment. Jewish customs persisted as Gentiles showed interest, diversifying the church. Paul played a pivotal role in disseminating Christianity among Gentiles, signifying a notable transformation. This transition marked a turning point as the early church, with a solid Jewish foundation, evolved into a diverse community.

The observance of feasts among Gentile believers likely blended cultural context and respect for Jewish heritage:

- **Sabbath Observance:** The extension of Sabbath observance to foreigners (non-Jews) within Israelite communities, as outlined in Exodus 20:8–11, 23:12, and Deuteronomy 5:12–15, provided a precedent for Gentile believers. While the Sabbath held spiritual significance, it also served as a day of rest and reflection, fostering a sense of unity among believers, both Jewish and Gentile.

- **Passover Participation:** Passover, one of the most significant feasts, allowed foreigners to participate, with certain conditions, as seen in Exodus 12:48–49. Gentile believers would likely have joined in the Passover celebrations, acknowledging the importance of this feast in commemorating God's deliverance from Egypt.

- **Feast of Weeks and Feast of Tabernacles:** Deuteronomy 16:11 and 16:14 highlight the inclusion of foreigners in the celebrations of the Feast of Weeks and the Feast of Tabernacles. Gentile believers, being part of the early Christian community, would have likely participated in these feasts alongside their Jewish counterparts.

- **Cultural Context and Unity:** Gentile participation in feasts, while not doctrinal, reflected cultural respect, unity with Jewish believers, and acknowledgment of a shared faith heritage.

The Council of Jerusalem

The Council of Jerusalem is pivotal moment in early Christian history. The Council, detailed in Acts 15, marks a significant turning point regarding Gentile inclusion and the practice of Jewish traditions within the early church. It embodies the negotiation between two major groups: traditionalist Jewish Christians and proponents of Gentile inclusion.

Traditionalist Jewish Christians valued adherence to the Mosaic Law, including circumcision and Jewish customs, as integral to their faith. They saw these practices as vital for maintaining their heritage and relationship with God, advocating for Gentile converts to adopt these customs fully.

In Acts 15 Paul, Barnabas and James argued against imposing Jewish customs on Gentiles, suggesting that faith in Christ alone was enough for salvation. They believed the Gospel's core transcended cultural and ceremonial laws, advocating for a focus on faith and moral living.

Bridging Cultures: James's Vision for Unity

James, with a heart for harmony, made a pivotal decision to ease the journey of Gentiles into the faith (Acts 15:13–21). He set forth a few key practices for them to follow, emphasizing the avoidance of idolatry, sexual immorality, consuming strangled animals, and blood. These measures were not about imposing burdens but about weaving a tapestry of fellowship between Hebrews and Gentiles within the church's embrace. James's guidance was more than a set of rules; it was an invitation to a shared moral ground, a commonality bridging diverse backgrounds. In James 15:20–21, he said,

"Therefore my judgment is that we should not trouble those of the Gentiles who turn to God, but should write to them to abstain from the things polluted by idols, and from sexual immorality, and from what has been strangled, and from blood. For from ancient generations Moses has had in every city those who proclaim him, for he is read every Sabbath in the synagogues."

Many commentaries suggest James was listing the Noahide laws (they come from the Talmud and are therefore extra-biblical). Genesis 9 is the foundation for later rabbinic interpretation (note: there is a lack of consensus regarding the precise number and specific directives, as well as which were originally given to Adam and which were later bestowed upon Noah). These include the rejection of idolatry, sexual immorality, and the eating of blood.

The guidelines set forth for the Gentiles were designed not as a burden, but as an open door to mutual respect and understanding. James's method was a deliberate act of kindness, aiming to weave the Gentiles into the fabric of the faith community. It acknowledged their distinct path, while also cherishing the shared values that unite all followers. Is it my opinion that this was a compassionate and merciful invitation, enabling the Gentiles to join in fellowship and gradually deepen their understanding of God's commands.

Fostering Connection Without Conformity

Our relationship with God goes beyond rituals - it's rooted in genuine connection. Practices like prayer and worship enhance this bond, not secure salvation. While observing holidays isn't compulsory, it offers insight into God's story and closeness with Him. Engaging these days revitalizes faith, like divine revelations enriching our spirits. They invite deeper interaction, improving our understanding of His will. As a father values time with his children, God uses feast days to foster intimacy and growth.

An Intimate Journey of Faith

Our observance of these feast days is not out of obligation but a joyous embrace of tradition and devotion. These moments allow us to deepen our communion with God, partaking in His divine plan and purpose. Just as children feel empowered to undertake significant challenges with their parents' support, celebrating these holy days encourages us on our spiritual journey, fostering meaning, purpose, and growth in alignment with God's seasons.

> *For to this you have been called, because Christ also suffered for you, leaving you an example, so that you might follow in his steps.*
> 1 Peter 2:21

Celebrating these holidays is intricately linked to our spiritual development and relationship with God. They offer a unique way to communicate with the Divine, drawing us closer and molding our character to reflect God's will during these observances and in our daily lives. Ultimately, participating in these feast days expresses our love for God—a sharing in His life and essence and a deepening of our connection with the Divine Presence that enriches our faith journey. This engagement transcends mere duty, embodying a joyful and fulfilling response to the love and grace bestowed upon us by our Heavenly Father.

Who Buried the Treasure?

Unearthing the Forgotten Feasts

Imagine a precious family heirloom, a treasure chest filled with valuable relics and ancient wisdom. Over time, as the family moves to a new country, they slowly lose touch with their heritage. Eventually they forget the importance of this heirloom and its link to their ancestors.

Similarly, the profound spiritual and prophetic insights of the biblical feasts are like that family heirloom. In the early days, when the family (the church) was closely connected to their roots (Judaism), they understood the value of this treasure chest and celebrated it with deep meaning. However, as time passed, the family experienced changes, moved to a different cultural environment, and lost touch with their heritage.

Following Traditions Blindly

You may have heard this story: a woman prepares a roast and cuts off the end before cooking it. When her husband asks why she does this, she replies that she learned it from her mother. The husband then asks the mother, who says she learned it from her grandmother. Finally, when asked, the grandmother reveals that she only cut the end off the roast because her cooking pan was too small to fit the whole roast.

The story's moral is that people often adhere to traditions or ways of doing things without knowing why they were started in the first place. It suggests that it's essential to understand the reasons behind our actions and not follow practices blindly. This story is often used in various contexts to encourage critical thinking and reassessment of customary practices.

The Jewish Early Church

The early church began as a sect within Judaism, predominantly made up of Jews who believed Jesus of Nazareth was the Messiah. Initially, the message of Jesus was spread mainly among Jewish communities. However, several key events and figures played a significant role in the transition of the church from a primarily Jewish context to a predominantly Gentile one.

The spread of Christianity in the Roman Empire, where Greek and Roman (Gentile) cultures were dominant, also influenced the shift. As more Gentiles joined, the cultural and religious practices of the church began to reflect a more Hellenistic (Greco-Roman) worldview.

Over time, these factors contributed to the gradual shift of Christianity from a Jewish sect to a predominantly Gentile religion, shaping its development and forming its distinct identity separate from Judaism.

Shift in the Second Century

By the second century, a new generation emerged and distanced themselves from their family's original customs and traditions. This process of de-Judaizing is like the family members deciding to leave their heritage behind and adopt new customs.

Gentile Christians began to dominate the church. This shift gradually removed Jewish customs, a process known as de-Judaizing. Anti-Semitism began to take root. The Gentile-led church sought to distinguish Christianity from Judaism. One significant change was altering the date of celebrating Christ's resurrection from the Jewish calendar (the third day of Passover on Nisan 17) to the Sunday that comes after the first full moon following the vernal equinox, eventually acquiring the pagan name Easter (Ishtarte). The early New Testament church did not celebrate Easter; instead, they continued to observe Passover with a renewed meaning and interpretation.

Changes in the Fourth Century

The Council of Nicea in 325 A.D., under Emperor Constantine, marked a turning point. Constantine's conversion to Christianity ended the persecution of Gentile believers and mixed Christianity with elements of paganism. Jewish believers faced pressure from their Gentile Christian peers to abandon their customs. Constantine even legislated against practices like observing the Sabbath on Saturday and celebrating Passover.

As Christianity distanced itself from its Jewish roots, anti-Judaism (anti-Semitism) began to take hold. Theological disputes between Christians and Jews intensified, leading to a rejection of Jewish practices, including the observance of biblical feast days.

Misinterpretations and Consequences

There is no longer Jew or Greek, there is no longer slave or free, there is no longer male and female; for all of you are one in Christ Jesus (Galatians 3:28). This verse, which emphasizes the idea that in Christ Jesus, all believers, regardless of their backgrounds, social status, or gender, are united as one, it was often misinterpreted to mean that Jewish Christians should abandon their heritage. This verse emphasizes the unity of Jews and Gentiles in Christ. The Bible acknowledges differences between various groups but stresses equality in God's eyes. Unfortunately, this misinterpretation led to further distancing from Jewish customs.

Replacement Theology

Replacement theology is an absurd teaching that suggests the Christian church replaces Jews as God's chosen people, a view historically linked to anti-Semitic attitudes. Some interpretations of Galatians 3:28 have fueled this notion, implying that the Christian covenant supersedes the Jewish covenant with God.

In Romans 11, Paul vehemently opposes replacement theology and clarifies Israel's ongoing significance:

- **Israel's Continued Role:** Paul emphatically states that God has not rejected His people (Romans 11:1), affirming Israel's continued place in God's plan.

- **The Olive Tree Analogy:** Using the metaphor of an olive tree, Paul illustrates the relationship between Israel (the original branches) and Gentile believers (grafted-in branches). This analogy (Romans 11:17–24) underscores that Gentiles are incorporated into God's promises without displacing Israel.

- **Partial Hardening and Future Redemption:** Paul speaks of a temporary hardening of Israel until the full inclusion of Gentiles (Romans 11:25–26), pointing to a future redemption for Israel and its ongoing role in God's plan.

- **God's Faithfulness:** Paul underscores the unchanging nature of God's gifts and calling (Romans 11:29), affirming God's continued covenant with Israel alongside His grace to Gentiles.

- **Call to Humility:** Paul warns against Gentile pride (Romans 11:18, 20–21), reminding them of their dependence on Israel's spiritual heritage, and emphasizing humility in their inclusion.

Galatians 3:29 reinforces that followers of Jesus are spiritual descendants of Abraham, inheriting the promises of God through faith in Christ. This verse signifies that the blessings promised to Abraham now extend to all believers, emphasizing the unity of believers in Christ as part of Abraham's spiritual family.

God is Doing a Marvelous Thing

Richard Booker said it so well in *Celebrating Jesus in the Biblical Feasts*:

But in these last days, God is doing a marvelous thing. He is breaking down the walls of hatred and misunderstanding that have divided the Jews and Christians. God is calling the Jewish people to return to their ancient homeland and to their covenant God. He is preparing them for the coming of the Messiah. At the same time, God is stirring in the hearts of Christians a holy love for the Jewish people and awakening them to the biblical Hebraic-Jewish roots of their Christian faith.

Many Christians are realizing that the origin of our faith is Jerusalem, not Athens, Rome, Geneva, Wittenberg, Aldersgate, Azusa Street, Springfield, Nashville, Tulsa, etc. As a result, Christians around the world are reaching out to the Jewish people in their communities, singing songs from the Hebrew Scriptures, rediscovering their Jewish roots, and celebrating the Sabbath and the Feasts of the Lord as fulfilled in Jesus. It is clearly God's appointed time to reconcile Jews and Christians in preparation for the coming of Messiah.[1]

Conclusion

The feasts of the Lord, given to Israel and grafted-in believers (Romans 11:17), serve as practical lessons about God and His plan for the world. Galatians emphasizes that all in Christ are heirs to Abraham's promises, connecting us to a rich spiritual heritage. Understanding this journey enriches our appreciation for the significance of biblical feasts, akin to rediscovering a priceless family heirloom amidst the twists of history.

---

1. Booker, Richard. *Celebrating Jesus in the Biblical Feasts Expanded Edition: Discovering Their Significance to You as a Christian.* Destiny Image, 2016.

Your Treasure Hunt

Jesus in the Biblical Holidays

- **1st Spring Holiday** — PASSOVER — Jesus' Death — Nisan 14
- **2nd Spring Holiday** — UNLEAVENED BREAD — Jesus' Burial — Nisan 14–22
- **3rd Spring Holiday** — FIRSTFRUITS — Jesus' Resurrection — Nisan 17
- **4th Spring Holiday** — SHAVUOT — Holy Spirit — Sivan 6
- **1st Fall Holiday** — FEAST OF TRUMPETS — Tishri 1
- **2nd Fall Holiday** — DAY OF ATONEMENT — Tishri 10
- **3rd Fall Holiday** — FEAST OF TABERNACLES — Tishri 15–22

CHARTING YOUR COURSE

Welcome to a journey through time and tradition, where we delve into the rich tapestry of the Bible's feasts, festivals, and fasts. We will traverse the ancient landscapes of Israel, exploring the sacred observances that defined the lives of the Israelites in the Old Testament era, and the enduring traditions that have shaped Jewish practices during and after the Gospel period. While there's an intersection between these lists, they are distinct in their nuances and significance.

A Yearly Companion for Spiritual Growth

My book is designed to serve as a timeless companion for your spiritual journey, especially during the sacred seasons of the biblical feasts. Each year, as these holy dates approach, you can use this book as a study guide to delve deeper into the rich symbolism, historical significance, and spiritual lessons tied to each feast. Whether you're observing alone, with family, or as part of a Bible study group, the insights and reflections offered will enhance your understanding and appreciation of these divine appointments.

By revisiting the chapters corresponding to each feast annually, you'll uncover new layers of meaning and personal relevance, making each celebration a fresh experience of spiritual renewal and growth. This cyclical approach not only enriches your faith but also strengthens the bonds of community as you share and explore these profound truths together. Let this book be your guide to experiencing the biblical feasts as vibrant, living traditions that illuminate your walk with God year after year.

If you're not familiar with these holidays from childhood, distinguishing among them can be challenging. I found it beneficial to categorize them into four spring holidays, three fall holidays, and two extra holidays. This book follows that structure, consistently revisiting the sequence: first spring holiday, second spring holiday, third spring holiday, fourth spring holiday, first fall holiday, second fall holiday, and third fall holiday. This repetitive method is designed to aid your understanding and retention.

The Sections and Chapters

This book is organized into ten-holiday sections. Each includes the following (or more):

1. **The Holiday Overview**: Each section begins with an introduction to the specific holiday, setting the stage for deeper exploration.

2. **Jewish Traditions of the Holiday**: Delve into the rich customs and rituals that have shaped Jewish practices over the centuries.

3. **How Sabbath Reveals Messiah**: Discover the connections between traditional observances and the life and mission of Jesus Christ.

4. **Celebrating Suggestions**: Practical ideas to bring these ancient celebrations into your modern life.

5. **Reflection Question**s: Thought-provoking queries to deepen your understanding and personal connection to each holiday.

6. **The Holiday Recipes**: Enjoy traditional recipes to fully experience the feasts in a tangible way.

Leviticus 23 Holidays

We'll start by exploring Leviticus 23, which details the weekly Sabbath and the seven annual holy days. Hanukkah and Purim, although not part of the seven feasts mentioned in Leviticus 23, are also included, celebrating events that happened well after the time of Moses.

- **The Weekly Sabbath:** A day dedicated to rest and spiritual renewal, observed from Friday evening to Saturday evening. It symbolizes the rest we find in Jesus, our eternal Sabbath, who offers a pause from life's burdens and a rest for our souls.

- **The First Spring Feast, Passover (Pesach):** This holiday commemorates the Israelites' liberation from Egyptian slavery, marked by the seder. It points to Jesus as our Passover Lamb, whose sacrifice brings liberation from the bondage of sin.

- **The Second Spring Feast, Feast of Unleavened Bread (Chag HaMatzot):** This seven-day feast following Passover represents purity and the hastened departure of the Israelites from Egypt. It symbolizes the sinless nature of Jesus and the urgency of accepting His salvation.

- **The Third Spring Feast, Firstfruits (Yom Habikkurim):** This feast, celebrated to offer the first fruits of the harvest, symbolizes Jesus's resurrection—the first fruits of those who have fallen asleep.

- **The Fourth Spring Feast, Feast of Weeks (Shavuot or Pentecost):** This festival celebrates the wheat harvest and the giving of the Law at Mount Sinai. It represents the outpouring of the Holy Spirit sent by Jesus, marking the birth of the church.

- **The First Fall Feast, Trumpets (Rosh Hashanah):** A time marked by the blowing of the shofar, signaling repentance; it foreshadows the return of Jesus, often associated with the sound of the trumpet calling believers to look for Him.

- **The Second Fall Feast, Day of Atonement (Yom Kippur):** This is the holiest day of repentance and atonement. It points to Jesus as our High Priest, who entered the Holy of Holies with His blood for our eternal atonement. (Technically, this is a fast rather than a feast.)

- **The Third Fall Feast, Tabernacles (Sukkot):** This feast commemorates the Israelites' journey in the wilderness and God's protection. It symbolizes Jesus as our true tabernacle, God dwelling among His people and providing shelter and guidance.

Two Extra Holidays

The biblical holidays above were established by God, but Scripture also references two extra holidays, Purim and Hanukkah, which were instituted and celebrated by the people of God.

- **Hanukkah:** Hanukkah, typically celebrated in December, is a Jewish holiday marking the Temple's menorah oil miracle and its rededication in Jerusalem.

- **Purim:** Purim, celebrated around February, is a joyful Jewish holiday marking the rescue of the Jews from a planned massacre in ancient Persia, as narrated in the book of Esther.

Three Pilgrimage Festivals

Passover, Feast of Weeks, and the Feast of Tabernacles are three pilgrimage festivals. All adult Jewish males were required to travel to Jerusalem for each celebration. Each of these three festivals aligns with critical agricultural periods in the land of Israel:

- **Passover** corresponds with the barley harvest season.

- **Feast of Weeks** coincides with the wheat harvest.

- **Tabernacles** signifies the end of the fruit harvest season.

Enhancing Faith Through Celebration

All these feasts of the Lord were given to Israel and grafted-in believers (Romans 11:17) to teach us, practically, more about God and His plan for the world. Galatians 3:29 states:

> *If you belong to Christ, then you are Abraham's seed,*
> *and heirs according to the promise.*

This emphasizes that all who are in Christ are part of Abraham's spiritual lineage and inheritors of God's promises. Israel was instructed to observe the feast days because they held the mysteries that God intended to unveil to His children in future years. God communicates to us through recurring imagery, patterns, and symbolic types that appear consistently throughout the Bible.

Join me on a thrilling journey as we explore and embrace the holy days in our spiritual lives. These days serve not as constraints of legalism but as beacons of light guiding us to freedom in the Messiah. Approach God with a teachable spirit, ready to embrace change. Walking closely with Him offers a life of constant renewal. Engaging with the Bible feast days is not just a commemoration of past events but a journey of transformation. These feasts open our eyes to new perspectives and deepen our understanding of God's plans. Fully commit to this adventure, growing increasingly aware of God's presence in every aspect of life.

Whether you want to incorporate these observances into your spiritual practice, family traditions, or community activities, these chapters provide a wealth of resources. You'll find creative and actionable ways to celebrate these holidays, from family-friendly ideas and recipes to reflective personal rituals and meaningful community engagements.

See Jesus as the vessel of our journey with God (Galatians 5:1), and consider celebrating these feasts as His winds push us toward His blessings. Leviticus 23 acts as our compass, leading us to reflect and grow closer to God. Let's open our hearts to God's Word, uncovering the profound truths it contains.

I hope you'll discover joy in these feasts, as many others have. They're more than rituals; they're insights into God's character and plans for us. May this exploration bring you and your family joy and a deeper understanding of your faith.

Agricultural Parallels

Harvesting Spritual Riches

A deeper appreciation of agriculture has greatly enriched my understanding of the Bible. Most of us today are distanced from nature in today's urbanized world, losing touch with the rich agricultural imagery often used in Scripture, like various harvests, such as wheat, olives, and grapes. This disconnect matters because divine revelation is intricately linked with Creation.

Jesus Himself frequently used natural elements in His parables (such as sheep, wheat, and vines) to reveal spiritual truths. Understanding that God is the Creator of both the natural and supernatural realms helps us see that principles in one often mirror truths in the other.

Ancient Israel: A Land of Faith and Diversity

Imagine ancient Israel, a land of diverse landscapes and rich cultural and religious practices. Here, amidst rolling hills and fertile plains, the Israelites' faith was closely tied to their land. Their divinely ordained feasts, established through Moses, marked the agricultural year and their spiritual rhythm.

Dual Significance of Feasts

Each feast had dual importance: agriculturally, they aligned with planting and harvest times; spiritually, they commemorated God's acts of faithfulness and deliverance. For instance, Passover was a spring festival and a powerful remembrance of the Exodus, central to Jewish history and identity.

Communal Celebrations and Transformations

These feasts were communal cornerstones, fostering unity and shared purpose. Picture the vibrant energy in ancient Jerusalem during these times as people from various backgrounds gathered to remember, celebrate, and give thanks. Over time, these feasts evolved with Jewish life, especially after the Temple's destruction, shifting from sacrificial rituals to prayer and personal holiness. Yet, their core as times for reflection, repentance, and renewal remained unchanged.

Nature's Rhythm in Ancient Israel

The ancient Israelites experienced cycles of rainy and dry periods rather than four distinct seasons. Early autumn rains prepared the ground for winter and spring showers, which nurtured crops to harvest. Summer brought thriving orchards and vineyards nourished by dew.

The rhythm of rain and sun governed harvests: barley and wheat from March to June and fruits like grapes, figs, and olives from August to November. Despite the bounty, challenges like famine and unpredictable rains tested the Israelites' resilience. In these trials, they found solace in God's care, contrasting with the distant gods of neighboring cultures.

Early and Later Firstfruits

The term "firstfruits" appears throughout the Bible, serving both literal and metaphorical roles, which might lead to confusion. Here's a clarification: "Firstfruits" are tied to the agricultural seasons of ancient Israel, reflecting both "early firstfruits" and "later firstfruits." The early firstfruits marked the beginning of the grain harvest, and the later firstfruits represented the broader range of agricultural produce. These offerings symbolized dedicating the first and best harvests to God, expressing gratitude and worship. Here is more clarification:

Early Firstfruits:

This is the third spring holiday, the Feast of Firstfruits, presented before the Lord in a wave offering ceremony during Passover/Feast of Unleavened Bread.

- Exodus 23:16, Exodus 34:22, Leviticus 23:10–11, Numbers 18:12, and Deuteronomy 26:1–11

- Refers to the very first ripened barley sheaf at the outset of the grain harvest in early spring

- Offered as the premiere firstfruits offering, marking the commencement of the barley harvest

- Represented by early crops like barley and wheat

- Signified new life and promise of the fuller harvest still to be gathered

Later Firstfruits:

Later firstfruits refers to the Feast of Weeks, the fourth spring holiday, which culminates with the offering of wheat bread.

- Leviticus 23:15–21, Numbers 28:26–31, 1 Corinthians 15:20–23, and Acts 2:1–4

- Refers to firstfruits offered from crops ripening weeks later i.e. grapes, olives, figs, etc.

- Offered at the end of spring and into summer

- Represented by fruits, vegetables, and grain crops maturing later

- Expanded upon the early firstfruits to eventually include all first produce

- Reinforced ongoing dedication of best to God

Both Firstfruits Revealed Christ as Messiah

The dual nature of firstfruits in Scripture helps reveal Christ's messiahship in a profound light.

- Early Firstfruits: Christ's resurrection symbolizes the initial offering of new life.

- Later Firstfruits: His ascension initiates the continuous gathering of believers.

Timekeeping in Ancient Hebrew Culture

In the tenth century BC, while kings measured years by their reigns, villagers' timekeeping revolved around the agricultural cycle, as seen in Ruth 2:23. Time was marked by sowing and harvesting, reflecting a profound bond with the land.

The Hebrew Calendar: A Lunisolar System

The Hebrew calendar is lunisolar, which is based on the moon's phases and the solar year. It consists of twelve or thirteen months, with the addition of a leap month in seven out of every nineteen years to keep the calendar in alignment with the solar year. The Hebrew months do not perfectly align with the Gregorian calendar months (used in the United States and most of the world) because they start on the new moon and can vary in length. Here is a general guide to how the Hebrew months typically coincide with the American (Gregorian) months, keeping in mind that the exact start and end dates of Hebrew months can shift within the Gregorian calendar:

1. Nisan (Nissan): March–April

2. Iyar: April–May

3. Sivan: May–June

4. Tammuz: June–July

5. Av: July–August

6. Elul: August–September

7. Tishrei: September–October

8. Cheshvan (MarCheshvan): October–November

9. Kislev: November–December

10. Tevet: December–January

11. Shevat: January–February

12. Adar: February–March

These alignments can vary slightly from year to year due to the lunisolar nature of the Hebrew calendar and its adjustments for leap years. In leap years, Adar is split into Adar I and Adar II, with Purim celebrated in Adar II.

Conclusion

Understanding their agricultural context is essential to appreciating the ancient Israelite feasts fully. These celebrations intertwined with the land's seasonal patterns, marking spiritual milestones and critical agrarian events. This perspective reveals the feasts, not just as religious practices but as integrations of daily life, survival, and gratitude for the earth's gifts. This link between faith, culture, and agriculture provides deeper insights into ancient rituals and their lasting influence.

COMPARING CALENDARS

	HEBREW	GREGORIAN	
1	Nisan	Mar/Apr	
2	Iyar	Apr/May	
3	Sivan	May/Jun	SPRING
4	Tammuz	Jun/Jul	
5	Av	Jul/Aug	
6	Elul	Aug/Sep	
7	Tishrei	Sep/Oct	
8	Heshvan	Oct/Nov	
9	Kislev	Nov/Dec	FALL
10	Tevet	Dec/Jan	
11	Shevat	Jan/Feb	
12	Adar	Feb/Mar	

Sabbath

The Weekly Holiday

SABBATH
THE WEEKLY HOLIDAY

OTHER NAMES:
Shabbat, Shabbos (Yiddish), Yom HaShabbat (Hebrew, "the day of the Sabbath")

BIBLE REFERENCE:
Genesis 2:2–3; Exodus 20:8–11; Leviticus 23:3; Isaiah 58:13–14; Mark 2:27–28

DATE OBSERVED:
Begins at sundown on Friday and ends at sundown on Saturday.

BRIEF INTRODUCTION:
The Sabbath is a time for spiritual rejuvenation and reflection, observed by ceasing work, engaging in family time, and participating in religious services and meals.

COMMEMORATES:
The Old Testament represents a day of rest and worship, echoing God's rest on the seventh day of Creation. In the New Testament, it symbolizes spiritual rest and renewal in Jesus.

Sabbath Overview

Brief Introduction: The Sabbath is a time for spiritual rejuvenation and reflection, observed by ceasing work, engaging in family time and meals, and participating in religious services.

Commemorates: The Old Testament represents a day of rest and worship, echoing God's rest on the seventh day of Creation. In the New Testament, it symbolizes spiritual rest and renewal in Jesus.

Other Names: Shabbat, Shabbos (Yiddish), Yom HaShabbat (Hebrew, "the day of the Sabbath").

Bible References: Genesis 2:2–3; Exodus 20:8–11; Leviticus 23:3; Isaiah 58:13–14; Mark 2:27–28.

Date Observed: Begins at sundown on Friday and ends at sundown on Saturday.

Preamble: Setting the Stage for the Feasts

Just as a concert's opening act sets the mood for the central performance, the initial verses of Leviticus 23 (1–3) prepare the reader for the profound significance of the seven feasts described later. These verses lay the essential groundwork like a concert's opening act might pause to establish critical traditions or rules, ensuring the audience's respect for the venue's culture.

In Leviticus, God instructs Moses to remind the Israelites of the Sabbath before introducing the main event—the seven feasts. This is a narrative break and a crucial reinforcement of a tradition foundational to the feasts. It helps attune the people to the importance of what follows.

The Sabbath: A New Rhythm of Life

The introduction of the Sabbath marked a pivotal change for the Israelites, transitioning from ceaseless toil under slavery, to experiencing a weekly day of respite. Embedded within the Ten Commandments, the Sabbath signified not just a mere ordinance but a fresh cadence of existence, symbolizing their passage from bondage to liberation. Grasping and valuing this period of rest was crucial for the Israelites to participate wholly in subsequent celebrations—akin to comprehending the customs of a concert, which ensures and amplifies the enjoyment of the event.

The Sabbath in Creation

Established during Creation, the Sabbath celebrates the universe's completion (Leviticus 23). Exodus 20:8–11 underscores it as a sanctification sign, a purposeful pause in God's plan: *In six days, the Lord made Heaven and Earth...and rested on the seventh day...*

Sabbath in the Wilderness

Moses emphasized the Sabbath as a reflection of God's rest, a reminder of His creative power and liberation from bondage, as stated in Exodus 31:13.

The Year of Jubilee

The land's Sabbath, as instructed in Exodus 23:10–11, is a Divine mandate for soil rejuvenation and ecological balance.

The Sabbath Delight

Isaiah and Jeremiah placed a significant emphasis on the observance of the Sabbath as a cornerstone of Israel's devotion to God, viewing it as a reflection of the nation's spiritual health. Isaiah 58 critiques the superficial observance of Sabbath rituals, arguing that such practices miss the essence of what the Sabbath should be—a "day of delight" characterized by two fundamental aspects:

First, genuinely honoring the Sabbath involves shifting focus from personal desires to joy in worshiping God. Isaiah rebukes the practice of performing outward acts of piety such as fasting while pursuing individual interests on the Sabbath. Authentic observance is about seeking God's presence and guidance, and acknowledging His sovereignty over our lives and time, offering a break from relying on our own strengths.

Second, Isaiah connects genuine Sabbath observance with a commitment to social justice—freeing those bound by injustice, and addressing the needs of the marginalized, including the hungry, poor, and afflicted. This view posits that proper rest and spiritual renewal are intertwined with emulating God's compassion and mercy, enriching our spiritual well-being through acts of kindness toward those in need.

Jeremiah echoes this sentiment, warning that neglecting the Sabbath and engaging in business as usual contributed to the community's moral decay. He argued that returning to observing the Sabbath was essential for spiritual healing and restoration, indicating that such practices could reverse their decline (Jeremiah 17:19–27). For both prophets, the Sabbath transcended mere rituals, to embody principles of integrity, empathy, and justice, and serving as a guide toward a more righteous and compassionate society.

Sabbath in the New Testament

The New Testament frequently references the Sabbath, reflecting its significance in early Christianity.

Teachings and Actions of Jesus

Jesus' interactions with the Sabbath, including healing on this day (Mark 3:1–6, Luke 13:10–17), demonstrate a focus on the spirit of the Law, emphasizing mercy and necessity.

In Mark 2:27–28, Jesus' declaration about the Sabbath underscores its intended benefit for people and his authority over Sabbath customs.

The Early Christian Community

References in Acts (13:14, 42–44, and 18:4) show that early Christians, including Paul, observed the Sabbath, using it for evangelism and teaching.

Colossians 2:16–17 positions the Sabbath as a precursor to the spiritual rest offered through Christ, indicating a shift toward a more spiritual interpretation.

Observing the Sabbath aligns us with God's intentions, teaching us to embrace spiritual renewal and live in harmony with the natural order. This exploration will continue in the "How Sabbath Reveals Messiah" chapter.

Jewish Traditions of Sabbath

A Day of Rest and Spiritual Discipline

Shabbat, also spelled as Sabbath in English, is a Hebrew word meaning "rest" or "cessation." It refers to the day of rest in Judaism that occurs from just before sunset on Friday evening until sundown Saturday night. Shabbat is observed weekly by Jews worldwide as a day of rest and spiritual rejuvenation, according to the fourth Commandment to remember it.

Shabbat is the most central ritual in Judaism, uniquely mandated within the Ten Commandments, and it stands as the foremost sacred day, surpassing even Yom Kippur in significance.

Shabbat as Bride and Queen

In Jewish tradition, Shabbat is personified as a bride or queen in Jewish literature, poetry, and music. An ancient rabbinic custom calls Shabbat the "bride of Israel."

Just as a wedding ceremony bonds husband and wife, Shabbat ushers in a sacred covenant each week between God and His people. The day is greeted joyfully with preparations befitting royalty. Songs on Friday nights welcome "Shabbat the Queen" and contain tender language that affectionately describes her beauty and the eagerness to unite with the beloved day. Foods, services, prayers, and customs seamlessly blend the celebration of Shabbat as both set-apart covenant and intimate personal encounters.

Jewish Fence Rules

Some explanation is helpful before detailing the rich traditions and practices surrounding the Jewish Sabbath celebration. "Fence Rules" are precautions rabbis instituted over time to avoid prohibited work on Shabbat day. They are not Bible mandates.

This concept of fence laws originates from the Mishnah, a compilation of Jewish oral traditions. They refer to prohibitions that rabbis and religious leaders created around the thirty-nine categories of forbidden creative work on Shabbat listed in the Torah. The goal was to "build a fence" around the Sabbath day laws to prevent them from being accidentally violated.

Imagine your back yard has an enormous hole that you don't know how to get rid of. How would you make your back yard safe for enjoyment? You'd likely build a barrier around the hole to prevent falls. In this metaphor, the hole symbolizes sin or the act of breaking a commandment, while the barrier constructed around it is akin to a fence law designed to safeguard against sin, to avoid the risk of transgressing the law. Some examples of rabbinic Jewish fence rules concerning Shabbat are:

- No cooking or baking, so no handling foods that could lead to that to work.

- There are no lighting or extinguishing flames, so no adjusting lamp wicks either.

- No writing, so no drawing or erasing.

- No sewing, so no handling of cloth scraps or needles.

- No planting or reaping, so no digging or watering plants.

- No kindling a fire, so no striking matches or turning electricity on/off.

- No carrying objects in public spaces outside one's home perimeter.

The fence rules created customs like preparing meals ahead of time, cleaning the house, and setting aside special dinnerware just for Shabbat use. They reduced the risk of mistakenly performing forbidden activities on the Sabbath. Over history, these precautions enabled rigorous Sabbath observance to permeate Jewish culture and community.

Adjustments to lights, appliances, and timers are completed beforehand to comply with Shabbat fence rules in preparation for Shabbat. This includes taking out the refrigerator light bulb to stop it from turning on, and organizing meals for the entire Shabbat period in advance.

The Sabbath Mode Refrigerator

My daughter recently purchased a new refrigerator. We were surprised to learn it had a "Sabbath Mode" feature. This setting allows the fridge or freezer doors to be opened and closed without activating the interior lights, sounds, or electronic controls.

We shared a lighthearted moment, joking about whether the refrigerator light matters to God, but this sparked a meaningful conversation. We discussed the fence rules our family adheres to, like teens avoiding the bedrooms of the opposite sex, and not being alone in a car with someone of the opposite sex unless they're married to them.

The well-intentioned Sabbath rules have grown increasingly complex over time. Despite being designed to enhance Sabbath observance and serve as a source of renewal, such restrictions have ended up becoming burdensome. This brings to mind the warning of the Savior about the Pharisees who would bind heavy burdens …grievous to be borne (Matthew 23:4), a reference to the elaborate fence laws they instituted. This context enriches Christ's invitation, "Come unto me, all ye that labor and are heavy laden, and I will give you rest" (Matthew 11:28), highlighting the promise of relief and rest from such burdens. Jesus challenged the religious leaders for imposing strict rules on others through severe legalism, lacking compassion.

A Typical Shabbat Celebration

By mid-afternoon on Friday, observant Jewish families start winding down their work week to embark on Shabbat preparations, treating the occasion with the anticipation of welcoming a cherished visitor. This involves tidying the home, personal grooming, dressing in fine clothes, setting the table with the finest dishes, and preparing a celebratory meal.

Shabbat commences at sunset, rooted in the Creation narrative from Genesis 1, which illustrates a day starting with the evening. The lighting of Shabbat candles by the woman of the household, no later than eighteen minutes before sunset, coupled with a blessing, signifies the onset of Shabbat. Two candles symbolize the commandments to remember (zachor) and observe (shamor) the Shabbat.

Following the candle lighting, families attend a concise evening service, considered brief at forty-five minutes by Jewish liturgical standards.

Upon returning home, the family settles into a lavish and leisurely dinner. It's a cherished tradition for parents to bless their children (see a beautiful example in the movie "Fiddler on the Roof"), followed by the head of the household conducting the Kiddush blessing to sanctify Shabbat with wine. This is succeeded by blessings recited over two braided challah loaves, symbolizing the sweetness and joy of the celebration.

The dinner, though without strict dietary mandates, often features stewed or slow-cooked dishes in observance of the prohibition on cooking during Shabbat.

The meal concludes with the Birkat Ha-mazon, or grace, after meals, performed more leisurely and joyfully than on regular days.

By the evening's end, often around 9 PM or later, the family enjoys time for conversation or Torah study before retiring for the night, fully immersed in the peace and sanctity of Shabbat.

Ending Shabbat

After dark on Saturday, the family performs the Havdalah or "separation" service. A unique braided candle marks the separation between sacred and ordinary. Spices symbolize the sweetness of Shabbat, which is now gone. A cup of wine culminates Havdalah as participants savor one more taste of the joyful Sabbath.

How Sabbath Reveals Messiah

Christ Our Sabbath Rest

SABBATH	JESUS
God blessed and made it holy.	God blessed Jesus as Beloved Son.
A day of rest commanded by God, Exodus 20:8–11.	Invites all to find rest in Him, Matthew 11:28–30.
Represents a covenant between God and His people, Exodus 31:16.	Establishes a New Covenant with His blood, Luke 22:20.
A time for spiritual reflection and renewal.	Povides constant access to spiritual renewal and peace.
A sign of God's sanctification Ezekiel 20:12.	Sanctifies believers, making them holy through His sacrifice Hebrews 2:11.
Ceasing regular work to focus on spiritual.	Laid down his "work" on seventh day in tomb.
Foretaste of eternal rest with God.	Entered eternal rest through resurrection victory.

A profound spiritual transformation occurs when one embraces the rest that Jesus offers. This concept transcends the physical cessation of work observed on the Sabbath day, and speaks to a more profound, more enduring rest found in Christ.

The proper Sabbath rest in Christ is about resting from our spiritual labor and striving. It's about understanding that our works do not achieve salvation and righteousness but are gifts received through faith in Jesus. In Matthew 11:28–30, Jesus invites all weary and burdened to come to Him for rest. This rest is a cessation from the works of the Law—from trying to earn God's favor through human effort.

Comparing the Sabbath with Jesus reveals profound connections between the practice of Sabbath observance and the person and work of Jesus Christ:

- Rest and Restoration with Sabbath: Instituted as a day of rest and cessation from work (Exodus 20:8-11), symbolizing God's rest after creation and offering physical and spiritual restoration.

- Rest and Restoration with Jesus: Offers rest for the soul to those who come to Him, saying, "Come to me, all who labor and are heavily laden, and I will give you rest" (Matthew 11:28-30).

- Holiness in Sabbath: A holy day set apart by God for reflection, worship, and renewal (Genesis 2:3).

- Holiness in Jesus: Sanctifies believers, setting them apart for God's purposes; He is our holiness (1 Corinthians 1:30).

- Freedom in Sabbath: Reminds the Israelites of their liberation from Egypt, celebrating freedom from slavery (Deuteronomy 5:15).

- Freedom in Jesus: Frees us from the bondage of sin and death, offering spiritual liberation and eternal life (John 8:36; Romans 8:2).

- Covenant in Sabbath: A sign of the covenant between God and Israel, symbolizing a special relationship (Exodus 31:16-17).

- Covenant in Jesus: Establishes a new covenant through His blood, inviting all into a personal relationship with God (Luke 22:20; Hebrews 8:6-13).

- Healing in Sabbath: Times of healing occurred on the Sabbath, pointing to God's desire for our wholeness (Mark 3:1-6).

- Healing in Jesus: Heals physically and spiritually, embodying God's power to restore us to wholeness (1 Peter 2:24).

- Provision in Sabbath: Encourages reliance on God's provision, as seen in the manna story (Exodus 16:22-30).

- Provision in Jesus: Teaches trust in God's provision for our needs (Matthew 6:25-34) and is Himself the "bread of life" (John 6:35).

- Eternal Rest in Sabbath: Foreshadows the eternal rest for God's people (Hebrews 4:9-10).

- Eternal Rest in Jesus: Is the fulfillment of that promise, offering eternal life and rest in the presence of God (John 14:2-3; Matthew 25:34).

These comparisons show how Jesus embodies and fulfills the Sabbath's themes, offering a more profound, more comprehensive rest and relationship with God that transcends the literal observance of a day.

Entering Rest through Faith

The book of Hebrews expounds on this, explaining that believers in Christ enter into His rest (Hebrews 4:3). This is a rest of faith, during which we place our trust in the completed work of Christ on the cross for our salvation and righteousness. We don't rely on our adherence to the Law or our good works, but on what Jesus accomplished.

Living in Sabbath rest in Christ means living in the freedom and peace that comes from being secure in our relationship with God, knowing we are loved, accepted, and forgiven. It involves walking in the Spirit daily, allowing Him to lead, guide, and work through us. Our actions and services become responses to God's love rather than attempts to earn His favor.

Sabbath Rest as a Lifestyle

Sabbath rest in Christ is not confined to a single day of the week; it becomes a lifestyle. It is about continually resting in God's presence and promises, finding peace and joy in our relationship, and being guided by His Spirit in all aspects of life.

The Community Aspect

In a communal sense, this rest also manifests in how we interact with others. It encourages us to extend grace, love, and forgiveness, just as we have received from Christ. It's about building relationships and communities grounded in the rest and peace of Jesus.

As we embrace Sabbath rest in Christ, we discover the incredible depth of His love and forgiveness. This revelation naturally leads us to extend the same grace and forgiveness to those around us. We find ourselves more patient, understanding, and compassionate in our relationships.

In our faith communities, this communal aspect of Sabbath rest becomes evident. It encourages us to build grace-filled relationships with our fellow believers. We discover how to share each other's burdens and support one another as we walk together on our faith journeys.

Jane's Journey to Sabbath Rest in Christ

Jane, a dedicated Christian, was overwhelmed and spiritually unfulfilled, despite her active involvement in church and relentless efforts to please God. After hearing a sermon about finding proper rest in Christ, Jane realized that her approach to faith was more about earning God's approval than enjoying a relationship with Him.

She began to see her church activities not as obligations but as expressions of love and gratitude for Jesus' sacrifice. This shift in perspective brought her a profound sense of peace and joy. Jane's service became joyful and stress-free, as she now understood that her identity and value are rooted in Christ's grace, not in her works.

Jane experienced a deeper connection with God, feeling loved and saved by grace. This new understanding also positively affected her interactions with others, making her more gracious and understanding. She started sharing her experience, encouraging others to find their rest in Jesus instead of their own efforts.

Jane's story is a testament to the transformative power of embracing Sabbath rest in Christ, shifting from a works-based faith to one that finds peace, assurance, and joy in the grace of Jesus.

In essence, Sabbath rest in Christ is about ceasing from our self-driven efforts to earn God's approval instead of resting in His grace, love, and mercy. It's about enjoying a relationship with God, based not on what we do, but on what Jesus has done for us. As we live in this rest, we find true peace, joy, and fulfillment that transcends any physical or ceremonial observance of the Sabbath.

Celebrating Sabbath

Rediscovering Its Significance

Honoring the Sabbath by resting aligns, not with becoming Jewish, but with emulating God. As God rested on the Sabbath, making it both blessed and holy, mankind is also encouraged to rest one day out of seven. Hebrews 4:9–11 highlights this, emphasizing that entering God's rest means ceasing from one's own work, just as God did. Unfortunately, many believers focus more on the term Sabbath and its Jewish connotations, rather than the concept of rest (menuach) and its blessings and holiness.

Identifying the Sabbath Day

The question of which day is the Sabbath is easily answered by simple arithmetic. According to Exodus 20:10, *the seventh day is the Sabbath.* By counting six days from Sunday, recognized as the first day of the week, we find that the Sabbath is Saturday. Biblically, the day begins at sundown, so the Sabbath starts on Friday evening and concludes at sundown on Saturday.

Initially, early Christians continued the tradition of observing the Sabbath, likely extending celebrations into early Sunday, as seen in Acts 20. However, to distinguish from Judaism, most of the church shifted to Sunday worship, a change later enforced by Constantine. Jesus and the apostles, however, observed the Sabbath as prescribed in the Hebrew Scriptures. Romans 14 advises, *Let every man be fully persuaded in his own mind.* This implies that following the Holy Spirit's guidance leads to freedom in God's instructions, avoiding legalism or sin.

Remember and Observe

We are encouraged to wholeheartedly rediscover the Sabbath, embracing the two intertwined commandments to remember and observe this sacred day of rest.

Far from legalism, Sabbath observance brings liberation - fostering trust in God's provision, connecting us to faith's Hebraic roots, enriching fellowship with both Creator and loved ones. Observing Sabbath unlocks blessings and renewed perspective. This timeless gift is no empty ritual, but a wellspring of spiritual vitality and understanding, containing profound truths that deeply nourish our soul.

- **Embracing a Rhythm of Grace:** The Sabbath, as highlighted in Exodus 20:8–11, teaches us about the rhythm of grace that God has woven into the fabric of life. By observing a day of rest, we learn to move in step with this grace, acknowledging that our lives are not sustained by relentless toil but by the unmerited favor of God.

- **Cultivating Trust in God's Provision:** The manna story in Exodus 16, where God provided for the Israelites on all days except the Sabbath, is a powerful reminder to trust in God's provision. Observing the Sabbath is a practical exercise in trusting that God will take care of our needs, even when we are not working to meet them ourselves.

- **Building Strong Family and Community Bonds:** The Sabbath offers an invaluable opportunity to strengthen family and community relationships. It's a time to gather, share, and nurture the bonds that sustain us. This practice echoes the biblical principle of fellowship as seen in Acts 2:46–47, where believers shared meals and time together with glad and sincere hearts.

- **Restoring Our Souls:** In the quiet of the Sabbath, there is a chance for deep spiritual renewal. Psalm 23:2–3 speaks of God leading us beside still waters and restoring our souls. The Sabbath can be like our still water, a time to be refreshed in the presence of the Lord, away from the demands and distractions of life.

- **Reflecting and Realigning with God's Will:** The Sabbath provides a space for reflection and reevaluation. It's a time to examine our lives, our choices, and our direction, ensuring they align with God's will. Psalm 46:10, *Be still, and know that I am God*, captures the essence of this introspective aspect of the Sabbath.

- **Modeling a Counter-Cultural Lifestyle:** In a world that often values productivity over people, the Sabbath stands as a counter-cultural statement. It's a declaration that our worth is not tied to our output. By observing the Sabbath, we model a different set of values—those of rest, reflection, and relationships. Priorities!

- **Learning the Art of Slowing Down:** The Sabbath teaches us the art of slowing down. In the words of Ecclesiastes 3:1, *There is a time for everything, and a season for every activity under the heavens*. The Sabbath is our time to slow down, to appreciate the simple joys of life, and to be fully present in each moment.

- **Practicing Humility and Letting Go of Control:** Finally, observing the Sabbath is an exercise in humility and surrender. It is an acknowledgment that the world continues to spin even when we are not at the helm; a reminder that ultimately, God is in control, not us.

My Struggle

I confess that practicing the Sabbath has presented its challenges for me. Being a mother of nine and somewhat of a workaholic, slowing down has always been a struggle. However, I've made an effort to incorporate Sabbath rest into my life, and I've found it to be truly rewarding. Here are a few strategies that have proven effective for me:

- **House Preparation:** I've established a routine of deep cleaning on Friday mornings. This ensures that the house is fresh and organized before I begin my Sabbath rest at sundown.

- **Laundry Management:** To avoid the stress of laundry piling up, I've designated Thursdays as my laundry day. This way I can start the weekend with a clean slate and a relaxed mind.

- **Special Sabbath Dinner:** We've also established a special dinner tradition on Fridays, with the intention of enjoying leftovers on Saturday. This not only eases the workload but also adds a sense of festivity to our Sabbath meals. It's a time when we come together as a family, sharing good food and precious moments.

- **Spiritual Nourishment:** I make it a point to set aside a pile of Bible study books and articles throughout the week. This collection becomes my source of spiritual nourishment during the Sabbath. It's a time when I eagerly dive into these materials, deepening my understanding and connection with my faith.

- **Family Bonding with Games:** Additionally, we've compiled a stack of board and card games that we reserve specifically for the Sabbath. These games provide a delightful way to engage with one another, fostering quality family time and relaxation and lighthearted fun.

Conclusion

Embrace the Sabbath as a joyful opportunity for grace, community, and renewal, realigning with God's rhythm amidst life's bustle. It's a glimpse of eternal peace, reminding us of Christ's care and our role in His Kingdom. Let the Sabbath deepen our connection to God's purpose, offering quiet joy and a hint of Heaven's promise and our Savior's unending love.

Sabbath Recipes
Recipes for Rest & Renewal

Challah Bread

Challah is a special braided bread traditionally eaten by Jews on Shabbat and significant Jewish holidays. Here are some key things to know about challah:

- The word "challah" comes from the Hebrew word meaning "portion" or "offering." A small piece of dough is usually set aside to be "offered" as a tithe when making challah.

- Typical challah has a golden, eggy, brioche-like texture. It is made with eggs, oil or butter, flour, sugar, yeast, and salt. The dough is braided before baking, often in various intricate patterns.

- Braiding challah symbolizes love and community. The various strands come together as one loaf, representing how individuals unite. Braiding also blesses food by increasing its quantity like God multiplied manna in the desert.

- Challah is central to many Jewish rituals surrounding Shabbat. At the Friday evening meal, challah is torn, not cut, as a nod to the day of rest and not "destroying" the wholeness of the bread. It is dipped in salt to add flavor and newness to life's blessings.

- Round challah is baked for the Jewish New Year to represent continuity and new beginnings in the year's cycle. Sweet challah with raisins is made on Rosh Hashana to signify wishes for a lovely New Year.

- So, in essence, challah is the quintessential bread of Jewish spiritual tradition, woven with meaning related to community, sustenance, and connection to God.

Challah Bread Recipe

Ingredients
4 cups all-purpose flour
½ cup sugar
2 tsp salt
1 package of active dry yeast
¾ cup warm water
2 large eggs
¼ cup olive oil
Egg wash (1 beaten egg with 1 tbsp water)

Instructions

- Combine flour, sugar, salt, and yeast in a large bowl.

- Mix warm water, one beaten egg, and oil separately. Add to dry ingredients.

- Knead until smooth, and let rise until doubled.

- Punch down, divide, and braid the dough. Let rise again.

- Brush with egg wash and bake at 375°F for 25–30 minutes until golden.

Chicken Soup

Ingredients
1 whole chicken, cut into pieces
3 large carrots, peeled and chopped
3 celery stalks, chopped
1 large onion, chopped
2 garlic cloves, minced
8 cups water
Salt and pepper to taste
Fresh parsley for garnish

Instructions

- Combine the chicken pieces, carrots, celery, onion, and garlic in a large pot. Add water.

- Bring to a boil, then reduce heat and simmer.

- Skim off any foam that rises to the surface.

- Simmer the soup for about 1–2 hours, or until the chicken is cooked through and the vegetables are tender.

- Remove the chicken pieces. You can shred the chicken, return it to the soup, or serve it separately.

- Season the soup with salt and pepper to taste.

- Garnish with fresh parsley before serving.

Enjoy this traditional challah bread and chicken soup for your Sabbath meal, bringing warmth, nourishment, and joy to your table. Shabbat Shalom!

Beef Brisket

Ingredients
3–4 pounds beef brisket
2 tbs olive oil
2 large onions, sliced
4 garlic cloves, minced
2 cups beef broth
1 cup red wine (optional; can be replaced with more beef broth)
1 can (14 oz) diced tomatoes
2 tbs tomato paste
2 tsp dried thyme
2 bay leaves
Salt and pepper to taste
Chopped parsley for garnish

Instructions

- Preheat your oven to 325°F (165°C).

- Season the brisket generously with salt and pepper.

- Heat olive oil over medium-high heat in a large or oven-proof Dutch oven. Add the brisket and sear on both sides until browned, about 3–4 minutes per side. Remove the brisket and set aside.

- Cooking the Vegetables: In the same pot, add the sliced onions and garlic. Cook until the onions are softened and golden. Return the brisket to the pot with the onions. Add beef, red wine (or additional meat), diced tomatoes, tomato paste, thyme, and bay leaves.

- Bring the mixture to a simmer, then cover the pot. Place the covered pot in the preheated oven. Cook for 3–4 hours or until the brisket is tender.

- Carefully remove the brisket from the pot and slice it against the grain. If desired, skim off any excess fat from the surface of the cooking liquid and remove the bay leaves. Serve the brisket slices with the cooking sauce spooned over the top. Garnish with chopped parsley.

This beef brisket is best enjoyed with family and friends as you gather around the Sabbath table. The slow-cooked, tender meat and rich, savory sauce create an exceptional dish perfect for a weekend feast. Shabbat Shalom!

Sabbath Questions

Illuminating Reflections

Reflecting on the Sabbath and its deeper meaning in light of Jesus' teachings can offer profound insights into how we live out our faith. Here are some questions to ponder:

1. **Understanding Sabbath Rest:** How does the concept of Sabbath, as observed from Genesis to Leviticus and expressed by Jesus, deepen your understanding of rest and worship in your life?

2. **Jesus and the Sabbath:** In what ways does Jesus' interpretation and observance of the Sabbath (Mark 2:27–28) challenge or affirm your current practice and understanding of Sabbath rest?

3. **Personal Application:** Reflect on your weekly routines. How might you incorporate a more intentional practice of rest and reflection as exemplified in the Sabbath?

4. **Spiritual Rest in Jesus:** Considering Jesus' invitation to find rest in Him (Matthew 11:28–30), how can you more fully embrace this spiritual rest in your daily life?

5. **Sabbath as a Sign of Sanctification:** Exodus 31:13 emphasizes the Sabbath as a sign of sanctification. How does keeping a day of rest set you apart in your spiritual walk?

6. **Community and Sabbath:** How does observing a Sabbath rest influence your relationships and interactions within your faith community?

7. **Sabbath in Today's World:** In a world that values constant busyness, what challenges do you face in observing a Sabbath rest? How can you address these challenges?

8. **Sabbath and Creation:** How does the Sabbath remind you of God's role as Creator and Sustainer, and how does this shape your view of the environment and stewardship?

9. **Joy and Delight in the Sabbath:** Isaiah 58:13–14 speaks of finding joy and delight in the Sabbath. How can you find joy in ceasing from your weekly labors?

10. **Jesus as the Ultimate High Priest:** Reflecting on Jesus' role as our High Priest (Hebrews 4:3), how does this enhance your understanding of the Sabbath as a time of spiritual renewal?

11. **Living in Sabbath Rest as a Lifestyle:** How can you extend the principles of Sabbath rest into your everyday life, beyond just one day a week?

12. **Sabbath and Mercy:** Jesus healed and showed mercy on the Sabbath. How can you use your day of rest to show mercy and love to others?

13. **Sabbath in Light of Eternity:** How does observing the Sabbath give you a foretaste of eternal rest in God's presence?

These questions are designed to help you delve deeper into the significance of the Sabbath and its fulfillment in Jesus, encouraging a lifestyle that reflects rest, worship, and a deeper relationship with God.

The Spring Holidays

PASSOVER
Commemorates the Israelites' liberation from Egyptian slavery, markes by the Seder meal. It points to Jesus as our Passover Lamb, whose sacrifice brings liberation from the bondage of sin

UNLEAVENED BREAD
A seven-day feast following passover represents purity and the hastened departure of the Israelites from Egypt. It symbolizes the sinless nature of Jesus and the urgency of accepting His salvation.

FIRSTFRUITS
Celebrated to offer the first fruits of the harvest, symbolizes Jesus's resurrection - the first fruits of those who have fallen asleep.

SHAVUOT
Celebrates the harvest and the giving of the Law at Mount Sinai. It represents the outpouring of the Holy Spirit sent by Jesus, marking the birth of the Church.

FOUR SPRING HOLIDAYS

In the tapestry of biblical celebrations, the four spring holidays—Passover, Unleavened Bread, Firstfruits, and Feast of Weeks—hold profound significance, especially in their reflection of Christ's life and ministry. Each of these holidays, rich in symbolism and tradition, points to key aspects of Christ's death, burial, resurrection, and the gift of the Holy Spirit.

Jesus frequently referenced the beginning—the Law of Moses (Torah, the first five books), and the Prophets (Jeremiah through Malachi) to unveil God's plan for humanity and provide clues to identify the Savior. For the Jews in his era, comprehending the Old Testament was vital to recognizing Jesus as their promised Messiah.

The crucifixion of Christ took place on the fourteenth of Nisan (Passover), and He remained in the tomb for three days (Feast of Unleavened Bread) until the end of the seventeenth day of Nisan (Feast of Firstfruits). As the rabbis often say, "coincidence is not a kosher word," emphasizing that there are no accidents or coincidences in God's kingdom.

1..Passover: The Symbol of Sacrifice

Passover, the first of these spring holidays, is a poignant representation of Christ's sacrifice. In biblical times, Passover involved the sacrifice of a lamb, which was a symbol of their deliverance from slavery in Egypt. This parallels Christ's role as the Lamb of God, whose sacrifice on the cross delivers humanity from the bondage of sin. Just as the blood of the Passover lamb protected the Israelites, Christ's sacrificial death offers protection and salvation to all who believe.

2. Unleavened Bread: The Emblem of Purity

Following Passover is the Feast of Unleavened Bread, a seven-day observance symbolizing purity and the absence of sin. In this feast, the removal of leaven (yeast) from homes represents the removal of sin. This holiday reflects Christ's burial and His sinless nature. Just as leaven is purged from homes, Christ's death purges sin, offering believers a path to spiritual purity.

3. Firstfruits: A Testament to Resurrection

The Feast of Firstfruits (Bikkurim), celebrated after the Sabbath following Passover, symbolizes the first harvest. It is a profound representation of Christ's resurrection. As the firstfruits are the first and best of the harvest, Christ, in rising from the dead, is the Firstfruits of all who have fallen asleep. His resurrection promises new life and hope, a first glimpse of the eternal harvest of souls.

4. Feast of Weeks: The Outpouring of the Spirit

Feast of Weeks (Shavuot or Pentecost) is celebrated fifty days after Firstfruits, at the end of the harvest, and commemorates the giving of the Law on Mount Sinai. In the Christian context, it aligns with the outpouring of the Holy Spirit on the disciples after Christ's ascension. Just as the Law was given on stone tablets at Sinai, the Holy Spirit writes God's laws on the hearts of believers, empowering and guiding us on our spiritual journeys.

Conclusion

These spring holidays form a beautiful, cohesive narrative that mirrors key events in Christ's life and mission. They are not just historical commemorations, but are alive with meaning and relevance, offering believers a rich understanding of God's redemptive plan through Christ. By observing and reflecting on these holidays, we can deepen our appreciation of the profound connection between the Old Testament feasts and the revelation of Christ's work in the New Testament.

Passsover

THE FIRST SPRING HOLIDAY

OTHER NAMES
Pesach, Paschal Feast, The Feast of Liberation, Chag HaMatzot, Chag HaAviv

BIBLE REFERENCE
Lev. 23:4–5; Ex. 12:1–4; Num. 9; 28:16–25; 2 Chron. 35:1–19; Ezra 6:19; Ezek. 45:21; Matt. 26; Mark 14; Luke 22; John 6:4; 11; 13; 19; 1 Cor. 5:7

DATE OBSERVED
Nisan 14 (March or April).

COMMEMORATES
Old Testament: it signifies the Israelites' freedom from Egyptian slavery. New Testament: it symbolizes Jesus' crucifixion, representing liberation from sin.

BRIEF INTRODUCTION
Celebrates the Israelites' liberation from Egyptian slavery, led by Moses. It centers on the ten plagues, particularly the final one where the angel of death "passed over" Israelite homes, symbolizing freedom, divine intervention, and the Jewish covenant with God.

Passover Overview

Brief Introduction: Celebrates the Israelites' liberation from Egyptian slavery, led by Moses. It centers on the ten plagues, particularly the final one where the angel of death "passed over" Israelite homes, symbolizing freedom, divine intervention, and the Jewish covenant with God.

Commemorates: Old Testament: it signifies the Israelites' freedom from Egyptian slavery. New Testament: it symbolizes Jesus' crucifixion, representing liberation from sin.

Other Names: Pesach

Bible Reference: Lev. 23:4–5; Ex. 12:1–4; Num. 9; 28:16–25; 2 Chron. 35:1–19; Ezra 6:19; Ezek. 45:21; Matt. 26; Mark 14; Luke 22; John 6:4; 11; 13; 19; 1 Cor. 5:7

Date Observed: Nisan 14 (March or April).

The Season of Transition: Spring and Renewal

As the world awakens from the dormancy of winter, Passover arrives, heralding the arrival of spring. Observed on the fourteenth day of Abib, later known as Nisan, this festival perfectly aligns with the transition from the rainy season to the burgeoning of new life in the growing season. It is a time marked by agricultural anticipation, where farmers and shepherds alike look forward to the promise of fertility and abundance that the land holds.

One of the Three Mandated Feasts

Three mandated holy days required all Jewish males to journey to Jerusalem: Passover, the Feast of Weeks, and the Feast of Tabernacles. Detailed guidelines for these feasts are outlined in Leviticus 23 and summarized in Numbers 28–29 and Deuteronomy 16. Among them, Passover holds particular significance, symbolizing not just a journey to Jerusalem, but a spiritual voyage through Jewish history, commemorating pivotal events.

The Symbolism of New Lambing

Passover holds particular resonance for the shepherd, coinciding with the new lambing season. This natural cycle of birth and renewal in the fields mirrors the broader theme of Passover—the birth of a nation—in a profound way. As the lambs enter the world, signaling new life and hope, they remind us of the miraculous emergence of the Israelites as a free and purpose-driven people.

Imagine a shepherd on the eve of Passover, tending to his flock under the starry sky. In the night's stillness, he witnesses the miracle of birth as young lambs take their first breaths. This cycle of life, so intertwined with the timing of Passover, becomes a living parable of the Exodus story.

Just as those lambs were born into a world of freedom, the Israelites emerged from the darkness of slavery into the brilliant light of liberty. The parallel between these lambs' birth and a nation's birth cannot be overlooked. It's a testament to the divine orchestration of nature and history, where the earth's seasonal rhythms synchronize with people's spiritual rhythms.

As he cares for his newborn lambs, the shepherd must reflect on the profound connection between the natural world and the spiritual realm. Passover serves as a reminder that the God who watches over the birth of each lamb also watches over His chosen people, guiding them to their new life as a nation.

In this way, the mirroring of natural and spiritual rebirth underscores the festival's profound meaning. Passover commemorates a historical event and invites us to witness the ongoing miracles of Creation and liberation, reminding us that just as the shepherd tends to his flock, our Creator watches over us with love and care.

The Passover Lamb

Central to the celebration of Passover is the Passover lamb—an emblem steeped in both agricultural and spiritual relevance. The choice of this unblemished and pure lamb, its sacrificial offering, and the act of marking the doorposts of the Israelites' homes with its blood, carry profound symbolism. The lamb, more than a religious symbol, is a testament to the pastoral life of the Israelites, mirroring their dependence on the land and its creatures for physical safety and sustenance.

This act of sacrifice and marking with blood was not merely a ceremonial observance, but a profound demonstration of faith and trust in God's provision and protection. Just as the lamb provided physical sustenance and safety, so did it symbolize God's promise of deliverance and guidance.

Spiritual and Agricultural Worlds

Passover is when the Israelites' spiritual journey and nature's cycles beautifully converge. It is a festival that marks a crucial transition, not just in the agricultural calendar but in the very identity of the Israelites. From the oppression of slavery to the hope of a land rich in resources and opportunities—a land "flowing with milk and honey"—Passover encapsulates the journey from despair to hope, from bondage to freedom.

Reflecting on Passover, we are reminded of the deep connections between our spiritual journey and the natural world. The festival is not just a remembrance of historical events but also a celebration of the rhythms of nature—of growth, renewal, and liberation. It reminds us that just as the land rejuvenates each spring, our spirits can also experience a rebirth, a freedom from the shackles of sin (burdens, limitations, restrictions) that bind us, whether in the fields of our daily lives or the sacred realm of faith.

Passover's Enduring Legacy

In the observance of Passover, we find a rich tapestry of meaning, interweaving the agricultural life of ancient Israel with their spiritual journey toward freedom and identity. It is a reminder of the eternal cycle of renewal and hope, and the enduring bond between the land, the people, and their faith. Passover stands as a beacon, inviting us to embrace the rebirth and liberation that each spring—and each act of faith—can bring into our lives.

God explicitly commands the Israelites to observe Passover as a lasting ordinance, a memorial to the miraculous liberation from Egyptian bondage. Exodus 12:14 states,

> *"This day shall be for you a memorial day,*
> *and you shall keep it as a feast to the Lord;*
> *throughout your generations,*
> *as a statute forever, you shall keep it as a feast."*

This command is not only a call to remember the physical liberation of the Israelites but also a profound invitation to reflect on spiritual freedom and redemption. By marking Passover "forever," this commandment emphasizes the timeless relevance of God's deliverance and the enduring covenant between God and His people. It's a yearly reminder of God's sovereignty, mercy, and the promise of liberation from all forms of bondage, urging each generation to recall and re-live the profound legacy of faith, resilience, and divine intervention in human history.

Forgotten then Restored

Centuries after God first instituted the Passover feast and commanded its perpetual observance, this sacrament had been widely forgotten by the Israelites for some time. By the days of Hezekiah, around 715 BC, the Passover rituals had not been properly performed for nearly 200 years - not since the era of Solomon who ruled from 970 to 930 BC. But Hezekiah sought to restore the divine Passover mandate, as Scripture records in 2 Chronicles 30. Verse 5 states, "They decided to send a proclamation throughout Israel, from Beersheba to Dan, calling the people to come to Jerusalem and celebrate the Passover to the Lord, the God of Israel. It had not been celebrated in large numbers according to what was written." This proclamation and the subsequent grand Passover celebration in Jerusalem showed a re-commitment to God's perpetual command for every Israelite generation to observe and keep the Passover feast in remembrance of His mighty works.

The First Passover

Blood on the Doorposts

The story of the first Passover and the Exodus from Egypt is a profound testament to faith and divine intervention, narrated in the book of Exodus. This historic event, over three thousand years old, continues to resonate, symbolizing a divine plan of redemption.

The backdrop of this narrative begins with Joseph, Abraham's great-grandson, who brought the Hebrews to Egypt (Genesis 37). Over time, the Hebrews, growing in number, were enslaved by a pharaoh who feared their rise. Moses, a Hebrew child saved by Pharaoh's daughter and raised as an Egyptian prince, became a central figure in this saga.

After killing an Egyptian to save a Hebrew and fleeing to Midian, Moses is called by God (Exodus 3) to lead his people to freedom. Despite his reluctance, Moses, with his brother Aaron, confronts Pharaoh, demanding the release of the Israelites. Pharaoh's refusal leads to the ten plagues, a series of divine punishments against Egypt.

The Ten Plagues

The Ten Plagues that God inflicted on Egypt before the Exodus were directed against the Egyptian gods, exposing their impotence against the one true God of Israel. Each plague mocked specific Egyptian gods:

1. **Nile Waters Turn to Blood (Exodus 7:14–25):** Challenging the Egyptian reverence for the Nile, this plague turned the source of life into death, questioning the power of Egyptian deities.

2. **Frogs (Exodus 8:1–15):** Frogs, revered in Egyptian mythology, became a curse, reversing their symbol from life to death.

3. **Lice (Exodus 8:16–19):** From the earth came lice, demonstrating God's dominion over the Egyptian Earth deities and showing His power in even the smallest creatures.

4. **Flies (Exodus 8:20–32):** The plague of flies, causing decay and disease, highlighted the distinction between the Egyptians and God's chosen people, Israel.

5. **Livestock Disease (Exodus 9:1–7):** Targeting Egypt's economic and religious heart, this plague showed the impotence of animal deities, and emphasized God's control over prosperity.

6. **Boils (Exodus 9:8–12):** Afflicting Egyptians with painful sores, this plague mocked Egyptian healing practices and deities, showing God's dominion over health.

7. **Hail (Exodus 9:13–35):** This destructive storm displayed God's supremacy over Egyptian weather gods, merging fire and ice in a fearsome display of power.

8. **Locusts (Exodus 10:13–19):** Devastating crops, the locusts demonstrated God's control over the natural world and the futility of Egyptian resistance.

9. **Darkness (Exodus 10:21–29):** The overwhelming darkness, in contrast to the light among the Israelites, symbolized the defeat of Ra, the Egyptian sun god, illustrating spiritual blindness.

10. **Death of the Firstborn (Exodus 11:1–10):** This was the final and most severe plague. The Israelites were spared by marking their doorposts with a lamb's blood, leading to the Passover ritual. Pharaoh's surrender following this plague allowed the Hebrews to depart Egypt.

Divine Compensation

The people of Israel labored as slaves in Egypt for hundreds of years, and the Egyptians exploited them and benefited from their suffering. Now that the people were finally free to leave Egypt, the Lord wanted them to be able to build their new life and not leave Egypt empty-handed after all that oppression.

The Lord said to Moses in Exodus 11:2: *"Speak now in the hearing of the people, that they ask, every man of his neighbor and every woman of her neighbor, for silver and gold jewelry."*

This was to make good on God's promise to give the Israelites favor with the Egyptians when he brought judgment on Egypt's gods and Pharaoh so Israel could go free (see Exodus 3:20-22). Their neighbors offering them gold and silver jewelry was partial "back pay" for all the Israelites' slave labor in Egypt over many generations.

This provided repayment after injustice and supplied the resources for building the Tabernacle and worship system God instituted in the wilderness. Exodus 12:35-36 summarizes: *"The people of Israel had also done as Moses told them, for they had asked the Egyptians for silver and gold...and they plundered the Egyp-*

tians." It was God-ordained compensation.

The Red Sea Miracle

As the Hebrews reached the Red Sea, they found themselves trapped, with the vast sea before them and Pharaoh's army rapidly approaching from behind. In this moment of fear and uncertainty, they witnessed the might of God: Moses, following divine instruction, stretched out his hand over the sea, and God miraculously parted the waters, creating a safe passage for the Israelites.

They crossed on dry ground, with walls of water on either side. As the Egyptian army pursued them, God intervened again. At Moses' command, the waters returned, engulfing and destroying Pharaoh's forces. This extraordinary event marked not only the Hebrews' dramatic escape from slavery but also a profound demonstration of God's power and His commitment to His people.

Passover: A Lasting Ordinance

The observance of Passover was established as an annual tradition, as commanded by God through Moses in Exodus 12. This celebration served as a time of remembrance and gratitude, commemorating the Israelites' liberation from slavery, and God's mercy. It was to be observed throughout generations as a lasting ordinance, reminding the Israelites of their covenant with God and His mighty acts of salvation. This annual observance reinforced the story's significance, ensuring that the lessons of faith, resilience, and Divine deliverance would be passed down through the ages, preserving the legacy of the Exodus for all time.

> *This day shall be for you a memorial day,*
> *and you shall keep it as a feast to the LORD;*
> *throughout your generations, as a statute forever,*
> *you shall keep it as a feast.*
> Exodus 12:14

Jewish Traditions of Passover

Tradition, Memory, and Identity

"Seder" is a term in Hebrew that translates to "order," signifying a sequence or arrangement. The Passover seder is a dinner commemorating the Israelites' exodus from Egypt and their liberation from slavery. This remembrance is achieved through a ritual meal where each element has symbolic significance, recalling the hardships of slavery and the joy of freedom.

In Exodus 12, specific foods are listed for the Passover meal. These include:

- A lamb, which is to be slaughtered and its blood used as a mark on the doorposts and lintel. The lamb should be roasted and eaten entirely
- Unleavened bread, known as matzah
- Bitter herbs

These foods are symbolic: the lamb represents the sacrificial offering, matzah symbolizes the Israelites' haste in leaving Egypt, and bitter herbs depict the bitterness of slavery. The following chapter details how these foods should be prepared and consumed during Passover.

Jewish Traditional Add-Ons

Throughout history, rabbis have enriched the Passover meal with additional elements. Before any concerns arise about the inclusion of these traditions, consider that Jesus Himself, during the Last Supper, adhered to the practice of the four cups (although He only drank three), a custom deeply embedded in the Passover observance of His era. These additions include:

- Green vegetables (a symbol of springtime, a tradition since the Temple era).

- A roasted egg (added in the late twelfth century—no one knows why, so our family decided to leave off the egg).

- Charoset (a mixture of apples and nuts, adopted around the first century).

- Four cups of wine, each with its own symbolic meaning (added during the time of Roman rule in Israel).

- A fifth cup, known as the Cup of Elijah (added during the medieval period). It is left untouched in honor of Elijah, who, according to tradition, will arrive one day as prophesied in Malachi 4:5.

Setting the Passover table is a ritual that combines tradition and symbolism. Central to the table is the seder plate, holding symbolic foods. Each item has a specific place and meaning, representing various aspects of the Exodus story. Additionally, there are cups for wine, symbolizing the four promises of redemption.

The table is often set elegantly to honor the significance of the occasion, with some families choosing to include a haggadah (see definition below) for each participant, guiding them through the seder rituals and readings. Thus, the Passover seder serves as a vivid, multi-sensory reenactment of a pivotal moment in Jewish history, ensuring that the lessons and experiences of the past are not forgotten.

A Passover Haggadah

A Passover haggadah is a text that outlines the order of the Passover seder. It includes various readings, prayers, blessings, and songs associated with the celebration of Passover. The haggadah serves as a guide through the seder, ensuring that all the traditions and rituals are performed correctly. It recounts the story of the Exodus from Egypt, which is central to the Passover celebration, helping participants remember and understand the significance of the holiday.

A special printable Passover haggadah that intertwines the story of the Exodus with the story of the resurrection is available for purchase at the Bible Journal Love Etsy shop. This haggadah presents a distinctive viewpoint, merging the traditional Jewish Passover narrative with elements that resonate with Christian believers, especially focusing on themes of resurrection. It aims to offer a thorough and enlightening approach for observers to celebrate Passover, while contemplating its profound link to foundational faith teachings and the concept of rebirth.

The Four Cups Tradition

The four cups of wine during Passover hold significant meanings. Each cup is a reminder of God's promises and the journey from slavery to freedom:

1. **Cup of Sanctification:** Marks the beginning of the seder and symbolizes God's promise to bring the Israelites out of Egypt.

2. **Cup of Plagues:** Drunk after telling the story of the Exodus, this cup remembers the ten plagues God sent to Egypt.

3. **Cup of Redemption:** Represents God's promise of redemption. This cup is taken after the meal and is often associated with the blood of the Passover lamb.

4. **Cup of Praise:** Concludes the seder, celebrating the Israelites' freedom, and thanking God for His blessings. (Jesus did not drink this cup. In Matthew 26:29 and Mark 14:25, Jesus remarks that He will not drink again of the fruit of the vine until He drinks it anew in the Kingdom of God, which most scholars interpret as Him refraining from the fourth cup.)

Miraculously, the four cups mirror the promises of Christ's ministry. He came to:

- Set us free

- Deliver us from bondage

- Redeem us through His ultimate sacrifice

- Usher in a future filled with hope and salvation

Within the seder is a moment of expectancy, a place set for the prophet Elijah. This cherished custom mirrors the anticipation of the Messiah's arrival, a promise splendidly fulfilled in Jesus, who boldly declared himself as the fulfillment of ancient prophecies.

In embracing the rich symbolism of Passover, we find ourselves part of a continuous story of faith and redemption. It's a story that affirms the enduring nature of God's promises and the transformative power of His love. This story guides us from the shadows of our past transgressions into the brilliant light of a redeemed and renewed life in Christ.

The Four Questions Tradition

Jewish tradition requires the youngest child at the table to ask, usually in song, four questions about why this night is different from all other nights. The origin of the four questions can be traced back to the Mishnah, compiled around 200 CE.

1. Why do we eat unleavened bread on this night when we eat leavened bread on all other nights?

2. Why do we eat only bitter herbs on this night when we eat all kinds of vegetables on all other nights?

3. Why do we dip our vegetables twice on this night when we do not dip our vegetables even once on all other nights?

4. Why do we eat our meals reclining on this night when on all other nights, we eat our meals sitting?

The leader answers each question, telling the Passover story.

Dayenu

"Dayenu" is a traditional song sung during the Passover seder. Its title means "It would have been enough for us," reflecting a deep sense of gratitude toward God. The song enumerates the numerous blessings and miracles the Israelites experienced, from the Exodus out of Egypt to the giving of the Torah and the building of the Temple in Jerusalem. After each blessing, the refrain "Dayenu" is sung, signifying that any single act of God's kindness would have been enough. This repetition emphasizes the overflowing gratitude toward God for all He has done. The song embodies a spirit of thankfulness, recognizing God's abundant generosity throughout history.

The Matzah and Afikoman

Central to the Passover celebration is the matzah, or unleavened bread. A special ceremony involving matzah takes place during the seder. Three pieces of matzah are placed in a matzah tash, a cloth holder with three compartments. The middle matzah is lifted and broken, and part of it is wrapped in a linen cloth to become the Afikoman, which is then hidden. This act is rich in symbolism and interpretation, with various explanations linking it to the patriarchs of Israel, the divisions of the Jewish people, or deeper scriptural meanings.

For thousands of years, Jews have observed the ceremonial breaking of matzah during the Passover seder, unaware of its symbolism related to Christ. The matzah, an unleavened bread, represents purity and is devoid of leaven, which biblically symbolizes sin. As we can see, the matzah's unblemished nature is seen as a representation of Christ's sinless life. The bread's stripes and piercings are seen as prophetic of Jesus' suffering and crucifixion. The ritual of breaking and wrapping the middle piece of matzah, known as the Afikoman, echoes the themes of sacrifice and redemption central to Jesus' crucifixion, burial and resurrection.

The Afikoman, a piece of matzah set aside and later "found" or brought back, symbolizes Christ's death and resurrection. It is hidden and then brought back, much like Christ was buried and then resurrected, making the Afikoman a symbol of hope and redemption in Christ.

The Song Hallel

As the meal finishes, everyone sips from their fourth glass of wine while singing and reciting psalms of praise. Psalms 113–118 are known as "Egyptian Hallel" psalms (Hallel means "praise Yahweh!").

Next Year in Jerusalem

At the conclusion of the dinner, guests say "L'shanah haba'a b'irushalayim!" This translates to "Next year in Jerusalem!"

Passover Steps

Passover seders, like Thanksgiving meals, bear the special imprint of those hosting. No two are identical. Tables may display china or paper plates, depending on preference. Families hand-pick rituals that interweave old-world symbols with contemporary meanings. The suggestions here offer ideas, but ultimately each Passover dinner is customized by the distinctive spiritual and cultural heritage of those gathered to commemorate their redemption story.

1. Lighting a Candle: Acknowledging God's sanctification and the lighting of festival lights.

2. Drinking the Cup of Sanctification: Recognizing God as the Creator of the fruit of the vine.

3. Eating Parsley Dipped in Saltwater: Symbolizing the bitter lives of the Israelites in Egypt.

4. Breaking the Afikomen: The middle piece of matzah, representing God's provision, and Jesus' suffering, death, and resurrection.

5. Eating Horseradish on Matzah: Observing the command to eat bitter herbs.

6. Eating Parsley with Charoset: Combining bitterness with the sweetness of hope in God.

7. Drinking the Cup of Plagues: Celebrating God's mercy and the gift of the Messiah. Put a drop of wine on the plate when each plague is read.

8. Eating the Afikomen: Symbolizing the unleavened bread and the body of Christ.

9. Drinking the Cup of Redemption: Gratefully acknowledging God's Creation.

10. Drinking the Cup of Praise: Reminiscent of Jesus' vow to abstain from the vine until the coming of God's kingdom.

Conclusion

The Passover seder intertwines ancient tradition and rich symbolism to retell the defining story of Jewish identity - God's deliverance of His people from slavery.

Through customized rituals rooted in the Exodus account, songs, food, and wine, Jewish families reconnect to foundational narratives of hardship, redemption and hope. The multifaceted seder experience imprints the imperative of remembering onto participants across generations. In commemorating their collective liberation from bondage, the Jewish people carry forward the etched memory of divine providence.

How Passover Reveals Messiah

Christ Our Passover Lamb

PASSOVER LAMB	JESUS
A physical lamb, a firstborn male, chosen without blemish	The Lamb of God, firstborn, perfect and without sin.
No bone were to be broken.	No bone were broken.
Sacrificed to atone for the sins of the Israelite people.	Sacrificed to atone for the sins of all humanity.
Blood, painted on doorposts, protected from the angel of death.	His blood offers spiritual protection from eternal death.
Passover lamb was a central part of the meal, commemorating deliverance from slavery.	At the Last Supper, He asked followers to remember His sacrifice for their salvation.
Deliverance was temporal, requiring annual commemoration.	Eternal salvation once-for-all provision for sin.
The Passover lamb was selected days before the sacrifice, set apart to be the means of deliverance.	Jesus was foretold and chosen before His birth, destined to die for the sins of the world.

The Passover events highlight the extent of God's commitment to liberate those He loves, underscoring the futility of human pride and idolatry. These events testify to His justice, mercy, and faithfulness, serving as a precursor to the ultimate redemption through Jesus Christ, our Passover Lamb.

A Joy and Privilege

The act of sacrificing the lamb during Passover symbolizes the profound precursor to redemption through God's Messiah. This observance honors a crucial moment in biblical history, celebrating the power of redemption. Passages in the Old Testament that emphasize the importance and joy of observing Passover include:

1. *This is a day you are to commemorate; for the generations to come you shall celebrate it as a festival to the LORD—a lasting ordinance.* Exodus 12:14

2. *On that day tell your son, "I do this because of what the LORD did for me when I came out of Egypt."* Exodus 13:8

3. *Observe the month of Aviv and celebrate the Passover of the LORD your God, because in the month of Aviv he brought you out of Egypt by night.* Deuteronomy 16:1

4. *He brought out his people with rejoicing, his chosen ones with shouts of joy.* Psalm 105:43

The New Testament refers to the concept of the Passover lamb primarily as a typology for Jesus Christ's sacrifice. The most direct references include:

- **John 1:29:** When John the Baptist sees Jesus, he says, "*Behold, the Lamb of God, who takes away the sin of the world!*" This declaration identifies Jesus as the sacrificial lamb, alluding to the Passover lamb as a symbol of salvation and deliverance from sin.

- **The Gospels:** The timing of Jesus' crucifixion during Passover is significant. The Gospels narrate the Last Supper, which was a Passover meal, linking Jesus' sacrifice with the Passover lamb. In John's Gospel, Jesus' death coincides with the time when the Passover lambs were being slaughtered in the Temple, further strengthening this association.

- **1 Corinthians 5:7:** The apostle Paul explicitly refers to Jesus as *our Passover lamb* who has been sacrificed. This statement draws a direct parallel between the sacrificial lamb of the Passover in Exodus and Jesus' sacrifice on the cross. It underscores the belief that just as the lamb's blood saved the Israelites from the final plague, Christ's blood saves believers from sin and death.

- **Revelation:** In the book of Revelation, Jesus is repeatedly referred to as the Lamb. For instance, Revelation 5:6 describes Jesus as *a Lamb standing, as though it had been slain*. These references are symbolic, depicting Jesus as a sacrificial lamb who brings salvation.

Passover Lamb and Jesus Christ

Here are key comparisons that illuminate how Jesus Christ embodies and transcends the symbolism of the Passover Lamb:

- **Spotless:** The Passover lamb in the Old Testament was required to be spotless, a symbol of purity and perfection (Exodus 12:5). This requirement prefigured Jesus in the New Testament, who is described as being without sin or blemish (Hebrews 4:15). Just as the spotless lamb was chosen for sacrifice, Jesus' sinless life positioned Him as the perfect sacrifice for humanity's sins, fulfilling the symbolism of the Passover lamb.

- **Male in its Prime:** The Passover lamb was specifically a male in its first year, signifying strength and vitality at its prime (Exodus 12:5). Jesus is presented as the Son of God, embodying spiritual strength and purity in His prime. Just as the chosen lamb was at its peak of life, Jesus' sacrifice as the Son of God came at a pivotal moment, marking Him as the ultimate unblemished offering for redemption.

- **Shed Blood:** The blood of the Passover lamb symbolized protection and deliverance for the Israelites (Exodus 12:7,13). This prefigured the New Testament, where Jesus' blood, shed during His crucifixion, signifies the New Covenant and the forgiveness of sins (Matthew 26:28), thus fulfilling and expanding upon the symbolism of the fulfillment and completion of His sacrificial role within the constraints of a single momentous day.

- **Reconciliation and Restoration:** Jesus' crucifixion goes beyond forgiveness, repairing the broken relationship between humanity and God. The Old Testament Passover lamb provided temporary protection but couldn't achieve this spiritual restoration.

- **Chosen before birth:** Unlike the Passover lamb selected on the 10th of Nisan, Jesus was chosen for His sacrificial role "before the foundation of the world" (Ephesians 1:4). This emphasizes the eternal nature of Jesus's preordained sacrifice and his role in God's plan.

- **No bones broken:** During Jesus's crucifixion, a prophecy from the Psalms was fulfilled when his bones were not broken (John 19:36; Psalm 34:20). This seemingly minor detail mirrors the instructions for the Passover lamb, where "no bone of it shall be broken" (Exodus 12:46). This parallel further reinforces the connection between Jesus and the fulfillment of the Passover symbolism.

Jesus Observed Passover

Jesus' observance of Passover, particularly during the Last Supper, infused traditional elements with new meaning, representing His body and blood. This act marked a new era of spiritual liberation. Jesus' instructions during the meal become a yearly reminder of both physical deliverance from Egypt and spiritual salvation through Him.

Da Vinci's Last Supper

Leonardo da Vinci's painting, "The Last Supper" stands as a monumental work of art, yet it diverges in several ways from the historical and biblical contexts it aims to represent. The painting infuses Renaissance artistic sensibilities into a scene from first-century Judea, leading to notable discrepancies:

- It depicts Jesus and the apostles seated at a high table, contrary to the era's custom of reclining at low tables during significant meals.

- The presence of leavened bread, whereas the Passover meal, which the Last Supper was, traditionally included unleavened bread.

- The setting appears to be during daylight, despite the Last Supper likely taking place in the evening.

- The attire of Jesus and the apostles is rendered in colorful togas, a reflection of Renaissance fashion rather than the simple, undyed wool tunics characteristic of the time of Jesus.

- The painting suggests the use of elaborate tableware, whereas historical evidence indicates the use of simple stone or clay vessels.

When analyzing Leonardo da Vinci's "The Last Supper," recognizing the role of preconceived notions is essential. We can greatly benefit from exploring and understanding our Jewish roots and heritage, as well as striving to comprehend the Bible within the context of its original cultural era. By familiarizing ourselves with the world in which the Bible was written, we enhance our grasp of its messages and teachings.

The Red Sea Metaphor

The Red Sea crossing, parallel to Jesus' baptism in the Jordan River, represents a journey from slavery to freedom, mirroring Christ's role in freeing humanity from sin. This event is a metaphor for Christ's saving grace, connecting historical deliverance with spiritual salvation.

Throughout the New Testament, the Exodus narrative, including the crossing of the Red Sea, is often seen as a typological precursor to salvation. The themes of liberation, God's deliverance, and the journey from slavery to freedom resonate with the New Testament's message of salvation through Christ.

- **1 Corinthians 10:1–2:** Paul draws a parallel between the experience of the Israelites and the Christian experience. He mentions how the Israelites were *baptized into Moses in the cloud and in the sea.*

- **Hebrews 11:29:** In the faith chapter of the book of Hebrews, the author mentions the Red Sea miracle as an example of faith. It states, *By faith the people passed through the Red Sea as on dry land; but when the Egyptians tried to do so, they were drowned.* This passage celebrates the faith of the Israelites who followed Moses and crossed the sea, highlighting it as a significant act of trust in God.

A Celebration of Deliverance, Past and Present

In conclusion, Passover is more than a historical remembrance; it is an active celebration of deliverance, both physical and spiritual. It calls us to recognize and rejoice in Christ's transformative sacrifice, inviting reflection on the profound implications of Jesus as our Passover Lamb. This narrative weaves together the liberation of the Israelites with our spiritual freedom in Christ, portraying God's unchanging plan of redemption.

Celebrating Passover

A Christian Passover Seder

The Passover seder is a cherished tradition commemorating the Israelites' Exodus from Egypt. Observing Passover can be a meaningful reflection of both the historical Exodus and the redemptive work of Christ. Don't worry about doing everything perfectly. When King Hezekiah decided to celebrate Passover after it had been neglected for many years (Chronicles 30), he postponed the festival to the second month (instead of Nisan 14). Though delayed, Hezekiah's celebration of Passover marked a significant religious reformation, bringing the people of Judah back to their religious roots, and emphasizing the flexibility within the Law to accommodate extraordinary circumstances for unity.

Haggadah

A haggadah is a text that guides you through the Passover meal, detailing each step of this important ritual. I have created a comprehensive, printable haggadah, available at the Bible Journal Love Etsy Shop for those interested in printing and creating copies (print, cut, and fold) for family members. It recounts the story of the Exodus from Egypt and integrates the narrative of Christ's sacrifice, offering a unique and enriching perspective on this traditional observance.

Preparing for the Passover Seder

Preparing for the seder involves selecting foods with significant biblical and symbolic meanings. Essential items include unleavened bread (matzah), representing the Israelites' quick departure from Egypt, and bitter herbs, symbolizing the bitterness of slavery. Other dishes may be added, in line with the tradition of avoiding leaven, to remember the Israelites' experience.

Setting the seder table:

- **Seder Plate:** While not mentioned in Leviticus, it holds symbolic foods like a lamb's shank bone, bitter herbs, charoset, and parsley.

- **Matzah:** Unleavened bread is a biblical requirement representing the haste of the Israelites' departure. A recipe is included in the Unleavened Bread section.

- **Wine or Grape Juice:** The four cups are a Jewish tradition (not a Bible mandate), symbolizing God's promises. Jesus drank from three of the four cups during the Last Supper. You can use four separate cups or pour liquid into each cup four times.

- **The Afikomen:** A piece of broken matzah symbolizing Christ's beating, death, burial and resurrection.

Passover Seder

The seder plate holds symbolic foods: a lamb's shank bone, symbolizing the Passover sacrifice, bitter herbs for the hardships endured in slavery, and a charoset, a sweet concoction, symbolizing the mortar used by the Hebrew slaves. These items are potent reminders of the Exodus story, seeing Christ as the ultimate Passover Lamb.

Meal Preparation

As the Bible instructs, prepare a meal with unleavened bread and bitter herbs. Other dishes can be included per your own tradition, considering the absence of leaven.

Passover Seder Steps

A free color-illustrated Passover Steps PDF is available for download at JesusintheBiblicalHolidays.com

1. **Kadesh (Cup of Sanctification):** The seder begins with the blessing over the first cup, setting the night as holy and commemorating God's promise.

2. **Handwashing (Urchatz):** Participants wash their hands as a symbol of purification and preparation for the sacred meal.

3. **Breaking the Matzah (Afikomen):** The leader breaks a piece of matzah, explaining its significance as a symbol of the Messiah's sacrifice, and then hides it.

4. **Parsley in Salt Water (Karpas):** Parsley is dipped in salt water, symbolizing the Israelites' tears during their enslavement.

5. **Breaking the Middle Matzah (Yachatz):** The middle piece of matzah is broken, with the larger piece designated as the Afikomen, symbolizing the Passover lamb, and then hidden.

6. **Storytelling (Maggid):** The story of the Israelites' slavery, deliverance, and God's response through plagues and the Passover lamb is recounted.

7. **Second Cup (Cup of Plagues):** Participants drink from the second cup, acknowledging the suffering in Egypt and symbolizing Christ's power to deliver from sin and death. Recall the ten plagues in Egypt, with a drop of wine placed on the plate for each plague.

8. **Handwashing with Blessing (Rachtzah):** Hands are washed again with a blessing in preparation for eating matzah.

9. **Blessing over Matzah (Motzi Matzah):** Blessings are recited over the matzah, representing the Israelites' swift departure from Egypt.

10. **Bitter Herbs (Maror):** Bitter herbs are eaten to remember the bitterness of slavery.

11. **Charoset Sandwich (Korech):** A sandwich made with matzah, maror, and charoset is eaten, symbolizing the mix of bitterness and freedom.

12. **The Meal (Shulchan Orech):** The meal is served and eaten.

13. **Finding the Afikomen (Tzafun):** The hidden Afikomen is found and then eaten, recalling the Passover and Jesus' sacrifice.

14. **Third Cup (Barech):** The third cup, the Cup of Redemption, is drunk, reflecting on Christ as the Lamb of God.

15. **Songs of Praise (Hallel):** Songs of praise are sung, and the fourth cup, the Cup of Praise, is filled and drunk, celebrating the resurrection of Jesus. In both Matthew 26:29 and Mark 14:25, Jesus makes a profound statement: *"But I say to you, I will not drink of this fruit of the vine from now on until that day when I drink it new with you in My Father's kingdom"*. Instead of proceeding to drink the fourth cup, Jesus refrained.

16. **Conclusion (Nirtzah):** The seder concludes with a prayer or expression of hope for redemption and peace.

Concluding our chapter on the Passover seder, we see how it beautifully connects the Exodus from Egypt to Christ's redemptive work.

PASSOVER SEDER ORDER

1. Kadesh (Cup of Sanctification): The seder begins with the blessing over the first cup, setting the night as holy and commemorating God's promise.

2. Handwashing (Urchatz): Participants wash their hands as a symbol of purification and preparation for the sacred meal.

3. Breaking the Matzah (Afikomen): The leader breaks a piece of matzah, explaining its significance as a symbol of the Messiah's sacrifice, and hides it.

4. Parsley in Salt Water (Karpas): Parsley is dipped in salt water, symbolizing the Israelites' tears during enslavement.

5. Breaking the Middle Matzah (Yachatz): The middle matzah is broken, with the larger piece designated as the Afikomen, symbolizing the Passover lamb, and hidden.

6. Storytelling (Maggid): The story of the Israelites' slavery, deliverance, and God's response through plagues and the Passover lamb is recounted.

7. Second Cup (Cup of Plagues): Participants drink from the second cup, acknowledging the suffering of the Egyptians and symbolizing Christ's power to deliver from sin and death. Recall the ten plagues in Egypt, with a drop of wine placed for each plague on the plate.

8. Handwashing with Blessing (Rachtzah): Hands are washed again with a blessing in preparation for eating matzah.

9. Blessing Over Matzah (Motzi Matzah): Blessings are recited over matzah, representing the Israelites' swift departure from Egypt.

10. Bitter Herbs (Maror): Bitter herbs are eaten to remember the bitterness of slavery.

11. Charoset Sandwich (Korech): A sandwich made with matzah, maror, and charoset is eaten, symbolizing the mix of bitterness and freedom.

12. The Meal (Shulchan Orech): The meal is served and eaten.

13. Finding the Afikomen (Tzafun): The hidden Afikomen is found and eaten, recalling the Passover and Jesus' sacrifice.

14. Third Cup (Barech): The third cup, the Cup of Redemption, is drunk, reflecting on Christ as the Lamb of God.

15. Songs of Praise (Hallel): Songs of praise are sung, and the fourth cup, the Cup of Praise, is filled and drunk, celebrating the resurrection of Jesus. In both Matthew 26:29 and Mark 14:25, Jesus makes a profound statement: "But I say to you, I will not drink of this fruit of the vine from now on until that day when I drink it new with you in My Father's kingdom." Instead of proceeding to drink the fourth cup, Jesus refrains.

16. Conclusion (Nirtzah): The seder concludes with a prayer or expression of hope for redemption and peace.

The Role of Communion

Do This in Remembrance

The First Serving of Bread and Wine

The first mention of bread and wine together in Scripture occurs long before the Last Supper—in fact, over four hundred years earlier! Genesis 14:17–24 tells of a meeting between Abram and a mysterious figure named Melchizedek, following a battle. This priestly king did something profoundly prophetic:

Melchizedek's Offering

Melchizedek brought out bread and wine to serve Abram. Centuries later, bread and wine would become the key symbols of Christ's Last Supper. This simple act points to Jesus in remarkable ways. As a royal priest offering sustenance, Melchizedek pictured Christ himself (Psalms 110; Hebrews 5–7), and his serving bread and wine to the patriarch Abram after victory signals Jesus' triumphant sacrifice delivering all nations from darkness.

King-Priest of the Cursed

Consider too Melchizedek's Canaanite lineage. Canaanites were under Noah's curse (Gen 9:25), yet Melchizedek blessed Abram, father of all faithful generations. This foreshadowed Jesus—who bore God's curse that all peoples might be blessed in Him (Galatians 3:13–14). Truly, Melchizedek and his bread and wine celebrated assured redemption!

Last Supper Fulfillment

The account carries Divine fingerprints. God twice names Himself "Most High...Possessor of Heaven and Earth"— nothing can prevent His full redemptive reign! So already by Genesis 14 the prophetic roots were set: evil was defeated despite the cost, and God's victory meal was coming for those once excluded. At Christ's climactic Last Supper, these truths blossomed fully: Satan's schemes utterly foiled, the children of promise welcomed into eternal joy! As we partake of the bread and wine today, we proclaim Christ the victor and happily share in that promised feast.

Now, as they were eating, Jesus took bread, and after blessing it broke it and gave it to the disciples, and said, "Take, eat; this is my body." And he took a cup, and when he had given thanks, he gave it to them, saying, "Drink of it, all of you, for this, is my blood of the covenant, which is poured out for many for the forgiveness of sins". Matthew 26:26

- **Transformation Through Communion:** As outlined in Romans 8:29, God's overarching aim is our transformation into Christ's likeness, a process significantly impacted by Communion. It's not merely a ritual, but a crucial element in our sanctification, setting us apart from worldly influences and nurturing our spiritual growth to reflect God's character. Communion deepens our relationship with Christ, allowing the Holy Spirit to shape our lives to mirror His image.

- **Strengthening Intimacy with God:** Partaking in Communion strengthens our faith, much like exercising a muscle enhances its strength. This spiritual exercise bolsters our belief in God's love and grace. As our faith grows stronger, it becomes a versatile tool, aiding us in life's challenges, and enabling us to extend love and compassion in various situations.

- **Representing Christ's Sacrifice:** The bread and wine represent Christ's body and blood, sacrificed for us. We unite ourselves with Christ through devout participation, signifying our integration into a profound spiritual fellowship.

Facets of Communion: A Spiritual Journey

- **Transformation:** Participation in Communion transforms believers into sacred spaces where God dwells.

- **Prayerful Communion:** Prayer before Communion fosters a personal and intimate dialogue with God.

- **Union with Christ:** Communion symbolizes our union, making us hosts of His divine presence.

- **Deepening Fellowship:** Communion is an intimate act of joining Christ in His kingdom pursuit.

- **Reflecting on Salvation:** Reminds us of Jesus' sacrifice and the hope of His return.

- **Compliance with Christ's Command:** Observing Communion is a continual renewal of our commitment to Christ's teachings.

- **Radiating Christ's Love:** The love received in Communion overflows into acts of charity and empathy.

- **Moral Responsibility:** Hosting God's presence calls for a life that honors this divine indwelling.

Communion Instructions Simplified

- **Frequency:** Early Christians regularly broke bread, as in Acts 2. While no specific frequency is mandated, regular participation, such as weekly or at least annually during Passover, is beneficial. I try to take Communion weekly.

- **Bread and Wine:** Reflecting the Last Supper's Passover context, unleavened bread and wine (or grape juice for various reasons) are used.

- **Location and Inclusiveness:** Communion can be held anywhere, emphasizing remembrance and fellowship. It's inclusive, with no age restrictions or prerequisites like Baptism.

- **Individual and Collective Growth:** It's vital for personal spiritual growth and fostering community.

- **Proper Observance:** Paul warns against improper Communion practices, as seen in 1 Corinthians 11:29. This calls for recognizing Christ's sacrifice, unity within the church body, and self-examination before partaking, ensuring a respectful and meaningful approach.

Divine Encounter and Deep Connection

- **Jesus as Mediator:** The key to understanding Jesus as a bridge is in the concept of sacrifice. Sin created a chasm between humanity and God, a gap that could not be bridged by human efforts alone. Jesus, through his sacrificial death, paid the penalty for sin, thus reconciling humanity with God (2 Corinthians 5:18–19). This act of atonement restores the broken relationship between humans and the Divine.

- **The Bread:** The bread is emblematic of the body of Christ. This parallels the moment at the Last Supper when Jesus broke matzah, offering it to His disciples as a representation of His body (Luke 22:19). In this act, the bread becomes more than a mere physical substance; it transforms into spiritual sustenance.

- **The Wine:** The Communion wine is a powerful symbol that connects us to God's enduring promise. Just as Abram's covenant with God in Genesis 15 showed the deep significance of sacrifice through a blood pact, the wine at the Last Supper reveals a profound truth. Jesus declared this wine to be His blood, a sacrifice for our sins, offering forgiveness and a fresh start under the New Covenant. This act not only fulfills the Old

- Covenant's promises but also shows God's constant faithfulness, bridging the past and present with His love and commitment.

- **Call to Reflect and Remember:** Each time believers partake in the bread of Communion, it's an invitation to reflect on the sacrifice of Christ, to remember His teachings, and to recommit to living a life in line with His example. This reflection is a form of spiritual nourishment, feeding the soul with the truths of the Gospel.

Conclusion

Communion transcends a mere ritual; it's a profound act of faith, remembrance, and fellowship, affirming our relationship with God and the Christian community. It's an observance of Jesus' sacrifice, celebrating our union.

Passover Recipes
A Feast of Remembrance

Passover Charoset

Charoset, often pronounced as "'har-o-set," derives its name from the Hebrew term "cheres," meaning "clay." This sweet condiment is a delightful blend of fruits, nuts, spices and honey.

Ingredients
3 medium apples, peeled, cored, and chopped
1 cup walnuts, finely chopped
½ cup sweet red wine (kosher for Passover
¼ cup honey
1 tsp ground cinnamon
½ tsp ground nutmeg

Instructions

- Combine the chopped apples and walnuts.
- Add the sweet red wine, honey, cinnamon, and nutmeg. Mix well.
- Refrigerate for at least an hour before serving.

Matzo Ball Kugel

Matzo Ball Kugel is a unique and flavorful casserole dish traditionally served during Passover.

Ingredients
4 sheets of matzah, broken into small pieces
4 large eggs
½ cup olive oil or melted schmaltz (chicken fat)
1 tsp salt
¼ tsp black pepper

1 cup finely chopped onions
1 cup grated carrots
½ cup finely chopped celery
¼ cup chopped parsley
½ tsp baking powder (ensure it's kosher for Passover)

Instructions

- Preheat the oven to 350°F (175°C) and grease a baking dish.

- Soak the matzah pieces in water until soft, then drain and squeeze out excess water.

- Beat the eggs with oil, salt, and pepper in a large bowl.

- Add the softened matzah, onions, carrots, celery, parsley. Add the baking powder to the egg mixture and mix well.

- Pour the mixture into the prepared dish and bake for about 45 minutes or until golden brown and set.

Roasted Lemon-Herb Chicken

A popular dish often served during Passover is roasted lemon-herb chicken. This dish is flavorful, relatively simple to prepare, and can be a delightful addition to the Passover meal. Here's a basic recipe:

Ingredients
Whole Chicken: About 4–5 pounds, washed and patted dry.
Lemons: 2–3 lemons, one for juicing and the others for stuffing inside the chicken.
Herbs: Such as parsley, rosemary, and thyme.
Garlic: 4–5 cloves, minced or whole, as per your preference.
Olive Oil: For brushing the chicken.
Kosher Salt and Black Pepper: For seasoning.
Vegetables: Optional, like carrots, onions, and potatoes, cut into large chunks.

Instructions

- Preheat the Oven: Set it to 375°F (190°C).

- Prepare the Chicken: Season the inside and outside of the chicken with kosher salt and black pepper.

- Rub the chicken with the juice of one lemon and olive oil.
  Stuff the cavity of the chicken with the remaining lemon (sliced), garlic, and a handful of fresh herbs.

- Prepare the Roasting Pan: If you're using vegetables, place them at the bottom of a roasting pan, creating a natural rack for the chicken to sit on. Place the chicken on top.

- Roast the Chicken: Roast in the preheated oven for about 1 to 1½ hours, or until the juices run clear when you cut between a leg and thigh. Baste the chicken occasionally with its own juices or a bit more olive oil for extra crispiness.

- Rest and Serve: Once done, let the chicken rest for about 10 minutes before carving. Serve with the roasted vegetables and garnish with additional fresh herbs.

- Optional: If you want a sauce, you can make a simple gravy from the pan juices. Skim off the excess fat, add a bit of chicken broth, and heat it in a pan, scraping up the browned bits for extra flavor.

The key to a flavorful roasted chicken is proper seasoning and not overcooking it. Use a meat thermometer to ensure the chicken is cooked through (the internal temperature should reach 165°F or 75°C).

Tzimmes

Tzimmes is a traditional Jewish stew often served during Passover.

Ingredients
Carrots: 1 pound, peeled and sliced into rounds or half-moons.
Sweet Potatoes: 2 large, peeled and cut into chunks.
Prunes or Dried Apricots: 1 cup, pitted and halved.
Honey or Maple Syrup: ⅓ cup for sweetness.
Orange Juice: 1 cup, freshly squeezed is preferable.
Lemon Juice: From 1 lemon.
Cinnamon: 1 tsp, ground.
Ginger: ½ tsp, ground (optional).
Salt: To taste.
Butter 2 tbs, cut into small pieces

Instructions

- Preheat the Oven: Preheat your oven to 350°F (175°C).

- Prepare the Ingredients: In a large mixing bowl, combine the sliced carrots, sweet potato chunks, and dried fruits.

- In another bowl, mix together the honey (or maple syrup), orange juice, lemon juice, cinnamon, ginger, and a pinch of salt.

- Pour the liquid mixture over the carrot and sweet potato mixture and toss to coat evenly.
  Transfer the mixture to a baking dish and dot the top with pieces of butter. Cover the dish with aluminum foil.

- Bake the Tzimmes: Bake in the preheated oven for about one hour. After one hour, remove the foil and continue baking for another 30 minutes, or until the vegetables are tender and starting to caramelize.

- Serve: Once done, remove from the oven and let it cool slightly. Tzimmes can be served warm as a side dish.

Notes: Tzimmes is a versatile dish, and you can adjust the sweetness or add other ingredients like raisins, nuts, or even a splash of orange liqueur for extra flavor. It can be made ahead of time and reheated before serving, which allows the flavors to meld together even more. For a savory twist, some people add a little bit of chopped onion or shallots to the mix before baking.

Unleavened Bread

See the Unleavened Bread Recipe chapter for an unleavened bread recipe.

Each of these recipes celebrates the unique flavors and traditions of Passover while adhering to the holiday's dietary restrictions. Enjoy!

Passover Questions
Illuminating Reflections

The Passover celebration, with its rich historical and spiritual significance, invites us to reflect on the themes of liberation, sacrifice, and divine intervention. As we explore the connections between the ancient Israelites' experience and the fulfillment of these symbols in Jesus Christ, these reflection questions are designed to deepen our understanding and encourage the practical application of these timeless principles in our daily lives.

1. Consider the Israelites' exodus from Egypt. How does this narrative of liberation from physical bondage mirror your spiritual journey from the bondage of sin?

2. What personal "Egypts" have you been delivered from, and how do you see God's hand in your liberation?

3. Consider the symbolism of the Passover lamb. In what ways does Jesus as the "Lamb of God" (John 1:29) deepen your understanding of sacrifice and redemption?

4. How does the unblemished nature of the Passover lamb enhance your appreciation for Christ's sinless sacrifice?

5. The Israelites marked their doorposts with the lamb's blood as a sign of protection. How can this act be seen as a symbol of Christ's safety in your life?

6. In what ways do you "mark" your life to show that you are under Christ's protection?

7. The unleavened bread, or matzah, is called the Bread of Affliction. How does this symbol of haste and simplicity influence your understanding of spiritual readiness and humility?

8. How does the simplicity of the unleavened bread inspire you to live a life free from the "leaven" of sin and excess?

9. Passover marks a time of agricultural renewal. How does this season of new beginnings resonate with your spiritual renewal?

10. How can you cultivate "new growth" in your faith and relationship with God during this season?

11. Reflect on Jesus' observance of Passover, notably the Last Supper. How does this deepen your understanding of Communion and the New Covenant?

12. How can you apply the principles of remembrance and thanksgiving, as demonstrated in the Last Supper, to your daily spiritual practice?

13. How does the Red Sea crossing, as a metaphor for baptism and deliverance, parallel your salvation experience through Christ?

14. What does "crossing the Red Sea" symbolize in your spiritual journey, and how do you navigate the "waters" of challenges and faith?

15. In what practical ways can you celebrate and honor the legacy of Passover in your life, recognizing Christ as your Passover Lamb?

16. How does the theme of deliverance in the Passover story inspire you to live a life of freedom and gratitude?

As we reflect on the rich themes and symbols of the Passover, may we be moved to a deeper appreciation for God's mighty acts of liberation and redemption. From the exodus to the cross, these timeless stories remind us of the great lengths God has gone to free us from bondage and shelter us with mighty protection. May the Passover Lamb and the unleavened Bread continuously nourish our spirits. And may this season of remembering help us walk in ever-increasing freedom, overflowing gratitude, and a faith renewed through reflecting on Christ our Passover.

Unleavened Bread

THE SECOND SPRING HOLIDAY

UNLEAVENED BREAD
THE SECOND SPRING FEAST

OTHER NAMES
Chag HaMatzot, Festival of Unleavened Bread, Feast of Unleavened Bread

BIBLE REFERENCE
Exo 12:8–11; 23:15; 34:18; Lev 23:5–6; Num 28:17; Deut 16:3; Mat 26:17–20

DATE OBSERVED
Nisan 15. It lasts for seven days (March or April).

BRIEF INTRODUCTION
The Feast of Unleavened Bread, succeeding Passover, commemorates the Israelites' Exodus from Egypt, symbolizing their transition from slavery to freedom and the journey to the promised land, with themes of liberation, purification, and casting off sin.

COMMEMORATES
The Old Testament signifies the Israelites' hurried departure from Egypt, resulting in the baking of unleavened bread due to time constraints. In the New Testament, it corresponds to Jesus' burial, aligning with the period of his entombment.

Unleavened Bread Overview

Brief Introduction: The Feast of Unleavened Bread, succeeding Passover, commemorates the Israelites' Exodus from Egypt, symbolizing their transition from slavery to freedom and the journey to the Promised Land, with themes of liberation, purification, and casting off sin.

Commemorates: The Old Testament signifies the Israelites' hurried departure from Egypt, resulting in the baking of unleavened bread due to time constraints. In the New Testament, it corresponds to Jesus' burial, aligning with the period of his entombment.

Other Names: Chag HaMatzot, Festival of Unleavened Bread, Feast of Unleavened Bread, Early Firstfruits

Bible Reference: Exodus 12:8–11; 23:15; 34:18; Leviticus 23:5–6; Numbers 28:17; Deuteronomy 16:3; Matthew 26:17–20

Date Observed: Nisan 15. It lasts for seven days (March or April).

The Exodus: A Journey of Liberation

The Feast of Unleavened Bread is rooted in the historical event of the Exodus when the Israelites were liberated from centuries of Egyptian bondage. This liberation was not just a physical release from slavery but also a spiritual awakening to a new identity as God's chosen people. The Exodus narrative recounts the miraculous interventions of God, from the plagues that beset Egypt to the parting of the Red Sea, demonstrating His power and commitment to freeing His people.

A Symbol of Hasty Departure

The eating of unleavened bread during this feast is a direct reminder of the Israelites' hasty departure from Egypt. In Exodus 12:17–20, we read about the instructions given to the Israelites to eat unleavened bread as a part of their Passover meal. This was because they left Egypt with such urgency that there was no time for their dough to rise. The unleavened bread, therefore, became a powerful symbol of this sudden transition from slavery to freedom, a vivid reminder of the night when they left their lives of bondage behind, embarking on a journey to a land promised by God.

In exploring the Feast of Unleavened Bread, it becomes essential to delve deeper into the symbolism of yeast (leaven) and unleavened bread, elements central to this commemoration, rich in spiritual and historical significance.

Yeast as a Symbol of Sin and Corruption

Yeast is often used symbolically to represent human pride, arrogance, false teachings, hypocrisy, and sinful behavior that can corrupt and lead people away from God's truth and righteousness. This symbolic use of yeast is rooted in its physical properties. Yeast causes fermentation, leading dough to rise by creating pockets of air. This process can represent how sin can permeate and inflate human pride, behavior, and society, often leading to moral decay. In the Exodus context, the Israelites' avoidance of yeast during their flight from Egypt can be viewed as a symbolic act of shedding the corrupt practices they had encountered in Egyptian society.

Here are a few key passages where yeast is used metaphorically in this way:

- **Matthew 16:6:** In this passage, Jesus warns his disciples about the *yeast of the Pharisees and Sadducees*. He is not referring to actual yeast used in bread but is using yeast as a metaphor for the teachings and influence of these religious leaders. Jesus cautions against their hypocrisy and false teachings.

- **1 Corinthians 5:6–8:** The apostle Paul uses yeast to symbolize malice and wickedness in this passage. He advises the Corinthian church to remove the "old yeast" (sinful behavior) so that they may be a "new unleavened batch" (pure and righteous). This metaphor encourages a life of moral purity and righteousness among believers.

- **Galatians 5:9:** Paul warns the Galatians, saying, *A little yeast works through the whole batch of dough*. Here he uses yeast to symbolize false teaching and legalism that can corrupt the true Gospel. He encourages them to resist such influences.

The Bread of Affliction and Purity

Unleavened bread, known as matzah, holds a dual symbolism. Firstly, it is referred to as the bread of affliction, a reminder of the haste with which the Israelites fled Egypt without the luxury of time to let their bread rise. This haste was a critical element of their escape and deliverance, emphasizing the urgency of their departure and the immediacy of God's intervention.

Secondly, unleavened bread symbolizes purity and the stripping away of sin. By removing yeast from their homes and consuming only unleavened bread, the Israelites symbolically cleansed themselves of the leaven of Egypt—the influences and practices incompatible with their renewed covenant with God. Eating unleavened bread becomes a poignant symbol of starting anew, free from the contamination of the past.

The Ritual of Cleansing: Removing Leaven

Cleansing one's home of all leaven before the feast—an act known as Bedikat Chametz—is a profoundly symbolic exercise. It involves a meticulous search for any trace of yeast or leavened bread, symbolizing a thorough examination of one's life to remove sin and moral impurity. This ritual reinforces the theme of purification and renewal central to the feast. What's fascinating is how Bedikat Chametz, deeply rooted in Jewish tradition, carries layers of meaning and symbolism pointing to Jesus and the Holy Spirit (explained in the chapter "Jewish Traditions of Unleavened Bread").

The Bread of Life

The symbolism of unleavened bread is seen in the light of Jesus Christ's teachings. Jesus referred to Himself as the Bread of Life (John 6:35), a reference that ties back to the idea of unleavened bread being pure and free from corruption. This symbolizes Christ's sinless nature and His role as our spiritual sustenance, free from sin's corruption (explained in detail in the chapter "How Unleavened Bread Reveals Messiah").

The Seven-Day Observance

The Feast of Unleavened Bread's seven-day period reflects the Israelites' transformation, symbolizing their journey from a past of sin and corruption towards a future aligned with God's intentions. This annual observance is both a commemoration of the Israelites' liberation and a means to educate younger generations about their heritage and God's miraculous deeds during the Exodus, symbolizing a spiritual journey towards renewal.

The Enduring Legacy of Unleavened Bread

The Feast of Unleavened Bread is more than a ceremonial observance. It is a time of remembrance, reflection, and spiritual renewal. It calls believers to remember the haste and urgency of the Israelites' departure from Egypt, and to reflect on their spiritual journey. This feast is a yearly reminder of the power of God to liberate and transform, echoing through time the eternal message of freedom from bondage and the journey toward a promised, divinely ordained future.

Jewish Traditions of Unleavened Bread

Beyond Matzah

The Feast of Unleavened Bread, or ag HaMatzah, holds a special place in the hearts of Jewish communities worldwide. This festival, deeply rooted in the historical exodus of the Israelites from Egypt, continues to be observed with rituals and customs commemorating the past, and offering profound spiritual insights for today.

Hag HaMatzah begins with searching for and removing all leavened bread from the home. This act is directly correlated to the swift departure of the Israelites from Egypt, as they had no time to let their bread rise. This physical cleansing transcends mere tradition; it symbolizes a spiritual purging, aligning with the commandments in Exodus 12:15 and Leviticus 23:6. The removal of leaven, or chametz, from the home is symbolic of the removal of sin and moral corruption from one's life.

Matzah: The Bread of Affliction

Jewish families consume matzah, an unleavened, simple, unadorned bread, during this week-long festival. Matzah serves as a poignant reminder of the *bread of affliction* eaten by the Israelites in their haste to escape bondage. This humble bread, made quickly without time for leavening, symbolizes the hardships endured during the journey to freedom and the simplicity of life that prioritizes spiritual values over material complexities.

Bedikat Chametz: The Search for Leaven

Bedikat Chametz is a traditional Jewish ritual performed on the evening before Passover. The term Bedikat Chametz translates to the "search for chametz," where chametz refers to leavened bread, or any food product made from wheat, barley, rye, oats, or spelt that has fermented. According to Jewish law, these items are prohibited during Passover.

The process of Bedikat Chametz involves a meticulous search for traces of chametz throughout the home. It's a symbolic act meant to ensure that the household is entirely free of leaven, aligning with the spirit of Passover, which commemorates the Israelites leaving Egypt in haste, without time for their bread to rise.

The ritual usually takes place after nightfall on the evening before Passover begins. The head of the household often conducts the search, traditionally done with a candle or flashlight, a wooden spoon, a feather, and a bag or piece of cloth.

Here is a brief outline of the process:

1. **Preparation:** The process begins with concealing morsels of bread or other leavened foods in various spots within the home for children or family members to discover. This engaging and instructive activity serves as a means of imparting the traditions and importance of Passover to children. To ensure that something is found during the search, small pieces of known chametz are placed around the house in advance, fulfilling the ritual's requirements.

2. **The Search:** Using the light from the candle or flashlight, the person searching looks for chametz in all corners of the home. This thorough search covers areas where chametz would likely to have been dropped or left throughout the year.

3. **Collecting Chametz:** As chametz is found, it is carefully swept up with the feather and placed onto the wooden spoon. The feather allows for a gentle and thorough collection of even the smallest crumbs.

4. **Disposing of Chametz:** Once all the chametz has been collected, it is wrapped in a cloth or bag. The next day it is traditionally burned in a ceremony called Biur Chametz, symbolizing the complete removal of chametz from the home.

5. This ritual, rich in symbolism, not only prepares the home for Passover but also serves as a spiritual exercise, prompting reflection on removing pride and sin (symbolized by chametz) from one's life.

Simplicity in Meals

The meals during the Feast of Unleavened Bread are marked by simplicity, mirroring the essence of the festival. Matzah, serving as a substitute for leavened bread, features prominently in various dishes, reminding participants of the unadorned yet satisfying nature of spiritual purity.

Reflections on Liberation and Renewal

Special services and Torah readings occur in Jewish communities throughout the week, focusing on liberation and spiritual renewal themes. This period is an opportunity to contemplate both the physical and spiritual journey from bondage to freedom, mirroring the Israelites' trek to the Promised Land.

Contemporary Significance

In observing the Feast of Unleavened Bread today, Jews are reminded of the timeless power of faith and the importance of historical remembrance. It presents an opportunity for introspection on one's spiritual journey, embracing a life characterized by simplicity, purity, and righteousness. This festival thus becomes a living narrative, intertwining past and present, and calling for a deeper understanding of faith and a closer walk with our Creator.

In sum, as celebrated today, the Feast of Unleavened Bread continues to be a powerful reminder of the enduring lessons from the Exodus story. It encourages the Jewish community and others who observe it to reflect on their spiritual roots and renew their commitment to a life that upholds the values taught by this time-honored tradition.

How Unleavened Bread Reveals Messiah

CHRIST OUR MANNA

UNLEAVENED BREAD	JESUS
Represents the removal of sin and impurity.	Jesus lived a sinless life, offering Himself as a pure sacrifice.
Passover requirement representing a quick departure, no rise time.	Passover fulfillment: deliverance from sin's bondage.
A reminder of deliverance.	Our Deliverer
Represents the absence of sin.	Jesus lived a sinless life.
During preparation, unleavened bread is striped and pierced.	Jesus' body was striped by whips and pierced at the crucifixion.
Afikoman is wrapped in a cloth or bag before being hidden.	Jesus' body was wrapped in linen before being placed in the tomb.
The Afikoman must be redeemed or back to the head of the household.	Christ is the Redeemer, offering Himself as a ransom for many.
God provided manna that sustained the Israelites while wandering in the desert.	Jesus is "bread of life" in John 6:35, spiritual sustenance, nutrition and satisfaction for eternity.

The Feast of Unleavened Bread is a joyful part of the Bible's rich traditions. This memorable holiday, beginning on the fifteenth day of Nisan overflows with meaningful symbols and rituals that shine a light on Jesus Christ's vital mission of salvation.

A Symbol of Christ's Purity

The unleavened bread, or matzah, used during this feast is devoid of leaven—a biblical metaphor for sin and moral corruption (1 Corinthians 5:6–8). In the same way, the absence of leaven in the matzah speaks profoundly to the sinless nature of Christ. He is the embodiment of purity, integrity, and holiness, untainted by the corruption of sin, much like the unleavened bread is free from the leaven's influence.

In the Gospel of John (John 6:35), Jesus declares Himself the Bread of Life. This profound statement gains even greater depth against the backdrop of the Feast of Unleavened Bread. Just as the matzah was a staple for the Israelites, sustaining them on their journey to liberation, so does Christ offer Himself the spiritual sustenance essential for our journey toward eternal life.

Moreover, Jesus symbolizes the manna provided by Heaven during the Israelites' wilderness journey. This bread from Heaven was a miraculous provision for physical sustenance, yet Jesus presents Himself as the true manna, offering spiritual nourishment that satisfies the deepest human soul's hunger.

The Physical Attributes of Matzah

The matzah, in its simple, pierced, and striped form, powerfully symbolizes Christ's redemptive suffering and agony and the depth of His sacrificial love; as the Messiah endured stripes for our sins and was pierced for our transgressions, His wounds brought us healing.

A Call to Sanctification and Holiness

The Feast of Unleavened Bread is a commemorative occasion urging believers to pursue holiness and sanctification, much like the Israelites' removal of leaven from their homes. We, too, aspire to lead lives marked by separation from sin and moral compromise, mirroring the Israelites' expulsion of leaven. This festival calls us to adopt a lifestyle that mirrors the purity and simplicity of Christ, allowing us to exist in the world without being contaminated by it.

Christ's Fulfillment of the Feast

In His death and resurrection, Jesus Christ brought the profound symbolism embedded in the Feast of Unleavened Bread to fruition. Like the unleavened bread, Christ's body did not undergo corruption in the grave (Acts 2:31). His resurrection signifies the ultimate victory over sin and death, capturing the essence of this feast's symbolism.

Embracing the Spiritual Riches

As we observe the Feast of Unleavened Bread, we can delve into its deeper spiritual meanings. It is a time to meditate on Christ's purity and simplicity, nourish our souls on Him as the Bread of Life and true manna from Heaven, and heed the call to a sanctified life. We are encouraged to depend on Jesus daily for our spiritual needs. This involves seeking his guidance, strength, and wisdom daily.

The unleavened bread stands as a lasting symbol of Christ's perfect sacrifice, a testament to His boundless love, and a guiding light for us to walk in His footsteps, liberated from the leaven of sin and imbued with the joy of His salvation.

Celebrating Unleavened Bread

Reflections and Teachings

The Feast of Unleavened Bread, an integral part of the Jewish liturgical calendar, extends beyond its historical significance, offering profound personal applications for believers today. This chapter explores how the principles embodied in this ancient festival can be woven into the fabric of our daily lives.

To apply the lessons of the Feast of Unleavened Bread, one must first understand its spiritual significance. The removal of leaven from the homes of the Israelites symbolizes a purging of sin and impurity. This act represents a conscious decision to eliminate the leaven of moral corruption, echoing the commandments in Exodus 12:15 and Leviticus 23:6. In our lives, this translates to a meticulous examination of our hearts and behaviors, identifying and eliminating attitudes and actions that hinder our spiritual growth.

Embracing Simplicity and Purity

Matzah during the Feast of Unleavened Bread calls for a life of simplicity and purity, urging a focus on spiritual over material values and joy in faith and community. It's a time for sanctification, living with integrity, honesty, and love, mirroring Christ's sinless nature. The Bedikat Chametz ritual symbolizes the Holy Spirit's role in purifying us from sin, akin to light exposing darkness. Forgiveness, a key teaching of Jesus, highlights the harm of holding onto unforgiveness and the cleansing power of mutual forgiveness, essential for spiritual health and growth. This underscores the need to remove spiritual "leaven" from our lives, promoting renewal and integrity.

Steps for The Search

1. **Preparation and Prayer:** Begin with a prayer time, asking the Holy Spirit to reveal any chametz in your life. This could be habits, attitudes, or actions that hinder your spiritual growth or relationship with God.

2. **The Search:** Use a candle or flashlight to represent Jesus' light. As you search your home for physical leaven, reflect on areas of your life that might need spiritual cleansing.

3. **Using the Feather and Wooden Spoon:** As you gather leavened products, use a feather and a wooden spoon (as in the Jewish tradition), symbolizing gentle guidance, and the support of the Holy Spirit in removing sin, and placing it on the wooden cross. Parallel this physical action with the introspection of sweeping away spiritual shortcomings.

4. **Disposal and Reflection:** Dispose of the collected items, symbolizing the casting away of sins. This can be accompanied by a prayer of repentance and a commitment to embrace a life following God's ways.

5. **Celebration of the Unleavened Bread:** Embrace the period of the Feast of Unleavened Bread by studying Scripture, particularly focusing on passages related to purification, sanctification, and the work of the Holy Spirit. Share unleavened bread as a family or community, reflecting on Jesus, the Bread of Life, who was without sin.

Living Out the Festival's Themes

To live out the themes of the Feast of Unleavened Bread, we should strive to embody its lessons in our daily routines and relationships. This could involve cultivating a spirit of humility, embracing opportunities for service and compassion, and seeking ways to extend the love and liberation we have experienced in Christ to others.

Conclusion

The personal application of the Feast of Unleavened Bread is a journey of ongoing transformation. It challenges us to continually purge the leaven of sin from our lives, to embrace simplicity and purity, and to commit ourselves anew to God's ways. In doing so, we honor the spirit of the feast and grow closer to embodying the principles it represents—freedom from bondage, spiritual renewal, and a life dedicated to following God's ways. Thus, this festival becomes a historical observance and a catalyst for personal growth and spiritual maturity.

Unleavened Bread Recipes
Flavors of Freedom

Matzah

Here's a simple recipe for homemade matzah, an unleavened bread suitable for Passover. Remember, matzah for Passover is made quickly to avoid fermentation, ideally in less than 18 minutes from start to finish (a rabbinical rule, not a biblical rule).

Ingredients
2 cups all-purpose flour
½ to ¾ cup water
1 tsp of kosher salt (optional)

Instructions

- Preheat your oven to 475°F (245°C). The stove must be scorching hot.

- Mix the flour and salt (if using). Gradually add water, mixing until the dough comes together. Be careful not to overmix or knead the dough too much.

- Divide the dough into small balls. On a well-floured surface, roll each ball as thin as possible. The thinner you roll the dough, the crisper your matzah will be. Aim for a thickness of about ⅛ inch or less.

- Use a fork to prick holes all over the surface of each piece. This prevents the dough from puffing up in the oven and ensures it stays flat.

- Place the rolled-out dough on a baking sheet, without parchment paper or greasing.

- Bake in the preheated oven for about 2 to 3 minutes, then flip and bake for another 2 minutes or until the pieces are lightly browned and crisp. Watch them closely, as they can burn quickly.

- Remove the matzah from the oven and let it cool on a wire rack.

- Serve your homemade matzah as a substitute for bread during Passover. Store any leftovers in an airtight container to keep them crisp.

Dutch Baby or German Pancake

Ingredients
3 eggs
½ cup all-purpose flour
½ cup whole milk
½ cup powdered sugar for dusting (optional)
2 tbs butter
1 tsp vanilla extract (optional)
Pinch of salt

Instructions

- Preheat the oven to 425°F.

- Melt the butter in a 10-inch cast iron or oven-safe skillet over medium heat. Swirl the pan to coat the bottom and sides.

- In a large bowl, whisk together the eggs, flour, milk, vanilla extract and salt until smooth and combined. Do not over-mix.

- Pour the batter into the preheated skillet with the melted butter. Immediately place the skillet in the oven.

- Bake for 15–17 minutes until puffed and golden brown. Do not open the oven during the baking time.

- Remove from the oven, dust with powdered sugar if desired, and serve immediately. The pancake will quickly fall, so transfer to plates right away to enjoy the oven-risen puff.
  Serve with fresh lemon juice and powdered sugar, maple syrup or fresh fruit toppings.

Unleavened Bread Questions

Illuminating Reflections

These questions are designed to help you delve deeper into the significance of the Feast of Unleavened Bread and its fulfillment in Jesus, encouraging a lifestyle that reflects the purity, liberation, and spiritual nourishment that He embodies.

1. How does the Feast of Unleavened Bread, commemorating the Israelites' exodus from Egypt, relate to your journey from bondage to freedom in your spiritual life?

2. In what ways can you identify with the Israelites' experience of a sudden transition from slavery to freedom? How does this inspire changes in your own life?

3. How does the symbolism of unleavened bread as purity and the casting off of sin resonate with your spiritual purification process?

4. What leavens in your life must you remove to embrace a purer, more Christ-like existence?

5. How can Bedikat Chametz (removing leaven) be applied metaphorically to your spiritual life? What steps can you take to cleanse your life from sin and impurity?

6. Reflect on Jesus' statement of being the Bread of Life. How does this deepen your understanding of the sustenance He provides in contrast to the temporary sustenance of the physical unleavened bread?

7. What action can you take to incorporate Jesus as your spiritual sustenance into your daily life and decisions?

8. How do you interpret the seven-day duration of the Feast of Unleavened Bread in the context of your spiritual journey? What does this period signify about growth and transition in faith?

9. What lessons can you learn from the Israelites' journey that apply to your spiritual walk today?

10. How can the themes of liberation, purification, and transition observed during the Feast of Unleavened Bread inspire your actions and choices in the present?

11. Consider practical ways to remember and celebrate God's provision and protection in your life, akin to the Israelites' remembrance during the Feast.

12. How does understanding Christ as the ultimate fulfillment of the Feast's symbolism affect your appreciation of His sacrifice?

13. What steps can you take to live a life that honors Jesus' sacrifice and embodies the purity symbolized by unleavened bread?

As we explore the rich biblical heritage of this holy season, may the Feast of Unleavened Bread nourish our spirits with its themes of liberation, purification, and remembrance. Through studying Christ's fulfillment of its symbols, may we walk in the newness of life, removing sin's leaven and feeding on the Bread of Heaven? Let this period of reflection establish practical patterns of embracing true freedom in Him, maintaining spiritual purity, giving thanks, and growing into His image. May we journey ever deeper into the abundance of His table, our lives reflecting the unleavened holiness we have received.

Feast of Firstfruits

The Third Spring Holiday

FEAST OF FIRSTFRUITS
THE THIRD SPRING HOLIDAY

OTHER NAMES:
Bikkurim, Reshit Katzir, Yom HaBikkurim,

BIBLE REFERENCE:
Exodus 23:19; Leviticus 2:12–14; 23:9–14; James 1:18; 1 Corinthians 15:20

DATE OBSERVED:
Starting on the second day of Passover, the 16th of Nisan (March or April)

COMMEMORATES:
This Old Testament feast marks the initial harvest, while in the New Testament, it symbolizes Christ's resurrection as the firstfruits of those resurrected.

BRIEF INTRODUCTION:
Linked with Passover and the Festival of Unleavened Bread, Firstfruits celebrates the barley harvest with an offering to God, symbolizing physical liberation and a spiritual harvest.

Feast of Firstfruits Overview

Brief Introduction: Linked with Passover and the Feast of Unleavened Bread, Firstfruits celebrates the barley harvest with an offering to God, symbolizing physical liberation and a spiritual harvest.

Commemorates: This Old Testament feast marks the initial harvest, while in the New Testament it symbolizes Christ's resurrection as the firstfruits of those resurrected.

Other Names: Bikkurim, Reshit Katzir, Yom HaBikkurim, Later Firstfruits

Bible References: Exodus 23:19; Leviticus 2:12–14; 23:9–14; James 1:18; 1 Corinthians 15:20

Date Observed: Starting on the second day of Passover, the sixteenth of Nisan (March or April)

Origins and Observances

The Firstfruits festival occurs during Passover and early spring, marking the beginning of the barley harvest in Israel. As the first agricultural harvest of the year, Firstfruits signifies new life and anticipation of greater harvests. It gets its name from the custom of bringing the initial, best portions of the barley crop as an offering of thanksgiving to God.

The significance of Firstfruits builds on Passover's redemption narrative. Passover represents deliverance from bondage, while Firstfruits signals a flourishing, fruitful life after liberation. Just as the first crops begin Israel's harvest season with the expectation of provision ahead, so too, Christ's resurrection as the "Firstfruits of those who have fallen asleep" (1 Cor 15:20) inaugurates our eternal life while anticipating full salvation yet to come.

Firstfruits thus links Passover's freedom from slavery to the ultimate hope of resurrection and life everlasting made possible by Jesus, the firstborn from the dead. By overcoming death, Christ's resurrection harvests a new creation and guarantees that we who belong to Him will also rise and reign (1 Cor 15:21-23).

Historical Significance

The Feast of Firstfruits represented a significant shift for the Israelites, contrasting their time in Egypt where Pharaoh claimed the fruits of their labor. This observance in the Promised Land symbolized their move from oppression to autonomy, marking their transition to a free, sovereign nation.

Spiritual and Agricultural Significance

Firstfruits is a metaphor for dedication and trust in God's provision, both agriculturally and spiritually. It involved a communal harvest and presentation of the first mature barley as a sacred offering. This practice highlighted the Jews' dependency on God for sustenance.

In the New Testament, Christ is portrayed as the firstfruits of resurrection, heralding a new era and the hope of resurrection for believers.

Enduring Significance

Reflecting on Firstfruits today reminds us of the importance of gratitude and dedication to God. It symbolizes our commitment to prioritize God in our lives, embodying trust in His provision, and acknowledging His sovereignty over Creation.

Jewish Traditions of Firstfruits

FIELD TO TEMPLE CEREMONIES

While the physical Temple no longer stands, the essence of the Firstfruits, a mitzvah in Judaism, is a commandment or law prescribed by God. It encompasses both religious obligations and moral conduct as outlined in the Torah, and the term is often used to refer to any good deed or act of kindness in various forms. The story of Bikkurim is now seamlessly integrated into the Passover haggadah. The seder plate, filled with symbolic items, mirrors the Bikkurim basket, transforming the Passover seder into a modern-day embodiment of the Firstfruits ritual. This is a time for recounting the Exodus and offering thanks to God.

During this time, the Israelites were mandated to journey to Jerusalem, bringing with them the premier yield of that year's harvest. In ancient times, consumption or sale of the season's new crops was forbidden until a symbolic sheaf of green barley had been presented and waved before the Lord by the priests, as stated in Leviticus 23:14.

The fundamental principle of Firstfruits—acknowledging the good (hakarat hatov)—remains crucial in Jewish tradition. It serves as a reminder to recognize God as the fountain of all blessings. Let's explore how the ancient Jews observed this tradition, including the Counting of the Omer.

Ancient Jewish Traditions

In the rich tapestry of Jewish history and worship, the ancient practice of offering firstfruits stood as a heartfelt expression of gratitude and recognition of God's provision. It was a vivid act of faith.

The mitzvah of Firstfruits originated in the fields of Israel. A farmer would mark the initial budding fruits by tying a reed around them, dedicating them as "first fruits." This was particularly significant for the seven species of plants Israel is known for (wheat, barley, grapes, figs, pomegranates, olive oil, and dates). The process of bringing these first fruits to the Temple, from Feast of Weeks to

Hanukkah, was filled with spiritual meaning.

The Journey of the Firstfruits to Jerusalem

The journey to Jerusalem with the first fruits displayed faith and community unity. The wealthy and the poor participated, with varying degrees of luxury in their offerings. The procession was a communal event, where people would gather and set out for Jerusalem, accompanied by the music of flutes and recitations of psalms.

Upon arrival in Jerusalem, a festive atmosphere welcomed the pilgrims. The offering of the first fruits in the Temple was a solemn act. The farmer and high priest would perform a ceremonial wave of the basket of produce, reciting a declaration highlighting Israel's history and God's faithfulness.

Food Traditions

During the Bikkurim celebration, the specific types of food served would typically include:

- **Fresh Fruits and Grains:** Since Bikkurim coincides with the start of the barley harvest, fresh grains and early fruits from the harvest were central to the celebration. This would include barley, wheat, and the first fruits of the season.

- **Seven Species of Israel:** Often the offerings would include the seven plant species mentioned in the Bible (Deuteronomy 8:8)—wheat, barley, grapes (or wine), figs, pomegranates, olives (or olive oil), and dates (or honey).

- **Bread and Baked Goods:** Freshly baked bread and other baked goods made from the new grain might be included, symbolizing the beginning of the grain harvest.

- **Vegetables and Legumes:** Depending on the local harvest and agricultural practices, a variety of vegetables and legumes might also be part of the feast.

- **Traditional Dishes:** In modern celebrations, traditional dishes specific to the cultural and ethnic backgrounds of the participants would also be included, often prepared using the fresh produce of the season.

Counting of the Omer

Agricultural Significance: The Counting of the Omer originates as an agricultural ritual in ancient Israel, marking the time from barley to wheat harvest. Beginning with an omer of barley offered on Passover's second day, it celebrates the season's first harvest and ends with the wheat harvest at Feast of Weeks

(Shavuot), reflecting gratitude for Divine provision.

Spiritual Reflection: Beyond its agricultural roots, this period serves as a time for introspection and spiritual preparation for the Feast of Weeks, which commemorates the giving of the Torah. Daily blessings and the omer count encourage anticipation, spiritual growth, and reflection on Torah values.

Customs: The Counting of the Omer is observed with traditions of semi-mourning and ethical study, particularly Pirkei Avot—a collection of rabbinical wisdom emphasizing moral conduct. These practices underscore a period of communal and personal improvement.

In Anticipation of Renewal: Beyond remembering the past, the Counting of the Omer and the study of Firstfruits express a yearning for the Temple's restoration and the resumption of its rituals. This anticipation strengthens faith and connection to Torah teachings, looking forward to a time of spiritual and physical renewal in God's perpetual benevolence.

How Firstfruits Reveals Messiah

Christ Our Firstfruits

FIRSTFRUITS	JESUS
First portion of crop harvest	God's firstborn son, Only begotten of Father.
Marks the start of the harvest season.	First to rise from the dead, inaugurating new life.
Symbol of Hope: Represents anticipation of the harvest to come.	Hope of Salvation: Jesus' resurrection as the guarantee of eternal life.
Acknowledgment of God's provision and faithfulness.	Embodiment of God's promise and faithfulness to humanity.
Demonstrates commitment of entire harvest yet to come.	Christ's resurrection inaugurates multitudes more being raised to new life
Firstfruits were the best produce offered to God	Jesus's whole life was dedicated and offered up to God, the first and best sacrifice.
Integral part of Mosaic Law, embodying obedience and devotion.	Fulfills and transcends the Law, revealing the spiritual essence of the New Covenant.

The offering of the firstfruits carries deep meaning, foreshadowing and illuminating the life and mission of Jesus Christ. This tradition of presenting the firstfruits symbolizes Jesus' resurrection, the first among all believers. Paul, in his first letter to the Corinthians, compares Christ to the first sheaf of barley harvested, indicating the beginning of a great and forthcoming harvest.

The Firstfruits ceremony involved the offering of the firstfruits and best produce of the harvest at the Temple as an expression of gratitude and acknowledgment of God's providence. This ritual was an act of trust, symbolizing the Israelites' dependence on God's continued blessings and provision. The very act of offering the firstfruits and not waiting until the full harvest was gathered was a profound expression of faith and reliance on God.

Christ as the Firstfruits of the Resurrection

The concept of firstfruits is given a new dimension in the resurrection of Jesus Christ. As Apostle Paul writes in 1 Corinthians 15:20:

> *But now Christ is risen from the dead, a*
> *nd has become the firstfruits of those who have fallen asleep.*

This powerful verse encapsulates Jesus' resurrection as the firstfruits of all future resurrections. Paul employs the familiar metaphor of firstfruits already established in the Old Testament—a concept readily grasped by his audience.

As the first crops to ripen, firstfruits held special significance. They represented the initial portion and a promise of greater abundance in the full harvest. Presenting firstfruits was an act of dedication and thanksgiving for all that God will provide.

Similarly, Jesus, as the first to rise from death, signals our coming resurrection. His defeat of death kickstarts God's total victory over death. Death no longer has the final say! Just as firstfruits came as the earliest preview of fields full of grain, Christ emerged first from the grave as a preview of countless more to follow in God's full harvest of resurrected people.

Paul envisions Jesus arising as a new type of firstfruits. Not simply produce, but the first person experiencing bodily resurrection into eternal, glorified life. As the firstfruits were set apart and offered back to God, Jesus was set apart in resurrection for God's glory. His resurrection guarantees ours as part of God's ultimate triumph over death. We can fully trust that Christ's firstfruits resurrection has opened the way for our own. What glorious hope and assurance this brings!

The agricultural firstfruits symbolism would have resonated profoundly with the early church. They grasped Jesus as the human embodiment of this concept—the first and best beloved Son raised as a preview of God's eschatological victory over the grave. The firstfruits vividly prefigure and point toward Christ, the ultimate firstfruits pledged to God.

The Dedication of Christ

During Firstfruits, the finest harvest was dedicated to God, mirroring Jesus Christ's life of dedication and ultimate sacrifice, embodying the perfect offering for humanity's redemption. This act was both a thanksgiving and a trust in God's future provisions. Jesus represents this divine provision, being the "Bread of Life" (John 6:35), fulfilling our spiritual needs and guaranteeing our eternal destiny.

Christ: The Fulfillment of the Law

The practice of Firstfruits, part of the Law given to Moses, finds its fulfillment in Jesus Christ. *He came not to abolish the Law but to fulfill it (*Matthew 5:17). In Him, the deeper spiritual meanings of the Law, including Firstfruits are revealed. Christ embodies the true essence of the Law—love, sacrifice, and total dedication to God's will.

Resurrection and Eternal Life

The Feast of Firstfruits is a powerful metaphor for understanding the work of Jesus. It teaches us about offering our best to God, acknowledging His provision in our lives, and living in a relationship of trust and dependence on Him. Bikkurim, in its essence, points to Jesus Christ—the firstfruits of a new creation, the ultimate offering and provision of God, and the fulfillment of the Law's deepest spiritual truths.

Firstfruits reminds us of the hope, assurance, and the new life we have in Christ. As believers, reflecting on Firstfruits invites us into a deeper appreciation of Jesus's sacrificial love and the profound truths of our faith.

Spiritual Symbolism

When the Israelites brought the first and best of their harvest to the altar, they were doing more than fulfilling a divine command; they were actively remembering and commemorating God's deliverance of their ancestors from bondage in Egypt and His faithful provision in bringing them into the Promised Land—a land flowing with milk and honey. This act was a tangible acknowledgment of God's sovereignty over all Creation and His abundant generosity.

Each time the Israelites presented their firstfruits, they were reaffirming their national history and identity. This was an act steeped in worship and gratitude, a celebration of God's continual care, and a public declaration of their trust in His ongoing provision.

Lessons from the Harvest

Biblical grain harvesting, unlike today's mechanized methods, was a labor-intensive task demanding patience and resilience, as farmers used sickles under the sun. This physical labor mirrored a spiritual journey, paralleling the diligence in our spiritual walk with God. The cycle of sowing, caring, waiting, and reaping reflects the spiritual disciplines of prayer, studying the Word, faith, and service, emphasizing that a fruitful spiritual life, like a successful harvest, requires careful planning, consistent effort, and patient waiting.

An Expression of Faith

The Israelites' act of offering the first and best of their produce to God was a profound expression of faith, recognizing that all blessings and fruitful harvests come from Him. This practice teaches a crucial lesson for believers today: offering our firstfruits—be it time, talents, resources, or service—affirms our trust in God's provision and prioritizes Him in our lives. The tradition of Firstfruits symbolizes gratitude, faith, and reliance on God, reminding us of His past deliverance, present provision, and future promises. Reflecting on this ancient practice encourages us to give our best to God and trust in His perpetual care, embodying a spiritual journey of remembrance, gratitude, and deepening faith.In the simple yet profound act of offering the firstfruits, we find a powerful metaphor for our spiritual journey. It is a journey marked by remembrance, gratitude, and faith—a journey that leads us closer to the heart of God.

Counting of the Omer

The Counting of the Omer and the period from Jesus' resurrection to Pentecost both symbolize a journey from physical liberation to spiritual revelation. They reflect transitions from the Exodus and resurrection, representing freedom from bondage and sin, to receiving the Law at Sinai and the Holy Spirit at Pentecost, signifying divine empowerment and guidance. These times are for anticipation, reflection, and preparation, leading to pivotal moments of divine encounter. This theme of moving from liberation to revelation highlights a deep connection in the relationship with God.

Celebrating Firstfruits
Gratitude and Recognition

Observing Firstfruits is an opportunity to reflect on the growth of our faith in Christ. We can draw inspiration from the barley that matures and ripens, just as our faith should mature over time. Here are practical steps to observe Firstfruits and grow in your faith.

Counting the Omer

Between Firstfruits and the Feast of Weeks (Shavuot) is a period known as the Counting of the Omer (Sefirat HaOmer). It lasts for forty-nine days, and each day is a time of reflection and spiritual growth. This counting is a tradition that connects Firstfruits to the Feast of Weeks, much like the way Christ's resurrection links to the outpouring of the Holy Spirit.

Waving the omer is a ceremonial practice associated with the biblical holiday of Firstfruits (Bikkurim). It involves the waving of a sheaf of newly harvested barley before the Lord as a symbolic gesture of gratitude and dedication.

Here's a description of how waving the omer is typically performed:

- **Gathering the Barley Harvest:** The journey begins with collecting a barley sheaf from the fields, symbolizing the inaugural harvest and heralding the start of the grain gathering season.

- **Binding the Sheaf:** The harvested barley is meticulously tied into a bundle, representing the finest early produce. The bundle needs to remain whole and flawless, epitomizing the purity of the initial offerings.

- **Presentation to the Divine:** In alignment with tradition, particularly during the Feast of Unleavened Bread, the barley sheaf is transported to a sacred site, historically the Temple in Jerusalem. This ritual is observed in synagogues or within Messianic communities in contemporary practices.

- **Ceremonial Waving:** A priest or appointed individual lifts the barley sheaf, conducting a ritual wave in all cardinal directions—east, west, north, and south—while facing the altar or congregation. This gesture is a poignant tribute to the Divine, recognizing His bounty and dominion over the crops.

- **Invocations and Gratitude:** Amidst the sheaf's waving, prayers and blessings are voiced, expressing gratitude for the earth's yield and soliciting Divine favor for the forthcoming harvest.

- **The Omer Countdown:** Following the sheaf's presentation, the Counting of the Omer commences, spanning forty-nine days until the Feast of Weeks. This period marks a spiritual expedition of introspection and development.

- **The Symbolism of Waving of the Omer:** This act is a powerful reminder of God's sustenance, His role as the supreme provider, and the significance of thankfulness within the rural traditions of ancient Israel. Furthermore, it underscores spiritual anticipation, mirroring the anticipation for the Law's revelation at the Feast of Weeks and the arrival of the Holy Spirit at Pentecost (Shavuot).

Despite variations in practice among Jewish and Messianic communities, the essence of this tradition remains intact, fostering a time of spiritual reflection and growth. To enrich this period, consider engaging in:

- **Scripture Meditation:** Reflect on specific Bible verses that resonate with renewal and spiritual evolution themes.

- **Character Studies:** Examine the narratives of biblical figures who underwent significant transformation, drawing parallels to your own spiritual journey.

- **Book Study:** Delve into biblical texts pertinent to the omer's themes, like Exodus or Psalms, exploring their relevance to gratitude and spiritual maturation.

- **Topical Studies:** Investigate spiritual themes such as gratitude or humility, examining biblical insights on these virtues.

- **Comparative Studies**: Analyze the connections between Old and New Testament teachings about omer's journey.

- **Bible Commentaries:** Utilize commentaries for a deeper understanding of relevant scriptures.

- **Group Discussions:** Share and discuss insights with others observing the omer, enriching your collective spiritual journey.

- **Devotional Readings:** Find daily devotional materials focused on the omer, offering guidance and reflection.

- **Study of Jewish Traditions:** Explore the historical and cultural backdrop of the Counting of the Omer.

- **Personal Journaling:** Document your reflections and spiritual growth during this period through journaling.

Conclusion

The Feast of Firstfruits blends faith with the natural cycle, emphasizing dedication and renewal. It teaches us to offer the first of our harvest and our lives to God, mirroring our commitment to prioritize Him. This act of offering, similar to presenting barley, marks our faith journey, where we grow spiritually, like seeds blossoming into life.

It draws a parallel between the nurturing of crops and our spiritual development, encouraging reliance on God and deepening our connection with Him. Moreover, this feast symbolizes renewal, reminding us of our faith's rebirth and growth potential. Celebrating God's past faithfulness and our future growth, the Feast of Firstfruits urges us to deepen our relationship with the Divine, showcasing the intertwined paths of faith, renewal, and spiritual growth.

Firstfruits Recipes
CELEBRATING NEW BEGINNINGS

The Feast of Fruitfruits is an occasion to celebrate with fresh, seasonal produce. Here are some recipes that could be fitting for such a celebration.

Barley and Fresh Herb Salad Recipe

This salad is healthy and full of fresh flavors, making it an excellent dish for any occasion.

Ingredients
1 cup pearl barley
3 cups water or vegetable broth
1 cucumber, diced
1 red bell pepper, diced
½ cup cherry tomatoes, halved
½ cup fresh parsley, chopped
¼ cup fresh mint, chopped
¼ cup fresh cilantro, chopped (optional)
3–4 green onions, thinly sliced
¼ cup olive oil
2 tbs lemon juice
1 garlic clove, minced
Optional: feta cheese, crumbled

Instructions

- **Cook the Barley:** Rinse the barley under cold water. In a medium saucepan, bring water or vegetable broth to a boil. Add barley and reduce heat to a simmer. Cover and cook for 30–45 minutes until the barley is tender and the liquid is absorbed. Remove from heat and let it cool.

- **Prepare the Vegetables:** While the barley is cooking, dice the cucumber and red bell pepper and slice the cherry tomatoes. Chop the parsley, mint, and cilantro.

- **Make the Dressing:** Whisk together olive oil, lemon juice, minced garlic, salt and pepper in a small bowl.

- **Combine the Salad:** Combine the cooled barley, cucumber, red bell pepper, cherry tomatoes, parsley, mint, cilantro, and green onions in a large bowl. Pour the dressing over the salad and toss well to coat.

- **Season and Serve:** Taste and adjust the seasoning with additional salt, pepper, or lemon juice. Sprinkle with crumbled feta cheese just before serving.

- **Chill (Optional):** For the best flavor, let the salad chill in the refrigerator for an hour before serving. This allows the flavors to meld together.
  Serve: Serve the salad chilled or at room temperature. It's perfect as a side dish or light lunch.

Stuffed Dates with Almonds and Honey

- **Ingredients:** Medjool dates, whole almonds, honey, and a pinch of cinnamon.

- **Preparation**: Slit the dates on one side and remove the pits. Insert an almond into each date. Drizzle with honey and sprinkle a touch of cinnamon. Serve as a sweet snack.

Olive Tapenade

Ingredients
1 cup pitted olives (a mix of green and black olives for varied flavor)
2 tbs capers, rinsed and drained
1–2 garlic cloves, minced
2 tbs fresh parsley, chopped
1 tsp fresh lemon juice
2–3 tbs extravirgin olive oil
Black pepper to taste
Optional: 1 tsp anchovy paste or 1–2 anchovy fillets (omit for a vegetarian version)

Instructions

- **Prepare the Olives and Capers:** If the olives are particularly salty, rinse them quickly under cold water. Drain them well, along with the capers.

- **Chop Ingredients:** Finely chop the olives, capers, and garlic. You can do this by hand for a chunkier texture or use a food processor for a smoother spread. If using a food processor, pulse to avoid turning it into a puree.

- **Mix Ingredients:** In a bowl, combine the chopped olives, capers, and garlic. Stir in the chopped parsley. Add the lemon juice and mix well.

- **Add Olive Oil:** Gradually stir in the olive oil until the mixture is spreadable but not too oily. If you're using anchovy paste or fillets, mix them in at this stage.

- **Season:** Add a bit of freshly ground black pepper. Taste and adjust the seasoning. Be cautious with salt, as the olives and capers already bring saltiness.

- **Serve:** Transfer the tapenade to a serving bowl. It can be served immediately, but letting it sit for an hour will enhance the flavors.

Serving Suggestions

- Use it as a spread on matzah, crusty bread or toast points
- Serve on crackers as an appetizer
- Use as a topping for grilled chicken or fish
- Mix it into pasta for a quick and flavorful sauce.
- **Storage:** Olive tapenade can be stored in an airtight container in the refrigerator for up to one week. The olive oil may solidify slightly when cold, so it's best to let it come to room temperature before serving.

Fig and Pomegranate Salad

Here's a delightful recipe for fig and pomegranate salad, perfect for enjoying during any special occasion:

Ingredients
6-8 fresh figs, quartered
1 cup pomegranate seeds
4 cups mixed greens (such as arugula, spinach, or baby kale)
½ cup crumbled goat cheese (feta)
½ cup walnuts toasted and chopped
3 tbs olive oil
2 tbs balsamic vinegar
1 tbs honey
1 tsp Dijon mustard
Salt and pepper to taste

Instructions

- **Prepare the Dressing:** Whisk together the olive oil, balsamic vinegar, honey, and Dijon mustard in a small bowl until well blended. Season the dressing with salt and pepper according to taste.

- **Assemble the Salad:** Combine the mixed greens, quartered figs and pomegranate seeds in a large salad bowl. Drizzle the prepared dressing over the salad and gently toss to coat the ingredients evenly.

- **Add Cheese and Nuts:** Sprinkle crumbled goat cheese and toasted walnuts over the top of the salad.

- **Final Touches:** Give the salad a final gentle toss to evenly distribute the cheese and nuts. Taste, and adjust the seasoning if necessary.
  Serve: Serve the salad chilled. It pairs wonderfully as a side dish with a variety of main courses.

Enjoy the sweet and tangy flavors of this salad, a perfect embodiment of the freshness and vibrancy of Bikkurim!

Firstfruits Questions

Illuminating Reflections

The Feast of Firstfruits, a time of offering and gratitude, invites us to contemplate this biblical festival's deeper spiritual meanings and applications. As we reflect on the themes of provision, dedication, and trust in God's provision, these questions aim to encourage a deeper understanding and practical application of the principles represented by the firstfruits in our lives.

1. How can offering the firstfruits be applied in your life today? What "firstfruits" can you offer God as a symbol of gratitude and trust?

2. Reflect on how offering the first and best of your resources, time or talents to God might change your perspective on stewardship and dependence on Him.

3. Considering the Israelites' offering of the firstfruits as an act of gratitude, how can you cultivate a more thankful heart for God's provisions in your own life?

4. What specific ways can you express your gratitude to God for His blessings, both big and small?

5. The Feast of Firstfruits commemorates the Israelites' journey from slavery to freedom. How does this historical event mirror the spiritual liberation you experience in Christ?

6. How can you celebrate and remember your own journey from bondage (sin, despair, hopelessness, etc.) to freedom in Christ?

7. Offering the firstfruits required the Israelites' trust in God's future provision. How can you demonstrate a similar faith in God's care and provision for your future needs?

8. Reflect on a time when you had to rely on God for provision. How did that experience strengthen your faith?

9. How does understanding Jesus as the Firstfruits of those raised from the

dead (1 Corinthians 15:20) enhance your understanding of the resurrection and eternal life?

10. In what ways can the concept of Jesus as the Firstfruits of the dead influence your daily walk with Him?

11. The Feast of Firstfruits was closely tied to the harvest. How can this symbolism guide you to seek a spiritual harvest in your own life, in areas such as personal growth, relationships, or ministry?

12. What steps can you take to nurture and cultivate areas in your life that need growth and maturing?

13. The Israelites offered their firstfruits in celebration of their physical and spiritual liberation. What does liberation in Christ mean to you personally?

14. Identify areas in your life where you have experienced or are seeking liberation through Christ.

15. How can the Feast of Firstfruits principles—gratitude, provision, dedication, and trust—be more fully integrated into your daily life and spiritual practices?

These questions are designed to help you delve into the significance of the Feast of Firstfruits and its fulfillment in Jesus, encouraging a lifestyle that reflects gratitude, trust in God's provision, and dedication to Him.

Feast of Weeks

The Fourth Spring Holiday

FEAST OF WEEKS
THE FOURTH SPRING HOLIDAY

OTHER NAMES
Feast of Weeks, Yom HaBikkurim, Atzeret Zman Matan Torateinu (the giving of the Torah), and Pentecost

BIBLE REFERENCE:
Exodus 34:22; Leviticus 23:15–22; Deuteronomy 16:9–12; Numbers 28:26

DATE OBSERVED
The sixth day of Sivan in the Hebrew calendar, typically falling in late May or early June.

COMMEMORATES
In the Old Testament, giving of the Torah at Mount Sinai and the wheat harvest. In the New Testament it is about the coming of the Holy Spirit.

BRIEF INTRODUCTION
Celebrates the wheat harvest and the receiving of the Torah at Mount Sinai, symbolizing spiritual harvest and the covenant with God. Traditionally observed with all-night Torah study and dairy foods, it links to ancestral roots and core Jewish tenets.

Feast of Weeks Overview

Brief Introduction: Celebrates the wheat harvest and the receiving of the Law at Mount Sinai, symbolizing spiritual harvest and the Mosaic covenant with God. Traditionally observed with all-night Torah study and dairy foods, it links to ancestral roots and core Jewish tenets.

Commemorates: In the Old Testament, giving of the Law at Mount Sinai, and the wheat harvest. In the New Testament it is about the coming of the Holy Spirit.

Other Names: Feast of Weeks, Yom HaBikkurim, Atzeret Zman Matan Torateinu (the giving of the Torah), Shavuot, and Pentecost

Bible References: Exodus 34:22; Leviticus 23:15–22; Deuteronomy 16:9–12; Numbers 28:26

Date Observed: The sixth day of Sivan in the Hebrew calendar, typically falling in late May or early June.

Feast of Weeks: Harvest, History, and Holy Torah

The Feast of Weeks is a multifaceted celebration within the tapestry of biblical feasts. It's a historical commemoration and a dynamic expression of God's ongoing work in our lives, embodying His grand plan of salvation.

The festival's roots are deeply intertwined with agriculture, as seen in the Bible's frequent use of farming language.

The concept of the firstfruits is central to understanding Feast of Weeks, a principle that extends beyond mere agricultural practices. In biblical terms, this symbolizes gratitude and hope, and the anticipation of future abundance.

Elements of the Feast of Weeks

- **Firstfruits:** Coinciding with Passover, this Feast of Weeks component symbolizes the harvest season's start, and represents an offering of thanksgiving for agricultural abundance.

- **Giving of the Laws:** Feast of Weeks additionally celebrates the event of the Law being given at Mount Sinai, a pivotal event in the Jewish faith. Leviticus 23:15–22 describes this as a transition from barley to wheat harvest, signifying new grain offerings to the Lord. The dramatic scene of Mount Sinai enveloped in thunder, lightning, and a trumpet's blast (Exodus 19:16–19) illustrates this historic moment when God revealed His Law and intentions to His chosen people.

Feast of Weeks is Pentecost

The Feast of Weeks is a pilgrimage festival when Jews were required to be in Jerusalem. Also known as Pentecost, the disciples convened in the city as Jesus had directed. During this gathering, the Holy Spirit dramatically descended upon them, signaled by a sound resembling a rushing wind and what appeared like tongues of fire on their heads.

This pivotal event happened fifty days after Jesus' resurrection and infused the disciples with the ability to speak in diverse languages.

It marked the inception of the Christian church, catalyzing the global dissemination of Jesus' teachings and leading to the conversion and baptism of thousands.

A Call to Divine Communion and Gratitude

The Feast of Weeks invites us to celebrate God's provision and His Law, while embracing the relationship He seeks with us. The festival encourages gratitude for both tangible and spiritual harvests. By offering our first fruits in devotion and service, we acknowledge God's sovereignty and our dependence on His blessings.

The festival is a vibrant tapestry of thanksgiving, expressed through joyous processions and sacred rituals, including the offering of barley sheaves at the Temple. This celebration transcends its agricultural roots, symbolizing a life of faith and hope in God's continuous blessings.

The Feast of Weeks is referenced in various biblical passages. These Scriptures collectively highlight the festival as a time of joyous celebration, community observance, and a reminder of God's enduring providence.

In conclusion, the Feast of Weeks is more than a date on the calendar; it's a significant spiritual event, inviting us to draw closer to God through His Word and Spirit. It celebrates life, trust, and the enduring relationship between God, humanity, and the land.

Jewish Traditions of Feast of Weeks

Honoring the Gift of the Law

The Feast of Weeks is a significant Jewish holiday marking the occasion of the Law being bestowed at Mount Sinai, occurring seven weeks after Passover. Today, Jews around the world observe this festival with various traditions and customs.

In ancient times, Jews journeyed to the Temple in Jerusalem to present the first fruits of their harvest as an expression of thankfulness. The Feast of Weeks is celebrated by Jews today with various customs and traditions that focus on its agricultural roots and significance as the time of the giving of the Law. Here are some of the critical ways the Feast of Weeks is observed in contemporary Jewish communities:

All-Night Torah Study

The all-night study session on the eve of the Feast of Weeks is called Tikkun Leil. It stands as a profound tradition within the Jewish community, offering a night of deep spiritual connection and communal learning. This practice intertwines historical roots with mystical significance, inviting participants to immerse themselves in a rich tapestry of Jewish wisdom.

- **Historical and Mystical Foundations:** Tikkun Leil, Shavuot's tradition, is steeped in historical anecdotes and mystical practices. On the eve of receiving the Law, the Israelites went to sleep early, only to oversleep. This event prompted the custom of staying awake all night, anticipating receiving the Law, symbolizing our continual readiness and eagerness to hear from God. The sixteenth-century Kabbalists of Safed further enriched this tradition, viewing it as a means of spiritual purification and preparation.

- **Diverse Textual Study:** The night of Tikkun Leil in the Feast of Weeks is dedicated to a broad exploration of Jewish texts, extending beyond the Torah to include the Talmud, Midrash, Halakha, philosophy, and

Kabbalah (mystical teachings). Many communities utilize a specially compiled Tikkun, which features excerpts from the entire spectrum of Jewish Scripture, offering a holistic approach to study.

- **Community Engagement:** Beyond individual study, Tikkun Leil in the Feast of Weeks fosters community, drawing together participants from varied backgrounds for a shared discovery and discussion night. This gathering is marked by an energizing atmosphere where lively debate and insightful dialogue flourish.

- **Educational Sessions:** The night is often punctuated with lectures and classes led by esteemed rabbis and scholars. These sessions delve into the nexus of the Feast of Weeks, Torah teachings, contemporary issues, and personal spiritual development, enriching the communal experience.

- **Spiritual Preparation:** The act of studying through the night serves as a spiritual journey, mirroring the anticipation and reverence of the Israelites at Sinai. It is a time of personal and collective renewal in our relationship with the Scriptures.

- **Concluding with Dawn Prayers:** The study session culminates in the morning prayer service, highlighted by reading the Ten Commandments. This moment resonates deeply with participants, symbolically reenacting the Sinai experience and reinforcing the eternal bond between the Jewish people and the Torah.

The Feast of Weeks epitomizes the vibrancy of Jewish learning and the unbreakable connection to our heritage, making it a cherished and enriching tradition for the Jewish community worldwide.

Reading the Book of Ruth

The tradition of reading the book of Ruth during the Feast of Weeks is profoundly symbolic and meaningful, as it intertwines the festival's themes with Ruth's narrative. Set against the backdrop of the harvest season, the story of Ruth resonates with the agricultural essence of the Feast of Weeks. As Ruth gleans barley in the fields, her actions mirror the wheat harvest celebrated during the ancient Feast of Weeks in Israel. This alignment of the story's setting with the time of the festival underlines the relevance and significance of reading the book of Ruth during the Feast of Weeks.

Milk and Honey Foods

A delightful aspect of modern Feast of Weeks celebrations is the enjoyment of dairy foods. Various explanations exist for this tradition, ranging from the idea that the Israelites, having just received the dietary laws, opted for dairy foods, which required less immediate preparation, to the symbolism of the land flowing with milk and honey. Cheesecake, blintzes, and other dairy delicacies have become synonymous with Feast of Weeks celebrations, adding a layer of culinary enjoyment to the spiritual observance.

Decorating with Flowers and Greenery

The tradition of decorating with flowers and greenery during the Feast of Weeks is deeply symbolic, tracing back to when Mount Sinai, in a barren desert, miraculously flourished as the Law was given to the Israelites. This blooming represents spiritual enlightenment at the receiving of the Law. By incorporating flora into the festival's decorations, Jewish communities honor this miraculous event, connecting deeply with the festival's historical and agricultural roots, and enhancing its celebratory and spiritual atmosphere.

Reading the Ten Commandments

The tradition of hearing the Ten Commandments during the Feast of Weeks is a central and meaningful practice. In synagogues worldwide, communities gather to listen to these foundational words, re-enacting their original delivery to Moses on Mount Sinai. This ritual transcends mere recitation; it is a collective journey back to a pivotal moment in Jewish history.

Standing together to hear the Commandments, congregants symbolically unite with their ancestors at Sinai, reinforcing the enduring bond between God and the Jewish people. This tradition honors a significant historical occurrence and acts as a potent symbol of the fundamental values of Jewish ethics and morality.

Involving children in this ceremony holds profound significance, reflecting the conviction that every Jew, young or old, inherits the Torah's legacy. This annual communal listening thus becomes a recollection of the past, a reaffirmation of faith, and an ongoing commitment to the values at the heart of Judaism.

Prayers and Services

During the Feast of Weeks, synagogue services are imbued with profound spiritual significance, prominently featuring the recitation of the Hallel, a series of joyful psalms of praise. These ancient melodies, sung with enthusiasm and devotion, resonate with thanksgiving, celebrating the joyous spirit of the festival. As congregants unite their voices in these sacred chants, they connect with a timeless tradition of worship where gratitude and celebration blend seamlessly. The Hallel, with its uplifting verses, embodies the jubilant essence of the Feast of Weeks, reflecting the communal elation in commemorating the giving of the Law.

Equally significant in the Feast of Weeks services is the Yizkor, a solemn memorial prayer for the departed. Recited on the festival's final day, Yizkor is a poignant reminder of the enduring bonds between the living and the departed. This reflective service invites congregants to honor the memory of loved ones, weaving a tapestry of remembrance and continuity. It is a moment that underscores the values imparted by the Torah, bridging generations in a solemn affirmation of life's fragility and the enduring impact of those who have passed. In this way, the prayers and services of the Feast of Weeks encapsulate the dual themes of jubilation and reflection, mirroring the festival's multifaceted nature.

Offering Firstfruits: Bikkurim

The Bikkurim tradition, or firstfruits offering, integral to the Feast of Weeks, has transformed from its ancient practice of presenting the harvest's first and best produce at the Jerusalem Temple, to modern adaptations that preserve its essence. With the Temple's absence, contemporary Jewish observance maintains the tradition's spirit through educational efforts and discussions, focusing on gratitude, the sanctity of the harvest, and divine blessings. Modern practices include creating displays of fruits and agricultural products in synagogues and homes, serving as a visual reminder of Bikkurim's significance. Additionally, acts of charity reflect the tradition's spirit, translating ancient gratitude into modern generosity and community support.

Conclusion

The celebration of the Feast of Weeks stands as a testament to the festival's timeless significance, weaving together the past and present, the tangible and the spiritual. It serves as a reminder of Divine generosity and the constancy of God's teachings. Engaging in synagogue services, participating in all-night study sessions, decorating with flowers, and enjoying dairy delicacies connect us to a tradition that spans millennia. Today's observance of the Feast of Weeks is more than a remembrance of historical events; it is an active expression of faith, a reaffirmation of the covenant between God and His people, and a vibrant celebration of the Torah's enduring presence in Jewish life and spirituality.

How Feast of Weeks Reveals Messiah

Christ the Bread of Life

FEAST OF WEEKS	JESUS
Celebrates the harvest and God's provision of physical sustenance	Represents spiritual sustenance and eternal life
Commemorates the giving of the Torah, symbolizing God's convenant with Israel	Embodies the New Covenant and the fulfillment of God's promises
Reflects physical nourishment and abundance	Offers nourishment that satisfies deeper existencial hunger
Marks the revelation of God's Law, a guide for righteous living	Provides guidance and understanding for spiritual and moral living
Comunity unites in gratitude and celebration	Believers unite in faith and fellowship around Jesus
Offering the first fruits as a sacrifice	Ultimate sacrifice for humanity's salvation
Time of renewal and strengthening of faith	Offers renewal of spirit and transformation of life

The Feast of Weeks transcends its origins as a mere festival to become a pivotal moment in the sacred narrative of salvation, highlighting the central roles of Jesus Christ and the Holy Spirit. What began as an agricultural festivity and a historical commemoration now unfolds in the New Testament as a vibrant tableau. It richly illustrates the character and mission of Jesus, elevating it from a conventional ritual to a lively and heartfelt celebration embraced by believers across the globe.

The Feast of Weeks prophetically anticipates the coming of Jesus. As the first fruits were offered in ancient times, Christ, the firstfruits of the resurrection, offered Himself to the Father (1 Corinthians 15:20). This offering paves the way for our resurrection and eternal life. Also known as Shavuot or Pentecost, marking fifty days after Jesus' resurrection, we celebrate this historical event and the dynamic presence of Christ through the Holy Spirit.

In John 6:35, Jesus declares, "I am the bread of life." This profound statement resonates deeply with the Feast of Weeks' themes, emphasizing spiritual sustenance and divine revelation. The Feast of Weeks' celebration of the harvest and God's physical provision parallels Jesus' offer of spiritual nourishment and eternal life, reflecting the fulfillment of God's promises.

Connections

- **Divine Provision:** The Feast of Weeks celebrates physical harvest and provision; Jesus embodies spiritual sustenance and eternal life.

- **Covenant and Promise:** The Feast of Weeks commemorates the giving of the Law and God's covenant with Israel; Jesus fulfills God's promises.

- **Nourishment and Sustenance:** The Feast of Weeks symbolizes physical abundance; Jesus offers spiritual nourishment, addressing deeper existential needs.

- **Revelation and Understanding:** The Feast of Weeks represents the revelation of God's Law; Jesus provides spiritual guidance and moral understanding.

- **Community and Unity:** The Feast of Weeks unites the Jewish community in celebration; similarly, believers unite around Jesus in faith and fellowship.

- **Sacrifice and Giving:** The Feast of Weeks' first fruits offering parallels Jesus' ultimate sacrifice for humanity's salvation.

- **Transformation and Renewal:** The Feast of Weeks marks a renewal of faith through the Torah; Jesus brings about spiritual transformation and renewal.

From Sinai to Pentecost

Many Christians view the term "Law" with apprehension, associating it with rigid and unnecessary rules. However, the Hebrew word often translated as "Law" is Torah, which carries a significantly different connotation. Deriving from the root word "yarah," meaning "to flow like water," Torah implies guidance. It figuratively means to show, teach, inform, or direct. Therefore, a more fitting translation of the Torah is "instruction," emphasizing its role in providing direction and teaching.

The law of the LORD is perfect, refreshing the soul. Psalm 19:7

The Bible consistently emphasizes that the Law is good, just, and righteous. Any negativity associated with the Law arises not from its inherent qualities but from its misuse or unauthorized additions by individuals (Deuteronomy 4:2).

So then, the law is holy, and the commandment is holy, righteous and good. Romans 7:12

Psalm 119:14 states, *I rejoice in following your statutes as one rejoices in great riches.* This verse is an extensive meditation on God's Law and commandments' beauty, perfection, and usefulness. To expand on this particular verse:

- **Joy in Obedience:** The psalmist equates following God's statutes with the joy of wealth, highlighting obedience to God as a source of deep happiness and contentment.

- **Valuing God's Word:** The verse places high value on God's statutes over material wealth, reflecting a mindset prioritizing spiritual over physical riches.

- **The Statutes as Guidance:** God's Laws guide a fulfilling and righteous life rather than arbitrary rules.

- **A Relationship with God:** The joy in the verse stems from a close, enriching relationship with God, fostered through obedience to His instruction.

- **Contrast with Earthly Riches:** The psalmist contrasts the enduring joy in God's Law with material wealth's transient and often unsatisfying nature.

Building on the sentiments expressed in the Bible about the value and joy found in God's commandments, we can explore how this reverence for the Law transitions into the era of grace introduced in the New Testament. This shift is beautifully exemplified in the transformation from the Feast of Weeks to Pentecost, where the celebration of the Law given at Sinai evolves into the celebration of the Holy Spirit's outpouring.

But whoever looks intently into the perfect law that gives freedom, and continues in it—not forgetting what they have heard, but doing it—they will be blessed in what they do. James 1:25

We should view God's Law as a source of wisdom and learning, an invitation to grow and flourish under His direction, much like a plant thriving by a stream of water. Let's delve into a comparative list highlighting aspects of Law and Grace as we move from the Feast of Weeks to Pentecost.

Harmony of Law and Grace

- **Judgement at Sinai:** Following the idolatry of the golden calf, three thousand men died (Exodus 32:28), reflecting the serious consequences of violating the Law.

- **Salvation at Pentecost:** Post-Holy Spirit outpouring, three thousand were saved (Acts 2:41), showing the transformative power of God's Grace.

- **Law at Sinai:** Mosaic Law upheld the principles of justice and adherence, emphasizing the goodness and righteousness of the Law.

- **Spirit at Pentecost:** The Holy Spirit leads to repentance and life, shifting our focus to spiritual growth.

- **External at Sinai:** The Law, delivered on stone tablets, highlighted obedience and external commitment.

- **Internal at Pentecost:** The Holy Spirit internally transforms, writing God's Laws on our hearts.

- **Law Established at Sinai:** The Law established Israel, laying a foundation for God's people.

- **Spirit of the Law at Pentecost:** The church is inaugurated under Grace, expanding this foundation to include all nations in harmony with the spirit of the Law.

- **God's Presence at Sinai:** God's presence was majestic and awe-inspiring but distant.

- **God's Presence at Pentecost:** The Holy Spirit's presence is intimate, indwelling believers.

- **Response at Sinai:** Israelites' rebellion led to judgment.

- **Response at Pentecost:** Response to Peter's message led to widespread salvation.

- **Community at Sinai:** Israelite community unified under the Law.

- **Community at Pentecost:** Christian church unified by faith in Christ and the Holy Spirit.

Embracing Spiritual Warfare

Receiving the Holy Spirit at Pentecost also heightens our spiritual warfare. As we draw closer to God, we become more visible targets of Satan. In this battle, we are called to don the whole armor of God (Ephesians 6:10–20), embracing Jesus as our High Priest and commander. This armor equips us to withstand spiritual challenges and walk confidently in faith.

A Call to Spiritual Harvest

The Feast of Weeks extends an invitation to participate in the spiritual harvest Jesus initiated. Empowered by the Holy Spirit, we are called to spread the good news and bring more people into God's family. It's a time of joy and gratitude, celebrating Jesus' sacrifice, resurrection, and the gift of the Holy Spirit.

Conclusion

Observing the Feast of Weeks allows us to connect with its rich symbolism and celebrate the fulfillment of these themes in Christ. It presents an opportunity to deepen our faith, engage in spiritual harvest, and anticipate a blessed future in the grace of our Lord Jesus Christ.

Celebrating the Feast of Weeks

FEAST OF WEEKS	PENTECOST
Law given fifty days after Passover	Holy spirit given fifty days after Passover
Three thousand men killed Exodus 32:28	Three thousand men saved Acts 2:41
Law written on stone Exodus 31:18	Law is written on our hearts Hebrew 8:10
Establishment of the covenant between God and Israel	Signifies a new covenant where God dwells within believers
Unified the Israelites with the Torah	Unifies diverse believers in the body of Christ
Transformed societal and moral structures	Transforms hearts and minds from within
Guidance through written laws	Guidance through internal prompting and conviction

Connecting Past and Present

As we explore practical ways to observe the Feast of Weeks, we'll discover how it beautifully intertwines with our faith and offers a deeper, more vibrant relationship with the Lord.

The Feast of Weeks, or Shavuot, as celebrated in Judaism, commemorates the giving of the Law at Mount Sinai. This festival takes on renewed significance as Pentecost, marking the outpouring of the Holy Spirit on the disciples. This transformational event empowered ordinary individuals to become bold witnesses of Christ, fueling the early church's growth.

Study the Day of Pentecost

One of the key takeaways from the Feast of Weeks is understanding and embracing the Holy Spirit's role in our lives.

Before Jesus ascended, He instructed His disciples within the context of a pivotal time. The disciples were already planning to be in Jerusalem for the Feast of Weeks celebration. During this time, Jesus instructed His followers to stay in Jerusalem and await the Comforter (His term for the Holy Spirit).

This directive came at a moment filled with anticipation and uncertainty following Jesus' resurrection. The promise of the Holy Spirit provided divine empowerment and guidance for the monumental task of spreading Jesus' teachings. This period of waiting was not merely a hiatus; it was a time rich with preparation, prayer, and communal solidarity, aligning with the spiritual significance of the Feast of Weeks.

By adhering to Jesus' command during the Feast of Weeks, the disciples showcased their obedience and faith, preparing the way for the momentous event of Shavuot/Pentecost. This juxtaposition of Jewish tradition and the nascent Christian faith highlights the deep historical and connections of both, underscoring the continuity and fulfillment of religious prophecy and practice.

Read the story of Pentecost in Acts chapter 2. This chapter provides a detailed account of the event, describing how the Holy Spirit descended upon the disciples. This event, often considered the birth of the church, signifies a shift from a ministry revolving around Jesus' physical presence, to a mission propelled by His followers, now unified and guided by the Spirit.

Studying the Ten Commandments

A personal study of the Ten Commandments is a profound way to deepen your relationship with God and grow in righteousness. It allows you to connect with the timeless wisdom of God's Word and integrate it into your daily life. May your study bring spiritual transformation and a closer walk with the Lord.

Sapphire Blue Stones

When God inscribed the Ten Commandments on Mount Sinai, He more than likely carved the profound edicts onto two tablets of sapphire-blue stone. Exodus 24:10 mentions that under God's feet there appeared to be a pavement of sapphire (something akin to lapis lazuli) as clear as the sky itself. God then told Moses to keep going up Mount Sinai until he received the stone tablets that God has prepared (Exodus 24:12). This imagery has led to the tradition that the tablets might have been made of a similar heavenly material, symbolizing the divine origin and purity of the commandments.

The choice of blue stone symbolizes rarity, regality, and value, which is why I selected blue for this book. It aligns with the notion that God would create something extraordinary—resilient, radiant, and imbued with His splendor—to convey His immutable commands.

God's Law

The law is good, and a perfect guide to right living. It serves as a definitive moral compass, distinctly separating right from wrong. The challenge, however, lies within us. Due to our flawed nature, sin cunningly blurs our moral vision, leading us to misconstrue evil for good and vice versa. Additionally, we exist in a world marred by sin. Being sinners in a sinful world, we encounter genuine ethical quandaries that complicate our ability to differentiate between right and wrong. The Law is never negative in the Bible, unless it is misused.

1. Walking in God's statutes keeps sickness away (Exodus 15:26)

2. Obeying God's decrees leads to many blessings (Deuteronomy 11:27)

3. Keeping the laws and decrees leads to prosperity (Joshua 1:8)

4. Delighting in the law leads to being like a fruitful tree (Psalm 1:2-3)

5. The law is perfect and refreshes the soul (Psalm 19:7)

6. God's commands are radiant and give light to the eyes (Psalm 19:8)

7. The law is supreme and brings great reward when kept (Psalm 19:11)

8. God's commands are just and faithfully endure forever (Psalms 111:7-8, 119:160)

9. God's good commandments bring peace and freedom (Psalm 119:165, James 1:25)

10. The law is holy, and the commandment is holy, righteous and good (Romans 7:12)

11. If you love me, keep my commands (John 14:15)

12. If you keep my commands, you will remain in my love (John 15:10)

13. His commands are not burdensome (1 John 5:3)

14. Now we know that the law is good, if one uses it lawfully. (1 Timothy 1:8)

15. The one who looks intently into the perfect law that gives freedom (James 1:25)

Timeline at Mount Sinai

The events below mark the critical moments of the Israelites at Mount Sinai, signifying the establishment of the Mosaic covenant, the revelation of the Law, and the challenges and reaffirmation of faith.

1. **Arrival at Sinai:** The Israelites reach Mount Sinai three months after leaving Egypt (Exodus 19:1).

2. **Preparation for Revelation:** God instructs Moses to consecrate the people for the Divine revelation on the third day (Exodus 19:10–11).

3. **Giving of the Ten Commandments:** God descends on the mountain amidst thunder, lightning, and trumpet sounds, and gives the Ten Commandments (Exodus 19:16–20; Exodus 20:1–17).

4. **Moses Receives Additional Laws:** Moses ascends to receive further laws and instructions, staying on the mountain for forty days and nights (Exodus 24:18).

5. **The Golden Calf Incident:** In Moses' absence, the Israelites worship a golden calf, which leads to Moses breaking the original tablets (Exodus 32:1–19).

6. **Moses Intercedes for the People:** Moses pleads with God not to destroy the Israelites for their idolatry (Exodus 32:11–14).

7. **Renewal of the Covenant:** Moses chisels new tablets, ascends Sinai again, and God renews the covenant, inscribing the commandments on the new tablets (Exodus 34:1–4, 28–29).

More Study Suggestions

- **Gather Resources:** Collect the necessary resources for your study. You'll need a Bible, notebook, journal, and perhaps a commentary or study guide to gain deeper insights.

- **Prayerful Approach:** Begin your study with a brief prayer, inviting the Holy Spirit to guide your understanding and applying the commandments. Ask for wisdom and discernment as you delve into God's Word.

- **Read the Commandments:** Open your Bible to Exodus 20:1–17 or Deuteronomy 5:6–21 and read the Ten Commandments slowly and attentively. Consider using different Bible translations to gain a broader perspective.

- **Reflect on Each Commandment:** After reading each commandment, take some time to reflect on its meaning and relevance in your life. Consider how it aligns with your beliefs and actions.

- **Learn About Blue Stones:** Read the verses about blue stones. Exodus 24:10, Ezekiel 1:26, Revelation 21:19, Job 28:5–6,16 and Isaiah 54:11 give biblical precedents for the possibility of the Ten Commandments engraved by God on rare blue sapphire stone tablets, reflecting the brilliance of His heavenly throne room and eternal kingdom foundations.

- **Journal Your Thoughts:** Use your notebook or journal to jot down your thoughts, questions, and personal reflections for each commandment. Write about any personal experiences related to these principles.

- **Explore Historical Context:** Research the context in which the commandments were given. Understanding the circumstances and the audience to which they were addressed can provide valuable insights.

- **Seek Practical Application:** Contemplate how each commandment can be practically applied daily. Think about specific situations where these principles can guide your decisions and actions.

- **Commit to Action:** As you conclude your study, commit to making practical changes in your life based on what you've learned—set goals for aligning your actions with God's moral standards.

Read the Book of Ruth

The book of Ruth is closely associated with the Feast of Weeks and offers profound insights into the themes of harvest, redemption, and God's faithfulness. Here's how you can practically incorporate this into your Shavuot observance:

- **Read the Book of Ruth Aloud**: Gather with friends, family, or fellow believers during the Feast of Weeks and read the book of Ruth aloud. You can take turns reading different sections or chapters. Allow the narrative to come to life as you hear the story of Ruth and Boaz.

- **Discuss its Significance:** After reading, discuss the key themes and lessons from the book of Ruth. Reflect on how God's providence and faithfulness are evident in the story. Share personal insights and applications.

- **Relate it to Your Life:** Consider how the story of Ruth relates to your journey of faith. Are there moments when you've experienced God's faithfulness, even in challenging circumstances? Use this discussion as an opportunity for personal and communal reflection.

Conclusion

As we observe the Feast of Weeks, let us embrace its full spiritual significance. Let it be a time of deep reflection on the role of the Holy Spirit, a celebration of our spiritual gifts, an affirmation of our unity in Christ, and a call to spiritual renewal. Shavuot/Pentecost is not merely a historical event; it's a present reality with profound implications for our lives as believers. It's an invitation to live a Spirit-filled life, actively participate in God's kingdom, and continually seek a deeper, more meaningful relationship with our Creator.

May this Feast of Weeks/Pentecost/Shavuot be a season of spiritual growth, service, and revival in your life and faith community. Embrace the beauty of this feast, and let it enrich your walk with the Lord.

Counting the Omer

COUNTING THE OMER	JESUS
The 49 days from Feast of Firstfruits and Shavuot (Pentecost)	The 49 days between Jesus' resurrection and Shavuot (Pentecost)
Progression from Passover to Shavuot	Progression from Jesus to Holy Spirit
Themes of liberation and revelation	Themes of liberation and revelation
Marking the journey from the Exodus to receiving the Torah at Mount Sinai	The transition from Jesus' resurrection to the birth of the Church
Transition from physical events to spiritual enlightenment and empowerment	Transition from physical events to spiritual enlightenment and empowerment
A time of reflection and anticipation for spiritual preparation and growth, leading up to receiving the Law	A time from sin's liberation through Jesus' sacrifice to empowerment by the Holy Spirit at Pentecost

Counting the Omer with Daily Verse

Counting the Omer is a spiritually enriching practice observed between Passover and Shavuot, symbolizing the journey from physical liberation to receiving spiritual Torah at Mount Sinai. This 49-day period offers a unique opportunity for personal growth and reflection.

Daily Counting

- **Count Each Evening:** The Omer is counted each evening after sunset, starting from the second night of Passover. Say the blessing: "Blessed are You, Lord our God, King of the universe, who has sanctified us with His commandments and commanded us concerning the counting of the Omer."

- **Announce the Day:** After the blessing, announce the count of the Omer. For example, "Today is the first day of the Omer." As the days progress, include weeks and days, e.g., "Today is twenty-five days, which are three weeks and four days of the Omer."

- **Read the Verse of the Day:** Utilize a Counting the Omer list below that includes a verse for each day. These verses can offer insights into themes of freedom, spiritual growth, and divine connection.

- **Study the Verse:** Contemplate or study the day's verse. Consider its historical context, spiritual implications, and how it relates to the journey of the Omer.

- **Journal:** Writing down your thoughts and reflections can deepen your engagement with the text.

- **Personal Prayer:** Following your reflection on the verse, spend some time in prayer. You can offer prayers of thanks, seek guidance, or express your desires for personal growth during this Omer period.

- **Reflect and Act:** At the end of your study and prayer, reflect on how you can apply the day's lessons in your life. Consider actions, changes in perspective, or conversations that might bring these insights to life.

- **Community Sharing:** If possible, share your reflections with a friend or family member who is also counting the Omer. This can enrich your experience through shared insights and support.

- **Look Forward to Shavuot:** As you progress through the Omer, keep in mind that this period culminates in Shavuot, celebrating the giving of the Torah. Let this anticipation infuse your daily counting with purpose and excitement for the spiritual revelation to come.

By following these steps, counting the Omer becomes more than just a ritual; it transforms into a journey of personal and spiritual development, enriched by the daily study of scripture and prayer.

Counting the Omer Verses

1. Leviticus 23:15: *You shall count seven full weeks from the day after the Sabbath, from the day that you brought the sheaf of the wave offering.*

2. Leviticus 23:16: *You shall count fifty days to the day after the seventh Sabbath. Then you shall present a grain offering of new grain to the Lord.*

3. Psalm 19:14: *Let the words of my mouth and the meditation of my heart be acceptable in your sight, O Lord, my rock and my redeemer.*

4. Psalm 139:23–24: *Search me, O God, and know my heart! Try me and know my thoughts! And see if there be any grievous way in me, and lead me in the way everlasting!*

5. Proverbs 3:5–6: *Trust in the Lord with all your heart, and do not lean on your own understanding. In all your ways acknowledge him, and he will make straight your paths.*

6. Isaiah 40:31: *But they who wait for the Lord shall renew their strength; they shall mount up with wings like eagles; they shall run and not be weary; they shall walk and not faint.*

7. Isaiah 43:18–19: *Remember not the former things, nor consider the things of old. Behold, I am doing a new thing; now it springs forth, do you not perceive it? I will make a way in the wilderness and rivers in the desert.*

8. Jeremiah 29:11: *For I know the plans I have for you, declares the Lord, plans for welfare and not for evil, to give you a future and a hope.*

9. Ezekiel 36:26: *And I will give you a new heart, and a new spirit I will put within you. And I will remove the heart of stone from your flesh and give you a heart of flesh.*

10. Matthew 6:33: *But seek first the kingdom of God and his righteousness, and all these things will be added to you.*

11. Matthew 22:37: *And he said to him, "You shall love the Lord your God with all your heart and with all your soul and with all your mind."*

12. Mark 1:14–15: *Now after John was arrested, Jesus came into Galilee, proclaiming the gospel of God, and saying, "The time is fulfilled, and the kingdom of God is at hand; repent and believe in the gospel."*

13. Mark 8:34: *And calling the crowd to him with his disciples, he said to them,*

"If anyone would come after me, let him deny himself and take up his cross and follow me."

14. Luke 9:23: *And he said to all, "If anyone would come after me, let him deny himself and take up his cross daily and follow me."*

15. 16. Luke 24:46–47: *And said to them, "Thus it is written, that the Christ should suffer and on the third day rise from the dead, and that repentance for the forgiveness of sins should be proclaimed in his name to all nations, beginning from Jerusalem."*

16. John 3:30: *He must increase, but I must decrease.*

17. John 6:35: *Jesus said to them, "I am the bread of life; whoever comes to me shall not hunger, and whoever believes in me shall never thirst."*

18. John 12:24: *Truly, truly, I say to you, unless a grain of wheat falls into the earth and dies, it remains alone; but if it dies, it bears much fruit.*

19. Acts 2:1–4: *When the day of Pentecost arrived, they were all together in one place. And suddenly there came from heaven a sound like a mighty rushing wind, and it filled the entire house where they were sitting. And divided tongues as of fire appeared to them and rested on each one of them. And they were all filled with the Holy Spirit and began to speak in other tongues as the Spirit gave them utterance.*

20. Acts 3:19: *Repent therefore, and turn again, that your sins may be blotted out.*

21. Romans 6:4: *We were buried therefore with him by baptism into death, in order that, just as Christ was raised from the dead by the glory of the Father, we too might walk in newness of life.*

22. Romans 12:2: *Do not be conformed to this world, but be transformed by the renewal of your mind, that by testing you may discern what is the will of God, what is good and acceptable and perfect.*

23. 1 Corinthians 5:7: *Cleanse out the old leaven that you may be a new lump, as you really are unleavened. For Christ, our Passover lamb, has been sacrificed.*

24. 2 Corinthians 5:17: *Therefore, if anyone is in Christ, he is a new creation. The old has passed away; behold, the new has come.*

25. Galatians 5:22–23: *But the fruit of the Spirit is love, joy, peace, patience, kindness, goodness, faithfulness, gentleness, self-control; against such things there is no law.*

26. Ephesians 2:8–9: *For by grace you have been saved through faith. And this is not your own doing; it is the gift of God, not a result of works, so that no*

one may boast.

27. Ephesians 4:22–24: *To put off your old self, which belongs to your former manner of life and is corrupt through deceitful desires, and to be renewed in the spirit of your minds, and to put on the new self, created after the likeness of God in true righteousness and holiness.*

28. Philippians 3:13–14: *Brothers, I do not consider that I have made it my own. But one thing I do: forgetting what lies behind and straining forward to what lies ahead, I press on toward the goal for the prize of the upward call of God in Christ Jesus.*

29. Colossians 3:1–2: *If then you have been raised with Christ, seek the things that are above, where Christ is, seated at the right hand of God. Set your minds on things that are above, not on things that are on Earth.*

30. Colossians 3:5: *Put to death therefore what is earthly in you: sexual immorality, impurity, passion, evil desire, and covetousness, which is idolatry.*

31. Colossians 3:8–10: *But now you must put them all away: anger, wrath, malice, slander, and obscene talk from your mouth. Do not lie to one another, seeing that you have put off the old self with its practices and have put on the new self, which is being renewed in knowledge after the image of its creator.*

32. 1 Thessalonians 5:16–18: *Rejoice always, pray without ceasing, give thanks in all circumstances; for this is the will of God in Christ Jesus for you.*

33. 2 Timothy 2:21: *Therefore, if anyone cleanses himself from what is dishonorable, he will be a vessel for honorable use, set apart as holy, useful to the master of the house, ready for every good work.*

34. Titus 3:5: *He saved us, not because of works done by us in righteousness, but according to his own mercy, by the washing of regeneration and renewal of the Holy Spirit.*

35. Hebrews 4:16: *Let us then with confidence draw near to the throne of grace, that we may receive mercy and find grace to help in time of need.*

36. Hebrews 10:22: *Let us draw near with a true heart in full assurance of faith, with our hearts sprinkled clean from an evil conscience and our bodies washed with pure water.*

37. James 4:8: *Draw near to God, and he will draw near to you. Cleanse your hands, you sinners, and purify your hearts, you double-minded.*

38. 1 Peter 1:3: *Blessed be the God and Father of our Lord Jesus Christ! According to his great mercy, he has caused us to be born again to a living hope through the resurrection of Jesus Christ from the dead.*

39. 1 Peter 2:2: *Like newborn infants, long for the pure spiritual milk, that by it you may grow up into salvation.*

40. 1 Peter 3:21: *Baptism, which corresponds to this, now saves you, not as a removal of dirt from the body but as an appeal to God for a good conscience, through the resurrection of Jesus Christ.*

41. 1 John 1:9: *If we confess our sins, he is faithful and just to forgive us our sins and to cleanse us from all unrighteousness.*

42. 1 John 2:6: *Whoever says he abides in him ought to walk in the same way in which he walked.*

43. 2 Peter 1:3: *His divine power has granted to us all things that pertain to life and godliness, through the knowledge of him who called us to his own glory and excellence.*

44. Revelation 21:5: *And he who was seated on the throne said, "Behold, I am making all things new." Also he said, "Write this down, for these words are trustworthy and true."*

45. Revelation 22:17: *The Spirit and the Bride say, "Come."' And let the one who hears say, "Come." And let the one who is thirsty come; let the one who desires take the water of life without price."*

46. Romans 8:14: *For all who are led by the Spirit of God are sons of God.*

47. Romans 8:28: *And we know that in all things God works for the good of those who love him, who have been called according to his purpose.*

48. 2 Corinthians 4:16: *So we do not lose heart. Though our outer self is wasting away, our inner self is being renewed day by day.*

49. Revelation 3:20: *Behold, I stand at the door and knock. If anyone hears my voice and opens the door, I will come in to him and eat with him, and he with me.*

50. Psalm 26:2: *Examine me, O Lord, and try me; test my heart and my mind.*

Feast of Weeks Recipes

Dairy Food Delights

The Feast of Weeks/Shavuot celebrates the giving of the Law at Mount Sinai and the wheat harvest in Israel. Traditional Feast of Weeks foods often include dairy dishes and springtime ingredients. Here are some recipes to help you celebrate the Feast of Weeks.

Classic Cheese Blintzes

A blintz is a type of Jewish stuffed pancake, traditionally served in Ashkenazi Jewish cuisine. Blintzes start with a crepe (thin pancake). Once it is cooked, it is filled, typically with a sweet cheese mixture or fruit compote, then folded to enclose the filling, and then pan-fried or baked to create a slightly crispy exterior.

Ingredients for the Crepes
1 cup all-purpose flour
1½ cups milk
2 eggs
1 tbs sugar
Pinch of salt
Butter for frying

Ingredients for the Filling
1½ cups cups ricotta cheese
½ cup cream cheese
¼ cup sugar
1 egg yolk
1 tsp vanilla extract

Instructions
~ **Make the crepe batter:** Whisk together flour, milk, eggs, sugar, and salt until smooth. Let rest for 30 minutes.
~ **Cook the crepes:** In a non-stick skillet, melt a little butter. Pour a thin layer of batter, swirling to spread evenly. Cook until edges lift, flip, and cook briefly on the other side. Repeat with the remaining batter.
~ **Prepare filling:** Mix ricotta, cream cheese, sugar, egg yolk, and vanilla until

smooth.

~ **Assemble blintzes:** Place a spoonful of filling in the center of each crepe. Fold the sides over the filling, then roll up from the bottom.

~ **Final cook:** Fry the blintzes in butter until golden on both sides. Serve with sour cream or fruit preserves.

Savory Spinach and Feta Quiche

Ingredients
1 pie crust
1 tbs olive oil
1 small onion, chopped
2 cups fresh spinach
1 cup feta cheese, crumbled
4 eggs
1 cup milk
Salt and pepper to taste

Instructions
~ **Pre-bake crust:** Preheat oven to 375°F (190°C). Line the pie crust with parchment and fill with pie weights. Bake for 10 minutes. Remove the weights and parchment.
~ **Cook vegetables:** In a skillet, heat the olive oil. Sauté the onion until translucent. Add the spinach and cook until wilted.
~ **Assemble quiche:** Spread the spinach mixture and feta cheese over the crust.
~ **Add egg mixture:** Whisk together eggs, milk, salt, and pepper. Pour over the spinach and feta.
~ **Bake:** Bake for 35–40 minutes, or until set. Let cool slightly before serving.

Sweet Cheese Kugel

Ingredients
12 ounces wide egg noodles
4 eggs
1 ½ cups cottage cheese
1 cup sour cream
½ cup sugar
½ cup raisins (optional)
1 tsp vanilla extract
Cinnamon and sugar for topping

Instructions
~ **Cook noodles:** Cook egg noodles according to package instructions; drain.
~ **Prepare kugel:** In a large bowl, mix the cooked noodles with eggs, cottage cheese, sour cream, sugar, raisins (if using), and vanilla.
~ **Bake:** Pour into a greased baking dish. Sprinkle with cinnamon and sugar.
~ **Final bake:** Bake at 350°F (175°C) for 45–50 minutes, until the top is golden and the center is set.

Honey Glazed Salmon

Ingredients
4 salmon fillets
¼ cup honey
2 tbs of soy sauce
1 garlic clove, minced
Juice of one lemon
Salt and pepper to taste

Instructions
~ Marinate salmon: In a bowl, mix honey, soy sauce, garlic, and lemon juice. Season the salmon with salt and pepper, and marinate in the mixture for at least 30 minutes.
~ Cook salmon: Preheat oven to 375°F (190°C). Place the salmon on a baking sheet and bake for 20 minutes or until cooked.
~ Serve: Serve the salmon with a drizzle of the cooking marinade and your choice of sides.

Enjoy these delightful recipes as you celebrate the Feast of Weeks and its rich traditions!

Feast of Weeks Questions

Illuminating Reflections

The Feast of Weeks, a festival rich in history and spiritual significance, offers an opportunity for profound reflection and application of its principles in our daily lives. As we explore the themes of harvest, revelation, and the coming of the Holy Spirit, these questions aim to deepen our understanding, and encourage us to live out the lessons of Shavuot practically and meaningfully.

1. How can the agricultural aspects of the Feast of Weeks inspire you to cultivate and harvest spiritual growth in your own life?

2. Reflect on a time when you experienced a spiritual harvest in your life. How did you see God's hand at work in that season?

3. Considering that the Feast of Weeks commemorates the giving of the Law, how can you incorporate the wisdom of God's teachings more fully into your daily life?

4. How does the Torah's guidance influence your decisions, actions, and worldview?

5. How does celebrating Shavuot/Pentecost deepen your understanding of the Holy Spirit's role in your life and the church?

6. How can you be more open to the guidance and empowerment of the Holy Spirit?

7. The Feast of Weeks is a time of thanking God for the harvest. What are some blessings in your life for which you can express gratitude to God?

8. How can you recognize and appreciate God's provision in your life's significant and minor aspects?

9. As The Feast of Weeks marks the receiving of the Law, how can you more

actively engage with the Bible to receive God's Word?

10. What steps can you take to share the teachings and insights you gain from the Bible with others?

11. The Feast of Weeks is traditionally a communal celebration. How can you foster community and unity within your faith group?

12. How does gathering with others to celebrate and learn from God's Word enrich your spiritual life and understanding of scriptural principles?

13. The Feast of Weeks points to future fulfillment in Christ. How does this perspective affect your hope and anticipation for God's promises?

14. In what areas of your life do you need to trust God more for His future fulfillment?

15. How can you embody the spirit of the Law (the essence and intention of Divine guidance) in your daily actions and relationships?

16. Consider the balance between Law and Grace in your life. How can you live in a way that honors God's commandments while embracing His Grace?

In conclusion, the Feast of Weeks invites us to delve into the depths of God's provision, His Word, and the transformative power of the Holy Spirit.

Fall Holidays

Blueprints of Faith

FEAST OF TRUMPETS
Also called Rosh Hashanah. A time marked by the shofar blowing, signaling repentance. It foreshadows the return of Jesus, often associated with the sound of the trumpet calling believers to Him.

DAY OF ATONEMENT
Also called Yom Kippur. The holiest day of repentance and atonement. This day points to Jesus as our High Priest who entered the Holy of Holies with His blood for our eternal atonement. Technically, not a feast day but a fasting day.

FEAST OF TABERNACLES
Also called Sukkot. Commemorates the Israelites' journey in the wilderness and God's protection. It symbolizes Jesus as our true tabernacle, God dwelling among His people and providing shelter and guidance.

Fall Holidays Overview

In the Fall Holidays chapters, we'll dive into the Jewish fall holidays, which are crucial to God's appointed times. Like their spring counterparts, these autumn celebrations are rich in spiritual significance, unveiling Christ's redemptive work and offering insights into spiritual fulfillment.

Spring's Fulfillment, Autumn's Promise

The fall holidays, prophetic in nature, hold promises yet to be fulfilled, unlike the spring holidays, which were realized in Christ's death and resurrection. The fall holidays are:

1. Feast of Trumpets (Rosh Hashanah)

2. Day of Atonement (Yom Kippur)

3. Feast of Tabernacles (Sukkoth)

Blueprints of Faith: Understanding the Seasons

Imagine looking at the blueprint of a house you've visited; you can easily recall its rooms, layout, and feel. This familiarity helps you grasp the design. In contrast, visualizing a house from its blueprint without visiting it can be challenging. This analogy helps us understand the spring and fall holidays in the biblical calendar.

The spring holidays are like a house we've walked through. We've experienced the reality of Christ's sacrifice and resurrection, making their significance easy to understand. These celebrations are like familiar rooms, filled with joy and understanding of what Jesus has done for us.

However, the fall holidays are akin to exploring blueprints of a house we have yet to visit. These holidays point to future events—the return of Christ and the establishment of His kingdom. They may seem more complex due to their unfulfilled nature, but they promise a glorious future. They encourage us to remain vigilant, seek reconciliation, and anticipate the Divine presence among us. Let's approach these prophetic holidays with hope and faith in what is yet to come.

The Forty-Day Journey of Reflection:

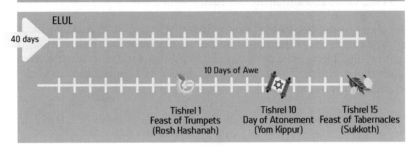

Teshuvah, a period of repentance and spiritual renewal, leads to the fall holidays. It includes:

- **The Month of Elul:** Thirty days dedicated to introspection and turning back to God.
- **The Ten Days of Repentance:** Beginning with Rosh Hashanah and ending with Yom Kippur, intensifying the focus on self-examination.

Together, these periods form a forty-day journey toward spiritual realignment.

Ten Days of Awe: High Holy Days

The Ten Days of Awe, from Rosh Hashanah to Yom Kippur, are a time of deep spiritual reflection, emphasizing forgiveness, human vulnerability, and the quest for moral betterment.

Feast of Trumpets: A Divine Alert

Yom Teruah, the Feast of Trumpets, marks the onset of the fall holidays, with shofars sounding as a spiritual alarm. It calls for self-examination and repentance in preparation for Yom Kippur. This feast also symbolizes the anticipation of Christ's return, reminding us to be prepared for this momentous event.

Day of Atonement: A Day of Redemption

Yom Kippur, the Day of Atonement, is the pinnacle of repentance and forgiveness. It reflects Christ's sacrificial role as our High Priest, who secures our forgiveness and reconciles us with God. This day is a profound time for heart-searching and turning away from sin.

Feast of Tabernacles: Celebrating Divine Fellowship

Sukkot, the Feast of Tabernacles, celebrates God's provision and presence with the Israelites in the wilderness. It symbolizes Christ's incarnation and indicates when God will dwell with us in His eternal kingdom. This feast encourages us to rejoice in God's care and anticipate our future with Him.

The fall holidays—marked by the Feast of Trumpets, the Day of Atonement, and the Feast of Tabernacles—illuminate the themes of awakening, redemption, and divine fellowship. They invite us to stay alert, embrace forgiveness, and celebrate God's enduring presence. These observances deepen our appreciation of Christ's mission and His promised return.

The Rapture and Second Coming

END TIME EVENT THEORIES

HOLIDAY	THEORY 1	THEORY 2	THEORY 3	THEORY 4
Feast of Trumpets (Rosh Hashanah)	Rapture	Second Coming	Rapture	Second Coming
Day of Atonement (Yom Kippur)	Second Coming	Judgment	Judgment	Judgment
Feast of Tabernacles (Sukkoth)	Millenium	Millenium	Eternity in Heaven	Eternity in Heaven

Prophetic Signposts

I've eagerly anticipated the return of Jesus for over four decades. It all began in the early 1970s when I learned about His promised return to Earth. The excitement that filled my heart was beyond words. I dove into books like *The Late Great Planet Earth* by Hal Lindsey, a well-known author of apocalyptic literature. During that time, the nightly news even featured Sun Myung Moon, a prominent religious leader, and I couldn't help but wonder if he might be the anti-Christ. The 1980s brought a resurgence of discussions about Jesus' return, with books like *88 Reasons Why The Rapture Will Be in 1988,* adding to the anticipation.

My perspective on the Second Coming shifted as I delved deeper into understanding the Old Testament patterns. Through extensive study and reading various viewpoints, I've come to hold a few firm beliefs:

- No one can predict the exact day or hour of Jesus' return, as stated in Matthew 24:36.

- His return will align with the patterns established in the Old Testament, likely occurring during one of the fall holidays.

- I've been pre-trib, mid-trib, and post-trib. All I know now is I have been wrong twice. :)

To help navigate the complexities of the Last Days and their connection, I've compiled various theories into the chart in this chapter that includes the Feast of Trumpets (Rosh Hashanah), the Day of Atonement (Yom Kippur), and the Feast of Tabernacles (Sukkot).

Harvesting Revelation

Eschatology, the study of the end times, has been a subject of profound interest and debate among Christians for centuries. The fall holidays—Rosh Hashanah, Yom Kippur, and Sukkot—are central to this discussion, each holding unique significance in the eschatological tapestry.

These fall holidays speak to Messianic anticipation of Jesus's return when the ultimate divine promises of final redemption, resurrection, and dwelling with God are finally fulfilled for his people, just as these holidays recall God faithfully fulfilling promises to past generations. The symbols and themes resonate with the biblical end-time prophecies of Christ's second coming.

The Feast of Trumpets (Rosh Hashanah)

One of the key events associated with Rosh Hashanah is the sounding of the shofar, which has captivated the imagination of many eschatologists. Some believe that the shofar blast will herald the return of Christ, an event commonly referred to as the Rapture. This view aligns with the idea that the last trumpet mentioned in 1 Corinthians 15:52 and 1 Thessalonians 4:16 is the shofar of Rosh Hashanah, signaling the gathering of believers to meet the Lord in the air.

Another perspective posits that Rosh Hashanah represents the beginning of the Tribulation period, a time of great turmoil and tribulation on Earth before Christ's return. This viewpoint emphasizes the connection between the Feast of Trumpets and the prophetic trumpets mentioned in Revelation, symbolizing Divine judgments.

The Day of Atonement (Yom Kippur)

Yom Kippur, the holiest day in the Jewish calendar, plays a significant role in eschatological interpretations. Some theologians believe that Yom Kippur foreshadows the day when Israel, as a nation, will recognize Jesus as the Messiah and experience national atonement. This event is seen as a precursor to the Second Coming of Christ.

Others associate Yom Kippur with the judgment seat of Christ, where believers' works will be examined and rewarded. This aligns with the idea that Yom Kippur represents a time of individual reckoning and purification before Christ's return.

The Feast of Tabernacles (Sukkot)

Sukkot, also known as the Feast of Tabernacles or Booths, is seen by some as a celebration of the Millennial Kingdom of Christ. This view posits that Sukkot signifies when Christ will establish His reign on Earth, and believers will dwell with Him in a symbolic sukkah or booth.

Others interpret Sukkot as a symbol of the ultimate ingathering of God's people, both Jews and Gentiles, into the Kingdom of God. This harmonizes with the concept of the final harvest and the fulfillment of God's promises to His chosen people.

Comparing and Contrasting Views

As we delve into these varying interpretations of the fall holidays, we must note that eschatological theology is multifaceted, and different scholars and believers hold various distinct viewpoints. While some emphasize the imminence of Christ's return, others emphasize the need for spiritual preparation and repentance during this season.

Amidst the turmoil of the 2020s, many have questioned why Christ's return seems delayed. Peter offers two answers: God's perspective on time differs from ours, as time is viewed against eternity, and God desires to provide salvation to as many as possible.

> *The Lord is not slow to fulfill his promise as some count slowness, but is patient toward you, not wishing that any should perish,*

> *but that all should reach repentance.*
> 2 Peter 3:9

We can't predict when God will bring about the final judgment. His delay is an act of mercy to provide salvation opportunities.

Conclusion

The fall holidays captivate Christians with their prophetic symbolism, offering insights into Christ's return and God's divine plan. Regardless of specific beliefs about the Rapture, the Millennial Kingdom, or Israel's restoration, these holidays serve as a profound framework for understanding end-time prophecies.

The Bible, particularly in Matthew 24:42–44 parables, Mark 13:33–37, and Luke 12:35–40, emphasizes the importance of vigilance and preparedness while awaiting Christ's return. This includes being responsible, patient, and charitable as critical aspects of our readiness.

Ultimately, although specifics regarding end-time events may remain unclear, the assurance of Jesus' eventual return in glory to judge and resurrect those who follow him is certain. This promise gives our earthly lives a more profound meaning and motivates us to stay faithful until His triumphant return.

Feast of Trumpets

THE FIRST FALL HOLIDAY

FEAST OF TRUMPETS
THE FIRST FALL HOLIDAY

OTHER NAMES:
Rosh Hashanah, The New Year, Yom Teruah, Day of Blowing the Shofar, Yom HaZikaron, Yom HaDin, The Day of the Awakening Blast, and The Day of the Sounding of the Shofar.

COMMEMORATES:
In the Old Testament, it marks the Jewish New Year, symbolizing a fresh start, introspection, and a time to renew one's faith and connection with God.
In the New Testament, it serves as a prophecy of a future events: some see the blowing of trumpets during this feast associated the Second Coming of Christ.

BIBLE REFERENCE:
Leviticus 23:23–25; Numbers 29:1; Ezra 3:1–6

DATE OBSERVED:
The first day of the Hebrew month of Tishrei (September or October).

BRIEF INTRODUCTION:
Marks the beginning of the Jewish New Year with resonant sound of the shofar (a ram's horn). Holds immense spiritual and symbolic significance, inviting reflection, introspection, and renewal, heralding the arrival of a new year filled with hope, repentance, and reconnection to one's faith.

Feast of Trumpets Overview

Brief Introduction: The Feast of Trumpets marks the beginning of the Jewish New Year and is characterized by the resonant sound of the shofar (a ram's horn). This ancient tradition holds immense spiritual and symbolic significance, inviting reflection, introspection, and renewal, heralding the arrival of a new year filled with hope, repentance, and reconnection to one's faith.

Other Names: Rosh Hashanah, The New Year, Yom Teruah, Day of Blowing the Shofar, Yom HaZikaron, Yom HaDin, The Day of the Awakening Blast, and The Day of the Sounding of the Shofar.

Bible References: Leviticus 23:23–25; Numbers 29:1; Ezra 3:1–6

Date Observed: The first day of the Hebrew month of Tishrei (September or October).

Commemorates: In the Old Testament, it marks the Jewish New Year, symbolizing a fresh start, introspection, and a time to renew one's faith and connection with God. In the New Testament, it serves as a prophecy of a future event: some see the blowing of trumpets during this feast associated with the Second Coming.

The New Year

The Feast of Trumpets, marking the Jewish New Year, is a day steeped in spiritual significance. Recognized as Rosh Hashanah ("Head of the Year"), it is a time of honoring God's authority, reflecting on judgment, and celebrating the world's Creation, as introduced in Leviticus 23:23–25. Despite occurring in the seventh month, Tishri, it is considered the "spiritual" New Year, a testament to its profound importance in Jewish tradition.

The Shofar: A Symbol of Spiritual Awakening

Central to this feast is the blowing of the shofar, a ram's horn, as commanded in Leviticus 23:23–25. This ritual, commemorating divine mercy and the Creation of the universe, awakens spiritual reflection and repentance.

The shofar's sounds carry deep symbolic meanings, from joy to sorrow. The Akedah (binding of Isaac), though a separate event (Genesis 22:1–19), enriches the themes of judgment and mercy associated with this day.

Diverse Roles of the Shofar

The shofar's significance extends beyond the Feast of Trumpets, playing various roles in Scripture:

- Announcing commandments (Exodus 19)

- Signaling war (Judges 3:27)
- Proclaiming the Jubilee year (Leviticus 25:9)
- Coronating kings (1 Kings 1:34)
- Symbolizing the regathering of Israel (Isaiah 27:13)
- Symbolizing the Messiah's arrival (Zechariah 9:14)

Prophetic Echoes in the New Testament

The shofar finds prophetic implications, especially in the book of Revelation, where trumpet blasts herald end-times events and God's ultimate victory (Revelation chapters 8 and 9). The last trumpet mentioned in 1 Corinthians 15:52 and 1 Thessalonians 4:16–17 further connects the Feast of Trumpets with themes of resurrection and Christ's return.

Tishrei 1: A Day of Many Meanings

- Traditions and interpretations within Jewish lore associate Tishrei 1 with several significant events:
- Creation of Adam and Eve: Marks the creation of the first humans.
- Day of Judgment: Believed to be when God judges and decides the fate of all beings for the coming year.
- Binding of Isaac: Recalled through Torah readings.
- Celebration of God's Sovereignty: Recognized as the coronation of God as king.
- Blowing of the Shofar: A call to repentance and renewal.

Personal Reflection and Application

The Feast of Trumpets invites us to spiritual vigilance and readiness. Let the shofar's call inspire us to live in anticipation of Christ's return and recommit to God's purposes. As we observe this sacred time, let it remind us of God's faithfulness and our call to repentance, linking us to the enduring rhythm of God's calendar and the prophetic fulfillment of His plans.

Jewish Traditions of Feast of Trumpets

Sounding the Call

The Feast of Trumpets is a triumphant day in Jewish tradition—a symphony of spiritual awakening, introspection, and the heralding of the Jewish New Year.

The Feast of Trumpets initiates the "Days of Awe"—ten days of repentance culminating in the Day of Atonement. It begins a deeply spiritual season for Jewish people to reflect and put things right with God.

The Call of the Shofar: A Central Ritual

The shofar's call, especially significant during Rosh Hashanah and Yom Kippur, is a mitzvah commanding attention and reflection. Prepared from a natural ram's horn, its sound during synagogue services awakens listeners to repentance, echoing the forefathers' sacrifices and symbolizing a return to God. In synagogues, the ba'al tekiah (master of the blast) skillfully performs this ritual, following specific patterns:

- **Tekiah:** A long blast symbolizing joy.
- **Shevarim:** Three short blasts for brokenness.
- **Teruah:** Nine staccato notes representing sorrow.
- **Tekiah Gedolah:** The concluding prolonged blast.

Binding of Isaac

The Binding of Isaac, also known as the Akedah, is traditionally associated with the Feast of Trumpets because it symbolizes themes of sacrifice, obedience, and redemption, which are central to the observance of the feast. The Binding of Isaac is connected to the Feast of Trumpets in several symbolic ways:

1. The story occurs in Mount Moriah, which later became the site of the Temple in Jerusalem, where sacrifices were offered on Trumpets and all biblical feasts. So, it foreshadows these future sacrifices.

2. Abraham's willingness to sacrifice Isaac was a test of his faith and obedience to God, which set the stage for God's future blessings and covenant with Abraham's descendants. These covenant themes relate to repentance and judgment, which are central ideas of Trumpets.

3. The ram that God provided as a substitute sacrifice for Isaac is seen as a foreshadowing of substitutionary atonement later fulfilled by Christ.

4. God intervened to spare Isaac at the last moment, portraying hope and life triumphing over death. This relates to the ultimate triumph over sin and despair that Trumpets points toward.

5. The Binding of Isaac carries notes of testing, covenant, repentance, substitution, and redemption that come to fruition in the final eschatological fulfillment of the Fall feasts. So, it is a fitting precursor.

In these ways, the Binding of Isaac serves as an archetypal backdrop that sets the stage and calls for the deeper, layered meanings of redemption embedded in the Feast of Trumpets.

God's Kingship

During Rosh Hashanah, psalms that proclaim God's sovereignty, such as Psalms 95–99, are often sung or read, emphasizing His authority and judgment. These psalms invite believers to recognize God as the ultimate ruler and judge, encouraging humility and devotion in a time of prayer and repentance. This observance directs Jewish hearts towards God's throne, reflecting on His faithfulness and seeking His grace for the future.

The Book of Life: Spiritual Significance

The Book of Life is symbolically connected to the Feast of Trumpets in a few key ways:

1. The 10 Days of Awe between Trumpets and the Day of Atonement are a time of repentance and seeking forgiveness before one's fate is sealed in the Book of Life. Trumpets begins this period of introspection and reckoning.

2. The trumpet blasts on the Feast of Trumpets are seen as wake-up calls to examine one's life and repent in preparation for the final judgment before the Book of Life is closed.

3. Judgment is a significant theme on Trumpets as God determines who will be remembered in the Book of Life and sealed for blessing, pro-

tection, and salvation. The books are opened as a divine investigation ensues.

4. Tradition holds that the Book of Life sets the course of one's life for the coming year on Trumpets. So divine judgments issue new decrees for each person for the year ahead.

5. The shofar blasts on Trumpets proclaim the future Day of Judgment when the Book of Life is finally complete, and all human destinies are sealed for eternity based on its record.

So, the introspection, judgment, and decree themes of the Feast of Trumpets tie closely to the biblical concept of the Book of Life as determining human courses, fates, and eternities.

Tashlich: Casting Away Sins

The ritual of Tashlich, conducted near flowing water, centers on the symbolic act of casting bread crumbs into the water, representing our sins. This practice, inspired by Micah 7:19, signifies a deep yearning for spiritual purification and new beginnings. Despite differences in how it's performed, the heart of Tashlich remains a profound expression of seeking forgiveness and harboring hope for the future.

Symbolic Foods

The feast's culinary traditions are steeped in symbolism:

- Apples in Honey: Representing a sweet new year.

- Round Challah: Symbolizing the continuity of Creation.

- Pomegranates: Denoting blessings and good deeds.

- Other foods like fish heads or lambs' heads symbolize leadership and strength for the year ahead.

How the Feast of Trumpets Reveals Messiah

Christ Our King

FEAST OF TRUMPETS	JESUS
The water pouring ceremony symbolizes God's provision of rain for the crops and remembers the water He supplied from the rock in the wilderness.	If anyone is thirsty, let him come to me and drink. Whoever believes in me, as Scripture has said, streams of living water will flow from within him" John 7:37-38.
The lighting of large menorahs that illuminated the Temple and surrounding areas, symbolizing God's presence and guidance.	During the feast, Jesus proclaimed, "I am the Light of the World" (John 8:12), indicating His role as divine guidance and presence in the world's darkness.
Tabernacles celebrates God's provision and protection in the wilderness,	Jesus is seen as the ultimate provider and protector of His people.
Dwelling in temporary shelters reflects God's closeness to His people during their journey	"The Word became flesh and made his dwelling among us." John 1:14, The Greek word for "made his dwelling" can also be translated as "tabernacled."

Imagine the sound of the shofar echoing through the hills of ancient Israel. This isn't just any sound; it's a divine alarm, a spiritual wake-up call. The Feast of Trumpets, or Rosh Hashanah, marks the beginning of a new year—a time for reflection and renewal.

This sacred echo reaches into the New Testament, where we find breathtaking parallels. Just as the shofar's blast pierces the air, so does the message of Christ pierce our hearts, reminding us of God's sovereignty, a theme deeply echoed in the life and teachings of Jesus. Each blast cries, "Prepare the way for the Lord!"

The Royal Proclamation

This feast symbolizes God's coronation as the sovereign king, a theme that resonates with Jesus' role in the New Testament. Like the shofar's call announcing a new era, Christ's arrival signifies the dawn of the Kingdom of God on Earth. This sound transcends a historical ritual, symbolizing a heavenly declaration of hope, salvation, and divine love.

The shofar's blast calls for introspection and repentance, mirroring Jesus' teachings emphasizing spiritual renewal. His life, parables, and sermons, notably the Sermon on the Mount and the parables of the Lost Sheep and the Prodigal Son, highlight the joy of spiritual awakening and repentance.

The Promise of Redemption and Judgment

In Jewish tradition, the Feast of Trumpets introduces the period leading to the Day of Atonement, focusing on God's redemption of Israel. This concept finds fulfillment in Jesus, who, through His sacrifice, bridges the Old and New Testaments.

While the feast symbolizes judgment, Christ's role as our advocate transforms this into a time of mercy and grace. It signifies a shift from judgment to divine forgiveness, encapsulating the essence of Christian belief in Jesus' intercession.

The Last Trumpet: A Future Hope

The Bible describes that trumpets will herald Jesus' return when he comes again in glory. Two key references are 1 Thessalonians 4:16-17 and 1 Corinthians 15:52:

1 Thessalonians 4 says, *The Lord himself will descend from heaven with a cry of command, with the voice of an archangel, and with the sound of the trumpet of God.* When Christ returns, a trumpet will accompany his appearance, sounded by a mighty angelic herald.

Similarly, 1 Corinthians 15 describes the *"last trumpet"* that will be blown when *the dead will be raised imperishable, and we shall be changed.* This trumpet signals Jesus' return and the resurrection of believers to new, immortal life.

The trumpet blast signifies the dramatic, decisive, public nature of Christ's second coming. Like a trumpet blast would assemble ancient Israelites, this rousing call rallies Christians, alive and dead, to assemble before God's glorious presence.

The piercing trumpet sound underscores the pivotal nature of this world-changing event. Christ's first coming was marked by humility and quiet servanthood, but his return will be heralded with power and celestial fanfare as he establishes his eternal kingdom on earth. All will hear and know that the Lord has come as King!

The apostle Paul's reference to a last trumpet at Christ's return aligns with the eschatological themes of the Feast of Trumpets. It foreshadows the triumphant return of Jesus, the resurrection of the dead, and the final victory over sin and death, weaving a tapestry of ancient tradition with future promise.

In the Feast of Trumpets, we find a beautiful revelation of our Savior, Christ the Lord—a magnificent tapestry of prophecy, promise, and purpose. So let us rejoice, for in this celebration, we glimpse the divine narrative unfolding across time and eternity.

Celebrating the Feast of Trumpets

TRUMPETS	MESSIAH
Heralds royal acknowledgment	Jesus is King Revelation 19:16
A call to repentance	Taught repentance Mark 1:15
A call to spiritual awakening	Rapture or Second Coming 1 Thessalonians 4:16
Trumpet assembled people for battle	JJesus is the Commander of the Army of God Revelation 19:11–16
Sounded during times of victory and triumph	Victory over death 1 Corinthians 15:55–57
A time to reflect on the concept of judgment	Jesus' final judgment Revelation 19:11–15

THEMES OF RENEWAL AND REPENTANCE

Rosh HaShanah, the Jewish New Year, carries profound symbolism that deepens our understanding of God's redemptive plan, and enriches our faith in Christ. As followers of Jesus, let's explore practical ways to embrace this holy day, recognizing its roots in Jewish tradition while discovering its relevance to our Christian faith.

The Shofar's Call

A central feature of Rosh HaShanah is the sounding of the shofar, a ram's horn. Sounding or listening to the shofar can be a poignant reminder of repentance and spiritual renewal for believers. Its blasts, echoing across time, draw us closer to God, stirring us to awaken to His presence, and prompting introspective reflection.

Whether attending a Messianic congregation's Rosh HaShanah service or observing at home, engaging in shofar sounds, Scripture readings, and worship songs deepens our connection to the Jewish roots of Christianity. A Bible study on the Feast of Trumpets could explore several themes:

- **Biblical Significance:** Delve into the biblical origins and significance of the Feast of Trumpets as outlined in Leviticus 23:23-25 and Numbers 29:1-6. Explore why trumpets were blown, the meaning behind the timing of the feast, and its connection to other Jewish festivals. Read all the chapters in this book on the Feast of Trumpets.

- **Prophetic Implications:** Investigate the prophetic significance of the Feast of Trumpets, particularly about eschatology and the second coming of Jesus Christ. Explore how the blowing of trumpets relates to the return of Christ, the resurrection of the dead, and the gathering of God's people.

- **Spiritual Preparation:** Reflect on the spiritual themes associated with the Feast of Trumpets, such as repentance, renewal, and readiness. Consider how believers can spiritually prepare themselves for the return of Christ and the fulfillment of God's promises.

- **Symbolism of Trumpets:** Examine the symbolic significance of trumpets in the Bible and Jewish tradition. Discuss how trumpets signal essential events, gather the people, and announce God's presence and how these themes relate to the Feast of Trumpets.

- Repentance and Reflection: This is a time for introspection and repentance. We can embrace this season by dedicating time to prayer, confession, and meditation on Scripture. This period becomes an opportunity for heartfelt reflection and seeking renewal in our relationship with God.

- Seek God's Blessing: As we observe Rosh HaShanah, let us earnestly seek God's blessings for the coming year. Pray for His favor, provision and protection, trusting in His continued guidance and the fulfillment of His promises.

Sharing New Year Cards

Sending Rosh HaShanah cards conveys prayers and blessings for a year of spiritual growth and joy. Through thoughtful messages, we can strengthen our bonds of love and faith within our community, reflecting our unity in Christ. Download a free PDF Rosh HaShanah card from the Bible Holidays Facebook Group.

Symbolism of Apples and Honey

Dipping apples in honey symbolizes a year filled with sweetness and blessing. Integrating this custom into our observance, we recognize God's blessings and express our hopes for a year of spiritual richness and joy, sharing this meaningful ritual with family and friends.

The Festive Meal

Gathering for a festive meal is a cornerstone of Rosh HaShanah. Christian families can come together, setting a table with fine dinnerware and white decor to symbolize purity and forgiveness in Christ. This shared meal emphasizes the importance of communion with God and fellowship with one another.

Conclusion

The Feast of Trumpets is a divine call, wrapping us in its spiritual essence to grow our faith, seek forgiveness, and look forward to Christ's blessings. It highlights God's ultimate authority and His longing to be close to us, echoed in the shofar's sound. This is a moment to ponder God's guidance and accept His peace.

God calls us to journey with Him towards a life marked by balance, leading us towards humility and purity. The shofar's call is a reminder of this path, nudging us to adopt humility and follow God's lead.

Feast of Trumpets Recipes

Sweet Beginnings: Apples and Honey

On Rosh Hashanah, apples and honey are traditionally served as a symbolic gesture for a sweet new year. The custom is simple yet meaningful. Here's how apples and honey are typically served during this celebration:

- **Sliced Apples:** Apples are washed, sliced, and arranged on a plate or serving platter. Some people may choose to leave the apples whole for individuals to slice themselves, but pre-sliced apples are more common for ease of serving.

- **Bowl of Honey:** A small bowl or dish of honey is placed alongside the apples. The honey should be pure and, ideally, new or fresh for the occasion, symbolizing the hope for a "sweet and fruitful" new year.

- **Blessing and Dipping:** Before eating the apple slices, a blessing is recited. The traditional blessing is the standard fruit blessing, "Baruch atah Adonai, Eloheinu Melech haolam, borei p'ri haetz," which means "Blessed are You, Lord our God, King of the universe, who creates the fruit of the tree." After this blessing, each apple slice is dipped into the honey.

- **Additional Prayer:** After dipping the apple in honey, it's common to add a special prayer for a good and sweet year, such as "May it be Your will, Lord our God and God of our ancestors, that You renew for us a good and sweet year."

- **Serving to Others:** The apples and honey are then shared among family members and guests.

Sweet Challah Bread

Ingredients

4–4½ cups all-purpose flour
½ cup warm water
½ cup sugar, plus extra for sprinkling
2 tsp active dry yeast
3 large eggs (1 for the dough, 2 for glazing)
¼ cup honey
¼ cup olive oil (plus extra for greasing the pan)
1 tsp salt
1 cup raisins (optional)
1 tsp cinnamon (optional)

Instructions

- **Prepare the Yeast Mixture:** In a small bowl, dissolve 1 teaspoon of sugar in ½ cup warm water.

- Sprinkle the yeast over the water and let it sit for 5–10 minutes until it becomes frothy.
  In a large mixing bowl, combine 4 cups of flour, ½ cup of sugar, and salt.

- Make a well in the center and add 1 beaten egg, honey, oil, and the yeast mixture. Mix to form a shaggy dough. If using, fold in the raisins and cinnamon at this stage.

- Knead the dough on a floured surface for about 10 minutes, adding more flour as needed, until the dough is smooth and elastic.

- Place the dough in a greased bowl, cover with a damp cloth, and let it rise in a warm place for 1.5 to 2 hours, or until it has doubled in size.

- **Shape the Challah:** Punch down the risen dough and divide it into 3–4 strands for braiding. For Rosh Hashanah, form a round loaf to symbolize the cycle of the year.
  Braid the strands and then bring the ends together to form a circle. Tuck the ends underneath for a neat look.

- **Second Rise:** Place the shaped challah on a baking sheet lined with parchment paper. Cover and let it rise again for about an hour, until it puffs up.

- **Preheat the Oven:** About 20 minutes before baking, preheat your oven to 350°F (175°C).

- **Glaze and Bake:** Beat the remaining 2 eggs. Brush the challah with the beaten egg, making sure to get into the crevices of the braid. Sprinkle with a little sugar for extra sweetness and shine.

- Bake in the preheated oven for 30–35 minutes, or until the challah is golden brown and sounds hollow when tapped on the bottom. Let the challah cool on a wire rack.

Enjoy your sweet Rosh Hashanah challah with family and friends, and may it bring sweetness to your new year!

Apple Honey Cake

This cake is adorable, decorated with little candy bees.

Ingredients
3 cups all-purpose flour
1 tsp baking powder
1 tsp baking soda
1 tsp ground cinnamon
¼ tsp ground cloves
¼ tsp ground allspice
½ tsp salt
1 cup vegetable oil
1 cup honey
1 ½ cups granulated sugar
½ cup brown sugar
3 large eggs
1 tsp vanilla extract
1 cup warm coffee or strong tea
½ cup orange juice
2 medium apples (peeled, cored, and chopped or grated)
Optional: ½ cup sliced almonds or chopped nuts for topping

Instructions

- Preheat your oven to 350°F (175°C). Grease a bundt pan or a 9x13-inch baking pan.

- **Combine Dry Ingredients:** In a large bowl, sift together the flour, baking powder, baking soda, cinnamon, cloves, allspice, and salt. Set aside.

- **Mix Wet Ingredients:** In another large bowl, whisk together the oil, honey, granulated sugar, brown sugar, eggs, and vanilla extract until smooth.

- **Combine Wet and Dry Ingredients:** Alternately add the dry ingredients and the coffee/tea and orange juice to the wet mixture, starting and ending with the dry ingredients. Mix until well combined. **Add Apples:** Fold in the chopped or grated apples into the batter.

- **Pour and Bake:** Pour the batter into the prepared pan. Sprinkle the top with sliced almonds or chopped nuts as desired. Bake for 45–55 minutes, or until a toothpick inserted into the center of the cake comes out clean.

- **Cool and Serve:** Let the cake cool in the pan for 15–20 minutes, then turn it out onto a wire rack to cool completely. Serve as is or dust with powdered sugar for an extra touch of sweetness.

Enjoy your apple honey cake! It's perfect with a cup of tea or coffee and captures the essence of the holiday with its sweet, comforting flavors.

Feast of Trumpets Questions

Illuminating Reflections

Reflecting on the Feast of Trumpets, also known as Rosh Hashanah, can offer profound insights into how we understand and live out our faith. This feast, rich in symbolism and tradition, invites believers to introspect, renew, and connect more deeply with their spiritual journey. Here are some reflection questions to help delve into the significance of the Feast of Trumpets and its fulfillment in Jesus, encouraging a lifestyle that reflects the principles outlined in Scripture:

1. **Awakening to Spiritual Realities**: How does the shofar sound during the Feast of Trumpets inspire you to awaken to your spiritual journey and needs?

2. **Introspection and Renewal:** How can you use this time to introspect and seek renewal in your faith and relationship with God?

3. **Embracing Fresh Starts:** The Feast of Trumpets marks a new year. How can you embrace this concept of a fresh start in your own life?

4. **Preparing for Christ's Return:** How does the theme of the Feast of Trumpets help you prepare for and anticipate the Second Coming of Christ?

5. **Reflection on God's Sovereignty:** What does the Feast of Trumpets teach you about God's sovereignty and your response to His divine authority?

6. **Understanding Judgment and Mercy:** How does the New Testament's portrayal of Jesus affect your understanding of judgment and mercy, as symbolized by the Feast of Trumpets?

7. **Personal Repentance and Forgiveness:** How can you practically apply the themes of repentance and forgiveness in your life during this season?

8. **Communal Observances and Unity:** Reflect on the importance of gathering with others to celebrate and learn from God's Word. How can communal observance enhance your spiritual experience?

9. **Balancing Celebration and Solemnity:** How can you balance the elements of celebration and solemn introspection in observing this feast?

10. **Anticipating Future Hope:** In what ways does the Feast of Trumpets encourage you to live with hope and anticipation for the future promises in Christ?

These questions are designed to help you explore the Feast of Trumpets' rich traditions and spiritual meanings. As you reflect on these questions, consider how they can influence your daily walk with Christ, encouraging a deeper commitment to faith, repentance, and anticipation of His return. Let this time be a catalyst for spiritual growth and renewed dedication to living out the principles of Scripture in your life.

Day of Atonement

THE SECOND FALL HOLIDAY

DAY OF ATONEMENT
THE SECOND FALL HOLIDAY

OTHER NAMES
Yom Kippur, Yom HaKippurim, Sabbath of Sabbaths, The Fast, The Day of Coverings.

DATE OBSERVED
The tenth day of the Hebrew month of Tishrei (September or October)

COMMEMORATES
The seeking of forgiveness, reconciliation with God, and atonement for sins through repentance, fasting, and rituals.

BIBLE REFERENCE
Leviticus 16; Leviticus 23:26–32; Numbers 29:7–11; Hebrews 9:7

BRIEF INTRODUCTION
The holiest day of the year, a time for solemn and significant Jewish day for reflection, repentance, and reconciliation through fasting, prayer, and introspection, symbolizing the pursuit of spiritual purity and redemption.

Day of Atonement Overview

Brief Introduction: The holiest day of the year, a time for solemn and significant day for reflection, repentance, and reconciliation through fasting, prayer, and introspection, symbolizing the pursuit of spiritual purity and redemption.

Commemorates: The seeking of forgiveness, reconciliation with God, and atonement for sins through repentance, fasting, and rituals.

Other Names: Yom Kippur, Yom HaKippurim, Sabbath of Sabbaths, The Fast, The Day of Coverings.

Bible References: Leviticus 16; Leviticus 23:26–32; Numbers 29:7–11; Hebrews 9:7

Date Observed: The tenth day of the Hebrew month of Tishrei (September or October).

A Time for Self-Examination and Repentance

The Day of Atonement, observed on the tenth day of Tishrei, stands as the pinnacle of spiritual introspection in the Jewish calendar. It marks the culmination of the Ten Days of Repentance, beginning with Rosh Hashanah.

The Heart of Atonement: Rituals and Observance

Leviticus 16 outlines the rituals performed on the Day of Atonement. It's recommended to familiarize yourself with it before proceeding with this chapter. The High Priest exclusively oversees the service, carrying out all tasks solo. Assistance or physical contact with him is prohibited until the entirety of the ceremony is concluded.

Central to this day were two goats: one sacrificed as a sin offering, and the other, the scapegoat, symbolically bearing the community's sins, sent into the wilderness. Beyond mere ceremony, this sacred ritual signified purification and unification with the Creator.

The day was marked by fasting, self-affliction, and complete rest, as described in Leviticus 23:27–32. It served as a sacred assembly dedicated to introspection and humility.

Reflecting and Repenting

Yom Kippur calls for a pause in daily routines, focusing instead on spiritual rejuvenation. This day of solemn rest allows individuals and the community to seek forgiveness and reconcile with God.

When you seek me, you will find me, provided you seek for me wholeheartedly.
Jeremiah 29:13

Each year during Rosh Hashanah, the sound of the shofar—a ram's The shofar's blast in worship calls believers to return to God, symbolizing unity as described in 1 Thessalonians 4:16–18. Its sound carries deep spiritual significance, urging contemporary faith followers towards reflection. The shofar, with its curved form, symbolizes humility and the importance of submitting to God's wisdom, echoing Solomon's advice in Proverbs 14:12 against self-reliance. It reminds us of God's promises for hope and well-being, as affirmed in Jeremiah 29:11, steering us towards obedience and trust in His plans.

In the spirit of the high holy days, we are called to seek God wholeheartedly, as encouraged in Jeremiah 29:13. This period of reflection and renewal is a time to align our hearts and minds with God's will, recognizing our limitations and the grace offered to us.

Fasting and Repentance

Isaiah 58 challenges the notion of outward rituals devoid of sincerity. Genuine fasting, as God desires, involves breaking the bonds of oppression and embracing acts of kindness and humility.

Righteousness through Faith

Romans 3:25–26 introduces the concept of atonement and righteousness through faith in Jesus, aligning with the essence of Yom Kippur. This passage underscores the idea of Divine reconciliation.

Yom Kippur's rich biblical roots offer a mercy, sacrifice, and redemption narrative. It invites introspection on personal shortcomings, and emphasizes a genuine, heartfelt approach to repentance. The high holy days, especially with the symbolic sound of the shofar, call us to a deeper understanding of our relationship with God and the humility required to walk in His ways.

Fulfillment in Christ

As depicted in Hebrews 9:7 and 9:24–28, Christ's sacrificial death and resurrection are seen as fulfilling the prophetic symbolism of Yom Kippur. Unlike the annual rituals performed by the Jewish high priest, Christ's singular sacrifice offers eternal redemption.

As we delve into the significance of these holy days, let their teachings transform our hearts and lives, drawing us closer to embracing God's love and grace.

Jewish Traditions of Day of Atonement

Prayer and Fasting

The Day of Atonement, Yom Kippur, is the holiest day in the Jewish calendar, is steeped in rituals that profoundly reflect God's character, and the deep, repentant relationship He seeks with His people.

Leviticus 16 outlines the detailed duties of the high priest on the Day of Atonement. Here's a brief outline of the High Priest's responsibilities on this day:

Preparation for the Ceremony

- **Ritual Cleansing:** The high priest undergoes a ritual bath to purify himself.
- **Sacred Garments:** He dresses in special linen garments, setting aside his usual priestly vestments.

Offering Sacrifices and Ceramony

- **Bull Offering for Personal Sin:** He offers a bull as a sin offering for himself and his household.
- **Two Goats for the Community:** He presents two goats before the Lord; one is for the Lord (to be sacrificed) and the other is the scapegoat (to be sent into the wilderness).
- **Casting Lots:** The high priest casts lots to determine which goat is for the Lord and which is the scapegoat.
- **Sacrificing the Lord's Goat:** He sacrifices the goat chosen for the Lord as a sin offering for the people.

- **Entering the Holy of Holies:** He enters the innermost sanctuary with the blood of the bull and the goat to sprinkle it on and before the mercy seat, making atonement for himself, his household, and the entire community of Israel.

- **Confessing Over the Scapegoat:** He lays his hands on the scapegoat, confessing over it all the iniquities of the Israelites, and then sends it into the wilderness, symbolically carrying away their sins.

- **Additional Offerings:** He makes a burnt offering for himself and the people.

- **Removing the Linen Garments:** He removes the linen garments, bathes again, and puts on his regular priestly garments.

- **Final Burnt Offerings:** He offers the burnt offerings on the altar to signify the completion of atonement and purification.

- **Cleansing of the Altar:** The high priest performs rituals to cleanse the altar, making it pure and holy once again.

- **Final Rituals:** He completes any additional rituals required to conclude the Day of Atonement ceremonies.

The High Priest: Mediator of Atonement

Central to Yom Kippur is the high priest, symbolizing the bridge between Israel and God. His multifaceted role represents mediation, atonement, and intercession:

- **Mediator Role:** As a mediator, the high priest entered the Holy of Holies to communicate directly with the Divine (Leviticus 16:15–16). This act represented the closest proximity to God's presence, permitted only on this one sacred day of the year.

- **Atonement Rituals:** The high priest performed rituals to atone for Israel's sins, including sacrifices and sprinkling blood on the Mercy Seat on the Ark of the Covenant, symbolizing cleansing and reconciliation (Leviticus 16:17).

- **Personal Purification:** Before Yom Kippur, the high priest underwent purification, symbolizing the sanctity required to approach God (Leviticus 16:14).

- **Scapegoat Ceremony:** The high priest oversaw the scapegoat ritual, symbolizing the removal of sins (Leviticus 16:21–22).

Fasting and Prayer: Emblems of Repentance

The twenty-five-hour fast on Yom Kippur is a profound spiritual practice:

- **A Time for Introspection:** The fast facilitates self-reflection from sundown to sundown (Leviticus 23:27–32).

- **Act of Repentance:** Fasting represents a physical expression of seeking humility and seeking forgiveness before God.

- **Spiritual Hunger:** The physical discomfort mirrors a more profound spiritual longing for righteousness and Divine connection.

- **Soul Detoxification:** This period encourages a break from worldly distractions, focusing on spiritual priorities.

- **Communal Solidarity:** Fasting fosters a sense of unity among those collectively seeking atonement.

- **Reinforcing Discipline:** The fast challenges and strengthens spiritual discipline and self-control.

- **Renewed Commitment:** Enduring the fast symbolizes a recommitment to faith and spiritual growth.

Wearing White: Garments of Purity

White attire on Yom Kippur holds deep symbolism:

- **Purity and Cleanliness:** White symbolizes the aspiration for spiritual purity (Ecclesiastes 9:8).

- **Renewal and New Beginnings:** The white garments reflect a chance for a fresh start and spiritual rebirth.

- **Equality Before God:** The simplicity of white attire emphasizes equal standing in seeking Divine mercy.

- **Mortality and Humility:** It reminds wearers of life's transience and the need for humility.

The Scapegoat Ritual

The scapegoat ritual, where two goats were selected: one was sacrificed to Yahweh and the other, the scapegoat, was sent into the wilderness carrying the sins of the people. The scapegoat is called Azazel, stemming from the original Hebrew translation meaning "the goat that departs." This concept of the scapegoat, first introduced in Leviticus 16, describes a goat designated to bear the sins of the Israelites, subsequently released into the wilderness as a symbol of sin being removed from the community.

This ritual foretells Jesus Christ's sacrifice, who, like the scapegoat, takes upon Himself the sins of humanity (Hebrews 9:28), offering a path to redemption and a restored relationship with God. Through this lens, the scapegoat becomes a powerful foreshadowing of grace, mercy, and the ultimate sacrifice for sin.

The Scarlet Ribbon

In the scapegoat ritual, a scarlet ribbon holds deep symbolic meaning. As detailed in the Mishnah (not in the Torah), a scarlet ribbon was tied to the scapegoat sent into the wilderness, signifying the sins of the Israelites. Additionally, a portion of this ribbon was affixed to the Temple door or a rock. The transformation of the ribbon's color from scarlet to white was seen as a sign of God's forgiveness, echoing the prophecy from Isaiah 1:18, *Though your sins are like scarlet, they shall be as white as snow.* This change was a visible indication of Divine absolution and purification from sin.

The miraculous event of the scarlet ribbon turning white ceased to occur forty years before the Second Temple's destruction in 70 AD. This period coincides with ' ministry and the subsequent years leading to the Temple's demise. Jesus, regarded as the ultimate sacrifice for sin, made the old sacrificial system unnecessary. This shift signifies a profound change in the way atonement was understood and practiced.

The mention of a scarlet ribbon may remind you of Rahab and the scarlet cord found in the book of Joshua (chapters 2 and 6). Both the scarlet ribbon and Rahab's cord symbolize the ways in which God offers salvation and rescue. While the scapegoat symbolizes the Israelites' atonement, Rahab's scarlet cord represents her faith and the preservation of her family from harm.

Neilah Service

The Neilah service is the concluding, climactic service on Yom Kippur, the Day of Atonement. It derives its name from the Hebrew word *nēʿīlā,* meaning "closure" or "locking," symbolizing the closing of the gates of repentance.

Key aspects of the Neilah service include:

- It is recited only once a year at the end of Yom Kippur as the sun begins to set. This marks the final opportunity to repent before the holiday ends.

- The service contains repeated pleas for forgiveness and mercy, including the heartfelt plea "Shema Yisrael," calling on God to hear his people. There is a sense of longing and urgency.

- The ark (Aron Kodesh) holding the Torah scrolls is kept open for the entire Neilah service, signifying the gates of prayer remaining open.

- The shofar is sounded with one final long blast at the end, marking the closing of the gates as Yom Kippur concludes.

- The service culminates with the declaration, "Next year in rebuilt Jerusalem!" expressing messianic hope for future redemption.

The Neilah service is profoundly moving, providing worshippers with an incredible finale filled with earnest yearning and the hope of reconciliation on the most sacred day of the Jewish calendar. The palpable sensations of the setting sun and closing gates add gravity to this pivotal moment.

How the Day of Atonement Reveals Messiah

CHRIST OUR HIGH PRIEST

HIGH PRIEST	MESSIAH
Mediator Between God and People Liviticus 8–10	Mediator Between God and People 1 Timothy 2:5–6
Teacher of the Law Deut 33:10	Teacher of the Law Matthew 5–7
Atonement for the Nation Numbers 15:25	Atonement for the World John 3:16
Temporary Sacrifice Leviticus 16:34	Ultimate Perfect Sacrifice Hebrews 9:28
Anointed with Oil Exodus 29:7	Anointed with Oil Hebrews 1:9
Religious Leade and Spiritual Guide Leviticus 21:10	Religious Leade and Spiritual Guide Luke 22:39–46
Sacrificed Blood of Animals Leviticus 16:15	Sacrificed His Own Blood Hebrews 9:12–15
Only a Symbol of the Real High Priest	Eternal High Priest Hebrews 4:14

The Day of Atonement, or Yom Kippur, resonates deeply within the Jewish tradition as a day shrouded in spiritual significance, and rich with ancient rituals. It is a sacred time when the high priest performed acts of atonement for the people—a shadow of the Messiah's role as the ultimate intercessor.

Sacred Duties of the High Priest

Once a year the high priest would enter the Holy of Holies, carrying the weight of Israel's sins. Garbed in pure white for humility and purity, he approached the Mercy Seat with the blood of a lamb, interceding for the nation's transgressions (Leviticus 16:15). This day was the only time when the high priest could enter the inner sanctum of the Temple, making it a profound moment of communion and supplication.

In his sacred duty, the high priest offered blood sacrifices, as commanded in Numbers 15:25, to atone for both unintentional sins and the collective transgressions of Israel. Each ritual, from the sprinkling of blood to the burning of incense, was a meticulous plea for God's forgiveness.

Christ as the Ultimate Sacrifice

Jesus is the embodiment of the high priest's role, offering not the blood of animals but His own as a sacrifice for sin (Hebrews 9:12–15). He is portrayed as entering the true Holy of Holies, not made by human hands, to mediate between God and humanity.

While the high priest offered the blood of goats and calves, Jesus offered his own blameless life as the ultimate sacrifice. As the perfect, blemish-free Lamb of God, Jesus' shed blood was sufficient to deal with sin once and for all (Hebrews 7:27). In contrast, the old covenant sacrifices provided ceremonial purification and temporary forgiveness, Christ's self-sacrifice brings genuine cleansing of conscience and open access to God.

Just as the high priest passed through the temple veil into God's presence, Jesus entered the true, heavenly Holy of Holies on our behalf, securing eternal redemption (Hebrews 9:12). His priestly inauguration was not in an earthly tabernacle, but in the very throne room of God. And he sits there perpetually, interceding before the Father as the definitive Mediator between the divine and human realms.

So while the Day of Atonement symbolized atonement and access to God through temple ritual using animal sacrifices, Jesus' superior priestly ministry points to the more significant, heavenly realities his death accomplished - realities that cleanse our conscience, bring us near to God and anchor our eternal salvation.

The Holy of Holies Veil Torn on the Day of Atonement

According to Day of Atonement tradition, the high priest was permitted to enter the Holy of Holies once a year on this most sacred day. He would pass beyond the temple veil into God's direct presence to offer sacrificial blood for atonement of sins. This ritual pointed toward reconciliation between God and His chosen nation.

The Gospels reveal that as Jesus succumbed to death on the cross, this heavy temple veil was dramatically torn from top to bottom. The timing and location carry deep symbolism: At the climax of history's ultimate sacrifice on Passover, the barrier to God's presence tore open at the precise time when the high priest would be performing Yom Kippur rituals behind that very veil.

As the mediator of the new covenant sealed in his blood, Jesus served as the Great High Priest, accomplishing eternally and for all people what this Yom Kippur ritual symbolized under the old covenant. His perfect sacrifice opened the way to God's throne permanently so that all who believe might boldly access our Heavenly Father.

God Grieved His Son

The significance of the torn veil in Jewish tradition is profound. Similar to the tradition of tearing garments to express grief, the torn veil symbolized our Heavenly Father grieving the loss of His Son.

The torn veil indicated that the old system of repetitive sacrifices by earthly priests had been gloriously fulfilled and transformed through Messiah's atoning work. The final sacrifice had been made; the ultimate high priest had entered the Most Holy Place once and for all.

The High Priesthood of Christ

Jesus fulfills and transforms the high priest's symbolism, offering Himself as the eternal mediator. He is described as the High Priest forever, according to the order of Melchizedek, a priesthood that is unending and perfect (Hebrews 7:17).

The Day of Atonement calls for deep introspection and repentance. The rituals and fasts observed physically manifest spiritual humility and the desire for atonement. Just as the high priest enacted purification rituals, Jesus calls for purity of the heart, inviting believers to sincere repentance and renewal of spirit.

God's Mercy Revealed in Christ's Sacrifice

Reflecting on the concept of atonement reveals the extraordinary measures God takes to bridge the gap between humanity and Himself. His relentless pursuit to save, deliver, and free us from the grip of self-absorption and spiritual adversaries underscores His profound desire to eliminate the hostility that alienates us from Him.

The divide between a wayward human spirit and a merciful Creator is both deep and complex. Human pride often boldly resists God's kindness. In their disillusionment, many reject God's benevolence, unaware of His constant work in their favor.

God identifies us as His children, and demonstrated this through a remarkable act of humility—His incarnation as a child. Despite this, He encountered hostility, exemplified by Herod's deadly schemes. Throughout His ministry, He faced constant opposition from religious leaders who failed to recognize His mission to bring humanity back to God. Despite His miraculous deeds and teachings, which unveiled His divine identity, He was falsely accused of embodying the evil He fought against.

His earthly journey was marked by multiple threats to His life. For instance, in Nazareth, He was confronted by a mob intent on killing Him; yet the culmination of His sacrifice, driven by His unwavering love for us, was still to unfold. In the throes of Gethsemane's anguish, betrayed by Judas and subjected to a mockery of justice leading to His brutal treatment and crucifixion, He willingly sacrificed Himself.

On the cross, He embodied mercy for all humanity. Despite having the power to save Himself, He chose to save us. The forgiveness He offers is costly, requiring the forgiver to bear the weight of the offense, anger, and bitterness in order to liberate the wrongdoer. This act of self-sacrifice at Calvary, where He took upon Himself the sins of all, offered liberation to every individual, transcending time and place.

The peace now established between God and humanity is priceless, achieved through the immense cost of His mercy. The assurance of our reconciliation with the Creator is unshakeable. Through His boundless grace, God paid the ultimate price to absolve our sins—a cost that no one else could bear.

The Day of Atonement's Lasting Echo

The Day of Atonement's ancient rituals find their echo in the life and sacrifice of Jesus Christ. Yom Kippur's traditions, including the high priest's solemn duties, become prophetic symbols pointing to Christ's redemptive work. For believers, these rituals are transformed into an enduring testament of Divine love and mercy, offering a path to reconciliation and a deeper relationship with God. Through the lens of these sacred traditions, we are invited to appreciate the continuous call for atonement and the profound promise of restoration that the Messiah brings.

Observing the Day of Atonement

Reflecting and Repenting

Tthe Day of Atonement stands as the holiest day within the Jewish tradition, devoted to repentance, prayer, and fasting. Observing elements of this day can provide profound spiritual insights and growth.

Embracing the Historical Context

Begin by immersing yourself in the origins and significance of Yom Kippur through a dedicated study of Leviticus 16. Understanding the biblical basis for the day's rituals—such as the high priest's role, the sacrificial system, and the profound symbolism of atonement—can deepen your appreciation for how these elements foreshadow the redemptive work of Jesus in the New Testament.

Fasting and Prayer

- **Structured Fasting:** Choose a specific start and end time for your fast. Reflect on its purpose, and commit this time to focus on spiritual needs over physical sustenance and comfort.

- **Guided Prayer Sessions:** Organize times of prayer throughout the fast. These can include personal repentance, intercession for others, and contemplation on the sacrifice of Christ. Use Psalms such as Psalm 51 for guided prayer.

- **Wearing White:** Wear white to symbolize purity and spiritual cleansing, mirroring the high priest's attire. This simple act is a visual and physical representation of your dedication to the day's observance.

- **Community Involvement:** If participating in a group observance, encourage all members to wear white to create a unified reflective atmosphere.

Reflective Bible Study

Set aside time for a focused Bible study on themes of atonement and forgiveness. Dive into passages such as Isaiah 53, Hebrews 9–10, and 1 John 1:9, and consider how they speak to the necessity of atonement and the character of God as both just and merciful.

Journaling for Reflection

- **Prompted Entries:** Use journaling prompts related to atonement, such as "What does atonement mean to me?" or "How do I experience forgiveness in my life?".

- **Reflect on Rituals:** Write a journal about the meaning behind Yom Kippur rituals and how they can relate to your spiritual practices.

Acts of Repentance and Reconciliation

- **Personal Inventory:** Make a list of relationships that require mending. Reach out to those you've wronged with a heartfelt apology.

- **Forgiveness Practice:** Write letters of forgiveness to those who have hurt you, releasing any bitterness as an act of your will, following Christ's example.

Acts of Charity

- **Community Service:** Engage in a local service project or organize an event to help those in need, reflecting the communal aspect of Yom Kippur.

- **Donation Drive:** Use the day to start a donation drive for a charity, emphasizing the giving aspect of atonement.

Personal Time of Solitude

Allocate a portion of Yom Kippur for solitude, free from daily distractions. Meditate on the nature of God's grace and listen for His guidance.

Community Gathering

- **Interfaith Observance:** Attend or host a service focusing on the themes of Yom Kippur, inviting people from various faith backgrounds to share in the experience.

- **Discussion Groups:** After the service, hold small group discussions to reflect on the observances and share personal insights.

Thanksgiving

End the observance with an expression of gratitude. Gather with others to share how the day has impacted your understanding and experience of God's mercy. Celebrate the assurance of forgiveness and hope through songs, prayers, and possibly breaking the fast together.

Conclusion

Observing elements of the Day of Atonement as a Christian deepens your spiritual walk, not through legalistic obligation but through meaningful practices that reflect repentance, grace, and redemption. It's a chance to connect with the roots of faith and understand the depths of God's love and forgiveness.

Day of Atonement Questions

Illuminating Reflections

These questions are for heartfelt reflection, inviting us to engage more deeply with our faith, understand the depth of God's love and mercy, and live out the transformative principles of atonement and redemption in our everyday lives.

1. How does the concept of atonement in Leviticus 16 deepen your understanding of forgiveness and reconciliation in your own life?

2. What does atonement signify to you personally, and how does this shape your perspective on sin and mercy?

3. Reflect on the role of the high priest as a mediator on the Day of Atonement. How does this enhance your appreciation of Jesus' role as the ultimate intercessor?

4. What insights can you gain from the high priest's rigorous preparations and exclusive access to the Holy of Holies?

5. Considering your shortcomings, how do you relate to having someone, like the high priest or Jesus, intercede on your behalf?

6. How can you apply the principles of confession and repentance, as demonstrated in the scapegoat ritual, to your daily life?

7. What current rituals or practices help you remember and appreciate Christ's sacrifice? Are there new practices inspired by Yom Kippur that you could adopt?

8. How can you incorporate a sense of humility and purity, symbolized by the high priest's white garments, into your spiritual practices and daily life?

9. What does it mean to you that Jesus is the *High Priest forever*? How does

this influence your approach to prayer and worship?

10. How does the eternal nature of Christ's priesthood provide comfort or assurance on your spiritual journey?

11. Reflect on the significance of the high priest's special garments and the separation of the Holy of Holies. What do these symbolize about holiness and your relationship with God?

12. How do the purity laws and sacred spaces in the Day of Atonement challenge or enrich your understanding of sacredness in your spiritual life?

13. What lessons about the cost of sin and the necessity of reconciliation can you draw from the various offerings on the Day of Atonement?

14. How does the recurring nature of these sacrifices highlight the persistent nature of human sinfulness and the need for ongoing spiritual renewal?

15. Reflect on how the New Testament, particularly in Hebrews, depicts Jesus fulfilling the high priest's role. What are the key similarities and differences?

16. How can you apply the principles of atonement and purification observed on this day to your spiritual disciplines and contemporary faith practices?

As we contemplate these profound questions, let us be inspired to deepen our spiritual walk, embracing the grace and mercy offered through Christ's eternal priesthood. May our reflections lead to a renewed commitment to live in the light of His love, carrying forward the lessons of atonement, forgiveness, and reconciliation in all that we do.

Feast of Tabernacles
THE THIRD FALL HOLIDAY

FEAST OF TABERNACLES
THE THIRD FALL HOLIDAY

OTHER NAMES:
Sukkot, Festival of Booths, Feast of Ingathering, Chag HaAsif (Festival of Gathering), and the Season of Our Joy.

DATE OBSERVED
From the 15th day of the Hebrew month of Tishrei to the 22nd day (September or October).

COMMEMORATES:
The forty-year wilderness journey of the Israelites after their exodus from Egypt. During this time, they lived in temporary shelters or booths (sukkot) as they traveled toward the Promised Land.

BIBLE REFERENCE:
Leviticus 23:34-43, Deuteronomy 16:13-15, and Zechariah 14:16-19

BRIEF INTRODUCTION
Sukkot, a cherished Jewish holiday, blends historical significance with joyful celebration.
It commemorates the Israelites' wilderness journey, highlighting God's protection and provision.

This festival, marking the fall harvest, fosters unity, reflection, and gratitude, as families gather in temporary booths to share meals and embrace joy and thanksgiving.

Feast of Tabernacles Overview

Brief Introduction: The Feast of Tabernacles, or Sukkot, is a cherished Jewish holiday that encompasses both historical significance and joyful celebration. It commemorates the Israelites' journey through the wilderness, where they dwelled in temporary booths, or sukkot, and experienced God's protection. This festival also marks the fall harvest season, fostering gratitude for God's provision. Sukkot is a time of unity, spiritual reflection, and the construction of booths, where families gather to share meals and embrace the spirit of joy and thanksgiving.

Commemorates: The forty-year wilderness journey of the Israelites after their exodus from Egypt. During this time, they lived in temporary shelters or booths (sukkot) as they traveled toward the Promised Land.

Other Names: Sukkot, the Festival of Booths, Feast of Ingathering, Zman Simchateinu (Time of Our Rejoicing), Chag HaAsif (Festival of Gathering), and the Season of Our Joy.

References: Leviticus 23:34–43, Deuteronomy 16:13–15, and Zechariah 14:16–19

Date Observed: From the fifteenth day of the Hebrew month of Tishrei to the twenty-second day (September or October).

Harvest of Blessings and Unity

This feast commemorates the forty-year period during which the children of Israel wandered in the desert, lived in temporary shelters, and celebrated harvest gatherings. The construction and dwelling characterize it in temporary booths or shelters (sukkot), which serve as a reminder of the Israelites' journey in the wilderness and God's continuous provision and protection. The holiday is marked by a series of rituals, including the waving of the lulav (frond of a date palm) and etrog (citron fruit), special prayers, and joyful processions.

Let's explore what the Bible reveals about the Feast of Tabernacles, or Sukkot, a festival rich in symbolism and Divine instruction.

The Instruction for the Feast

Our journey begins in Leviticus 23:33–43, where God commands the Israelites to observe the Feast of Tabernacles.

These are the appointed feasts of the LORD, which you shall proclaim as times of holy convocation, for presenting to the LORD food offerings, burnt offerings and grain offerings, sacrifices and drink offerings, each on its proper day, besides the LORD's Sabbaths and besides your gifts and besides all your vow offerings and besides all your freewill offerings, which you give to the LORD.

On the fifteenth day of the seventh month, when you have gathered in the produce of the land, you shall celebrate the feast of the LORD seven days. On the first day shall be a solemn rest, and on the eighth day shall be a solemn rest. And you shall take on the first day the fruit of splendid trees, branches of palm trees and boughs of leafy trees and willows of the brook, and you shall rejoice before the LORD your God seven days. You shall celebrate it as a feast to the LORD for seven days in the year. It is a statute forever throughout your generations; you shall celebrate it in the seventh month. You shall dwell in booths for seven days. All native Israelites shall dwell in booths, that your generations may know that I made the people of Israel dwell in booths when I brought them out of the land of Egypt: I am the LORD your God. Leviticus 23:33–43

Starting on the fifteenth day of the seventh month, after the harvest has been gathered, the Israelites are to celebrate the Lord's festival for seven days. The first and eighth days are days of sacred assembly, marked by rest and unique offerings. God instructs the people to live in booths for seven days as a reminder that He made the Israelites live in temporary shelters when He brought them out of Egypt. This commandment invites us to remember and celebrate God's provision and protection.

A Time of Joy and Thanksgiving

In Deuteronomy 16:13–15, the Feast of Tabernacles is framed as a time of joy and thanksgiving.

You shall keep the Feast of Booths seven days, when you have gathered in the produce from your threshing floor and your winepress. You shall rejoice in your feast, you and your son and your daughter, your male servant and your female servant, the Levite, the sojourner, the fatherless, and the widow who are within your towns. For seven days you shall keep the feast to the LORD your God at the place that the LORD will choose, because the LORD your God will bless you in all your produce and in all the work of your hands, so that you will be altogether joyful.

The Israelites are instructed to celebrate their festival for seven days after gathering the produce of their threshing floor and winepress. This celebration is to be a joyful expression of gratitude for the bounty of the harvest and God's blessings. It reminds us to be thankful for God's abundance in our physical and spiritual lives.

The Sacrificial Observances

Numbers 29:12–38 details the sacrificial observances to be made during the Feast of Tabernacles. Over the seven days, various offerings will be made, including burnt offerings, grain offerings, drink offerings, and sin offerings. These sacrifices underscore the importance of approaching God with reverence, and they point forward to Jesus Christ, the ultimate sacrifice for our sins.

In the New Testament

In the New Testament, Jesus observed the Feast of Tabernacles in John 7:37–39. On the festival's last and most significant day, Jesus stood and said loudly, *"Let anyone thirsty come to me"* and He spoke of the Holy Spirit, whom believers in Him would later receive. Here, the Feast of Tabernacles takes on new meaning as it points to Jesus, the source of Living Water and the coming of the Holy Spirit.

Prophetic Importance of Sukkot

Zechariah 14:16–19 prophesies that all nations will one day celebrate Sukkot in Jerusalem, recognizing God's sovereignty. This highlights the festival's enduring and universal significance.

Embracing Sukkot's Joy

As we reflect on Sukkot, let's embrace the joy integral to this feast, rooted in God's provision. This joy transcends circumstances, reminding us of our lasting relationship with God through Jesus. Celebrating Sukkot encourages us to share this joy and gratitude with others.

Jewish Traditions of Feast of Tabernacles

Tracing the Historical Roots

This festival, celebrated joyously in the Jewish community, invites us to reflect on God's provision and faithfulness, drawing us closer to our shared spiritual heritage.

Building the Sukkah

One of Sukkot's central traditions is the sukkah's building, a temporary booth or shelter. This practice, rooted in Leviticus 23:42–43, is a poignant reminder of the Israelites' journey in the wilderness, where they dwelt in makeshift shelters under God's protection.

God provided three essential directives for the celebration of Sukkot.

- The first of these is detailed in Leviticus 23:40, where it is commanded to gather foliage from beautiful trees—palm branches, boughs from leafy trees, and willows by the brook—using these items to rejoice before the Lord for seven days.

- The second directive, found in Leviticus 23:42, instructs that all native-born Israelites are to build and dwell in a temporary shelter, known as a sukkah (singular) or sukkot (plural), for seven days.

- The final instruction is outlined in Deuteronomy 16:13–14, emphasizing the importance of joyful celebration during the Feast of Booths. This celebration, occurring after the harvest from the threshing floor and wine vat, is a communal affair involving not just family members but also servants, Levites, strangers, orphans, and widows within the community.

As we think about the sukkah, let it remind us of our reliance on God's provision and care. The fragility of these structures symbolizes our transient life on Earth, while their open walls and roofs invite us to trust in God's more excellent shelter.

The Four Species

The Four Species are a set of four plants mentioned in the Torah as part of the Feast of Tabernacle. The Four Species hold deep symbolic meanings in Jewish tradition. These species each represent different spiritual concepts.

1. **Etrog (Citron):** The etrog is a citrus fruit similar to a lemon but larger and with a bumpy surface. It is known for its fragrance and taste, representing individuals who possess both Torah knowledge (taste) and good deeds (fragrance). Symbolically, it represents the heart, the center of understanding and wisdom.

2. **Lulav (Date Palm Branch):** The lulav is a long, straight palm branch, often with two shoots at the top. It bears fruit (dates) but has no scent, symbolizing those who study the Torah (fruit) but do not perform good deeds (lack of fragrance). The lulav physically resembles the human spine in its shape and structure. It symbolizes upright behavior and leadership.

3. **Hadas (Myrtle):** The hadas consists of a myrtle branch with leaves growing in three clusters along the branch. The myrtle has a pleasant fragrance but no taste, representing those who perform good deeds (fragrance) but do not study Torah (lack of taste). It is also often seen a symbol of the eyes, representing enlightenment and vision.

4. **Aravah (Willow):** The aravah is a willow branch with neither taste nor smell, symbolizing those lacking both Torah learning and good deeds. It represents the mouth, symbolizing speech and expressing thoughts and prayers.

When these Four Species are held and waved together during Sukkot, they symbolize the unity of different types of individuals in the community, each contributing their unique qualities to the whole. This action also signifies a prayer for an abundant harvest and is a physical demonstration of rejoicing before the Lord.

In a broader spiritual sense, the Four Species represent the need to serve God with all aspects of our being—heart, spine (backbone or strength), eyes (vision or intellect), and mouth (speech)—and emphasize the importance of unity within the community, where each individual, regardless of their level of learning or piety, is valued as part of the collective.

The Water-Drawing Ceremony

The Water-Drawing Ceremony, or Simchat Beit HaShoeivah, celebrated during Sukkot in the Second Temple era, was a ritual of deep spiritual and agricultural significance. Participants drew water from the Pool of Siloam to pour as a libation on the Temple altar, expressing gratitude for God's provision of water, crucial for life and agriculture. More than a plea for rain, it symbolized total dependence on God for sustenance, merging physical and spiritual sustenance. Characterized by unparalleled joy, music, and dance, it celebrated the communal sharing of God's blessings, linking water, a vital resource, with Divine wisdom and blessings. Although no longer performed literally, its spirit endures in Sukkot prayers and reflections, reminding us of the joy in God's presence, spiritual nourishment, and hope for redemption, thus keeping its essence alive across time.

Pool of Siloam

During Christ's time, the Pool of Siloam gained significance, as its water was used for a special ceremony during the Feast of Tabernacles. Every morning of the festival, a priest would fetch water from the pool, pouring it on the Temple's altar amid the people's jubilant chants. On the eighth day this ritual ceased, and it was then that Jesus made a profound declaration, offering "living water" to all who thirst. His words echoed Isaiah, illustrating salvation's joyous abundance.

With joy you will draw water from the wells of salvation. Isaiah 12:3

In John 9, Jesus heals a blind man by instructing him to wash in the Pool of Siloam, linking the act to His identity as the Sent One from God. Although the original pool's grandeur has diminished, its significance remains in biblical history as a place used by kings, priests, and the Messiah Himself.

The invitation to partake of the Living Water Jesus offers still stands, symbolizing spiritual illumination and salvation, as depicted in Revelation 22:17.

Hospitality and Joy: The Essence of Sukkot

Hospitality is a crucial aspect of Sukkot, as it is a time for welcoming guests into the sukkah. This tradition of ushpizin (Aramaic for "guests") reflects Abraham's welcoming of strangers, emphasizing the values of generosity and fellowship. Moreover, Deuteronomy 16:14–15 calls for joy and celebration during this festival. As we think about this joy, let's embrace the spiritual pleasure of communing with God and sharing in fellowship with others.

Hoshana Rabbah: The Time of Final Sealings

The seventh day of Sukkot carries special significance as Hoshana Rabbah which translates from Hebrew as "the great supplication" or "the great saving plea." It carries this name because on this seventh and climactic day of the Feast of Tabernacles, prayers take on an intense, urgent tenor.day ties back to Jesus' intense prayers in Gethsemane to save humanity from death and secure redemption. His sacrifice answers these urgent pleas for salvation.

The shofar blowing on this solemn day is believed to be the final trumpet blast, closing the annual period God allots for repentance and atonement since Rosh Hashanah ten days prior. As the last day of the High Holy Days season, Hoshana

Rabbah takes on an air of expectancy and finality. This connects to descriptions in the New Testament of trumpets accompanying Christ's return and the final judgment (Matthew 24:31; 1 Corinthians 15:52; Revelation 11:15).

Prayers intensify on this day, repeatedly pleading the phrase "Save us!" as divine decrees are sealed over every person's life in the coming year. It is taught that the books recording each person's deeds over the past year are now closed, as their judgment is finalized on this climactic seventh feast day. The urgent pleas to "Save us!" on this day point toward humanity's need for a Savior and Messiah. Jesus is the one who ultimately saves people from judgment and seals the book of their eternal destiny with his atoning sacrifice.

The day prior was Simchat Torah, full of joyful dancing with the Torah scrolls that contain God's instruction for righteous living. Hoshana Rabbah now contrasts that jubilation with the severity of righteous judgment soon to be enacted based on one's adherence to the law.

As the last festal day goodness can tip judgment's scales before the books close, tradition prescribes spending Hoshana Rabbah as a day of persevering prayer, interceding for mercy and atonement. At the same time, the door of grace remains open the narrowest crack.

Conclusion

As we explore the Jewish traditions of the Feast of Tabernacles, let's embrace the profound spiritual lessons they offer. These traditions connect us to our Jewish roots and enrich our understanding of God's provision, protection, and desire for fellowship with His people. Let this time of Sukkot inspire us to dwell in His presence with gratitude, to celebrate our unity in diversity, and to seek the Living Water that sustains us eternally.

How the Feast of Tabernacles Reveals Messiah

Christ Our Dwelling

TABERNACLES	JESUS
Tabernacles is celebrated during the seventh month, aligning with Jesus' birth around the same period.	Jesus' arrival coincides with the festival of Tabernacles, emphasizing His birth during a season of pilgrimage and celebration.
Tabernacles commemorates God protecting the Israelites as they wandered in the wilderness, dwelling with them in temporary shelters.	Jesus embodies the profound concept of Emmanuel, which translates to "God with us." He "tabernacled" among humanity by taking on human flesh.
Tabernacles symbolizes the sheltering presence of God among His people, emphasizing His care and protection throughout their journey.	Jesus embodies the ultimate provision and sustenance as the mirroring Tabernacles' focus on God's provision during the wilderness journey.
The Feast of Tabernacles is associated with the fall harvest.	Jesus referred to Himself as the Bread of Life (John 6:35) and was born in Bethlehem, which means "House of Bread." He ushers in the great harvest of souls.
The Feast of Tabernacles celebrates the fruits of vineyard and olive grove.	Jesus is the "true vine" (John 15:1) and his name Messiah means "anointed one," relating Him to olive oil used for anointing priests and kings.

Jesus, through His infinite grace, sets us free from guilt and leads us into a life filled with gratitude and freedom. This transformation is a testament to His commitment to us, as He reshapes our character and turns our past struggles into a foundation for a fruitful future. In our darkest moments, Jesus brings the light of joy, redeeming the once barren fields of our lives into lands of abundant blessing.

This transformative power of Jesus is at the heart of the Feast of Tabernacles, or Sukkot, a time when we celebrate Jesus' desire to tabernacle among us. Just as the Israelites lived in temporary shelters during their wilderness journey, relying on God's provision, we too are reminded of our dependence on Jesus. He chooses to dwell within us, guiding us day by day, just as He guided the Israelites.

In His tabernacling presence, Jesus asks for our obedience to His teachings. Embracing His commands leads us to a life of contentment and wonder at the miracles He works in us. Freed from the folly of our old ways and the chains of self-centeredness, we discover the joy of living in harmony with Jesus' will.

Repeatedly, Jesus invites us to find rest and renewal in Him, offering a life of abundance and freedom from the weariness of self-preoccupation. He calls us to live our lives in union with Him, promising that His steadfast commitment to us will be matched by our devotion to His path.

As we reflect on the Feast of Tabernacles, let's embrace how it reveals Christ to us in these ways:

- **The temporary booths** remind us of His incarnation.

- **The water ceremony** speaks of Him as the living water.

- **The lights** of the festival reflect His role as the Light of the World.

- **The harvest celebration** foreshadows the ingathering He will accomplish.

The Temporary Booths

- **Temporary Dwellings:** During Sukkot, Jews construct and live in sukkot, which are temporary, fragile structures with a roof made of natural materials. These booths serve as a reminder of the Israelites' forty-year journey in the wilderness, living in temporary shelters and depending on God's provision and protection.

- **Jesus's Incarnation:** God taking on human form and dwelling among humans can be paralleled with the symbolism of the sukkah. Just as the sukkah is a temporary dwelling, so was Jesus's time on Earth in human form. The Gospel of John (1:14) states, *The Word became flesh and made his dwelling among us,* which some translations render as "tabernacled" among us, directly connecting with the concept of Sukkot.

- **Vulnerability and Humility:** The sukkah's fragile nature reminds us of the vulnerability and humility of Jesus's earthly life. Despite being Divine, He chose a life subject to the limitations and hardships of the human condition, symbolized by the temporary and exposed nature of the sukkah.

- **God's Presence and Protection:** Sukkot celebrates God's continual presence and protection, just as Jesus's incarnation represents God's presence in the world. The booths are a tangible reminder of the need for God's shelter and guidance in one's life.

- **Joy and Celebration:** Despite its temporary nature, the sukkah is also a place of joy and celebration, reflecting the joy in Christ's coming and the salvation it brings. The festive nature of Sukkot aligns with the celebration of Jesus's birth and His impact on humanity.

The Water Drawing Ceremony

The WaterDrawing Ceremony (also know as Water Libration Ceremony or Simchat Beit HaShoeivah), was an integral and joyous part of the ancient Feast of Tabernacles (Sukkot). Held at the Temple in Jerusalem, this ceremony has profound symbolic significance, especially when viewed through the lens of theology as it relates to Jesus Christ.

This act was more than a mere ritual; it was a vibrant, celebratory affair accompanied by music, dancing, and great rejoicing. The ceremony was a plea for rain, essential for the upcoming agricultural year, and a reminder of God's provision of water in the wilderness for the Israelites.

- Living Water: In the New Testament, particularly in the Gospels, Jesus speaks of Himself as the source of "living water." In John 7:37–38, during the Feast of Tabernacles, Jesus declares, *"If anyone thirsts, let him come to me and drink. As the Scripture has said, he who believes in Me will flow rivers of living water out of his heart."* This statement aligns closely with the Water Drawing Ceremony, symbolizing Jesus as the spiritual source of life and sustenance.

- **The Holy Spirit:** The reference to Living Water is often interpreted as a symbol of the Holy Spirit. Just as the water was poured out during the ceremony, Jesus, through His life and death, would pour out the Holy Spirit upon humanity, offering refreshment and new life to all who believe in Him.

- **God's Provision and Salvation:** The ceremony symbolizes God's continuous provision and salvation. Just as the Israelites depended on God for water in the wilderness, we look to Jesus for spiritual nourishment and salvation.

- **Fulfillment of Prophecy:** Jesus' participation and declaration during the Feast of Tabernacles is seen as a fulfillment of Old Testament prophecies and the embodiment of rituals like the Water Drawing Ceremony. It signifies that the traditions and symbols of the Old Testament find their ultimate meaning in Him.

The Light of the World: Illuminating God's Truth

One of the critical themes of Sukkot is light, which can be seen as a powerful representation of Jesus Christ being the Light of the World. On the opening day of the Feast of Tabernacles, four large menorahs (candelabra), each reaching a height of seventy-five feet, were erected within the precincts of the Women's Court in the Temple.

- **The Illumination of the Temple:** During Sukkot in ancient times, a significant ceremony called the Illumination of the Temple was held. The large menorahs were lit casting a bright light that symbolized the Shekinah Glory of God—His divine presence. Jerusalem would be illuminated by these lights, symbolizing the spreading of divine light and truth.

- **Jesus as the Light of the World:** In the New Testament, Jesus declares Himself as the *Light of the World* (John 8:12). This statement was made during the Feast of Tabernacles, making it profoundly significant. Just as the lights in the Temple illuminated Jerusalem, Jesus's presence brings spiritual light and clarity to a world often shrouded in spiritual darkness.

- **Guidance and Protection:** The light during Sukkot also recalls the Pillar of Fire that guided the Israelites through the desert at night during their exodus from Egypt. Similarly, Jesus, as the Light of the World, is seen as a guiding force, leading believers through life's challenges and deserts, providing direction, comfort, and protection.

- **Revelation of Truth:** Light is often associated with truth and revelation. The illumination during Sukkot symbolizes God's revelation to Israel. Jesus, as the Light reveals the truth about God and His plan for salvation, dispelling the darkness of sin and ignorance.

- **Universal Impact:** The light from the Temple menorahs was not just for Israel but was a symbol of enlightenment for all nations. This reflects the belief in Jesus as a Savior, not just for Jews but for the entire world, bringing God's Light and salvation to all humanity.

Harvest Celebration

The Feast of Tabernacles marks a time of joy and gratitude for God's provision, paralleling the imagery in Matthew 9:37–38, where Jesus speaks of gathering believers from every nation into God's Kingdom. This aligns with the spiritual harvest depicted in Sukkot, reflecting Jesus's vision of universal unity under God's sovereignty.

Jesus and the Ingathering of Nations

Jesus frequently emphasizes gathering people from all nations into God's Kingdom, mirroring the Sukkot gathering on a spiritual level. His inclusive vision aligns with the essence of Sukkot—a celebration of universal joy and unity.

- **Harvest Festival:** Sukkot serves as a harvest festival, symbolizing both agricultural gatherings and the gathering of people in Jerusalem to celebrate God's blessings.

- **Tabernacles and Dwelling Together:** During Sukkot, Jews dwell in temporary booths, symbolizing life's transience, and preparation for eternal life under God's reign. Jesus's teachings often echo this transient life, emphasizing unity under God's sovereignty.

- **Prophetic Fulfillment**: Prophetic visions in the Old Testament foresee all nations worshiping God in Jerusalem during Sukkot, symbolizing Jesus's role in uniting people and fulfilling the promise of universal salvation and worship.

- **A Symbol of Hope and Inclusivity:** Sukkot's themes of harvest and gathering symbolize hope and inclusivity, echoing Jesus's teachings on the openness of the Kingdom of God to all believers.

- **Christ's Reign Over All Nations:** Zechariah 14:16–19 prophesies that all nations will celebrate the Feast of Tabernacles in Jerusalem, recognizing Christ's kingship. This points to Christ's future reign over all nations, symbolized by the Feast of Tabernacles.

The Feast of Tabernacles commemorates God's faithfulness, and signifies our future hope in Christ's ultimate victory and establishment of His kingdom on Earth. Let us hold these truths close, deepening our understanding and appreciation of Jesus, our Savior and King.

Was Jesus Born During Tabernacles?

Christ's Birth

TABERNACLES	JESUS' BIRTH
One of the three major pilgrimage festivals when Jews travel to Jerusalem.	These pilgrims would either pass through or stay in Bethlehem.
Celebrated by dwelling in temporary tabernacles.	God tabernacling with humanity.
Tabernacles includes water libation ceremony.	Jesus offers Living Water.
Commemorates Israel's wilderness journey.	Jesus' birth marks the start of salvation's journey.
Emphasizes community and gathering.	Jesus' birth unites Heaven and Earth.
Tabernacles theme is harvest.	Jesus represents the harvest of souls.
Tabernacles looks forward to the Messianic age.	Jesus' birth initiates the Messianic age.

While the tradition places the celebration of Christmas on December 25th, intriguing evidence and scriptural interpretation suggest Jesus might have been born during Sukkot, the Feast of Tabernacles. This period is marked by significant events and practices that align with the details surrounding His birth:

- **Deciphering Holy Timelines:** Understanding the timing of Jesus' birth comes from studying John the Baptist's conception and birth. Elizabeth was six months pregnant with John when Mary conceived Jesus (Luke 1:24–27). Given John's conception around Passover, this places Jesus' birth approximately six months later, around the Feast of Tabernacles.

- **Roman Census:** The Feast of Tabernacles is one of the pilgrimage feasts when all male Jews must go to Jersulaem. According to Luke, Joseph and Mary traveled to Bethlehem due to the decree from Caesar Augustus that a census should be taken of the entire Roman world. As Joseph and Mary were both of the line of David, they had to return to Bethlehem, the town of David. It is very possible that this census coincided with the pilgrimage Feast of Tabernacles, when Jewish families would already be traveling to Jerusalem. This could explain the overcrowding and the lack of accommodation for Mary and Joseph (Luke 2:7).

- **Temporary Booths:** The Feast of Tabernacles involves dwelling in sukkot, temporary booths, commemorating the Israelites' journey from Egypt. This parallels the circumstances of Jesus' birth in a stable—a temporary, humble abode.

- **Fall Lambing Season:** The Feast of Tabernacles coincides with the fall lambing season, aligning with the presence of shepherds in the fields during Jesus' birth (Luke 2:8–20), indicating a birth time outside the cold winter months.

- **Fulfillment of Feasts:** The timing of Jesus' conception, possibly during Hanukkah, with His birth nine months later at the Feast of Tabernacles, reflects a symbolic fulfillment of the Jewish feasts—from the Festival of Lights to the celebration of God's dwelling among His people.

- **Celebration of God's Presence:** Sukkot celebrates God's dwelling among His people, a theme that resonates with Jesus' birth. The term "Immanuel" (God with us) reflects this Divine presence, as announced by the angels.

- **Good News of Harvest:** The Feast of Tabernacles is a harvest festival of joy and thanksgiving. The angelic announcement of Jesus' birth as "good news" mirrors this theme, heralding the Messiah's arrival as a time of spiritual harvest and salvation.

- **Universal Invitation:** The Feast of Tabernacles emphasizes inviting all nations to celebrate, prefigures the universal nature of Jesus' birth announcement, meant for "all the people," symbolizing God's inclusive plan of salvation (Zechariah 14:16, Galatians 3:28, and Revelation 7:9).

- **God Dwelling with His People:** Sukkot finds its ultimate expression in Jesus. John 1:14 uses the language of dwelling or tabernacling to describe the Word becoming flesh, highlighting Jesus as God incarnate, dwelling among humanity.

- **Prophecy Fulfillment:** Christ willingly descended to Earth and humbled himself to take the form of a lowly servant—being born in a stable to a poor family and in the ultimate act of humble obedience (Philippians 2:7–8). The timing of Jesus' birth during Sukkot fulfills prophecy and embodies the symbolism of Jesus as the Light of the World, dispelling darkness and offering eternal life to all.

These connections between Jesus' birth and the Feast of Tabernacles offer a rich tapestry of biblical fulfillment, symbolism, and divine orchestration, inviting believers to see the profound ways in which God's plans and promises are woven through the fabric of scripture and history.

Celebrating the Feast of Tabernacles

Embracing Joy and Reflection

The Feast of Tabernacles, or Sukkot, is a joyful festival commemorating God's provision and protection during the Israelites' forty years in the wilderness. Observing Sukkot can be a meaningful way to connect with the Jewish roots of our faith and deepen our spiritual understanding. Here are some practical suggestions for those interested in building a sukkah, engaging in the ritual of the Four Species, and other activities to enhance spiritual growth and understanding.

As we build our temporary shelters, we are reminded of the transient nature of our earthly journey and the enduring joy found in our relationship with Jesus. He tabernacles among us, offering protection, provision, and the promise of eternal life.

Building a Sukkah

- **Understand the Sukkah:** Learn about the significance of the sukkah, a temporary booth or hut representing the fragile dwellings the Israelites lived in during their desert journey from Egypt to the Promised Land. It symbolizes dependence on God and His provision.

- **Construct a Sukkah:** Build a simple sukkah in your back yard or community space. It doesn't have to be elaborate; the key is its temporary and fragile nature. Use natural materials for the walls and roof, leaving spaces to see the sky, reminding us of God's Creation and our reliance on Him.

- **Decorate With Purpose:** Decorate your sukkah with items representing God's blessings, such as fruits, vegetables, and crafts. This can be a fun family activity, and each decoration can serve as a reminder to give thanks for God's provision.

- **Fellowship and Hospitality:** Use the time of Sukkot to practice hospitality, inviting friends and family to your sukkah. Share meals and fellowship, celebrating the community and God's provision.

- **Prayer and Worship:** Dedicate time for special prayer and worship sessions in your sukkah, focusing on thankfulness for God's protection and provision.

- **Engage in Service and Giving:** Sukkot is a time of joy and thanksgiving. Participate in acts of service or charity, sharing the joy and blessings you have received with others.

Bible Study Ideas

- **Study Booths or Shelters:** Read Leviticus 23:42-43, Nehemiah 8:13-18, and Hebrews 11:8-9 to examine the symbolic meaning of temporary dwellings.

- **Reflect on Creation:** Read the Creation story in Genesis and reflect on the beauty of God's Creation. You can adapt this ritual by bringing together different elements of nature and using them as a focus for prayer and reflection on God's diverse Creation.

- **Reflection on Jesus as Our Shelter:** Reflect on how Jesus provides shelter and safety in our lives, akin to the symbolism of the sukkah. Discuss or journal about how this understanding impacts your faith. Psalm 61:3; Psalm 91:1-2; Isaiah 4:6; Isaiah 25:4; John 10:9; 2 Corinthians 5:1 present God and Jesus as our refuge, shelter, shade, strong tower, and eternal heavenly dwelling protecting us from danger, storms, heat, enemies, and the failure of earthly shelters.

- **Jesus as the Fulfillment of Tabernacles:** Study John 1:14 and John 7:1-9, considering how themes like God's dwelling and living water point to Christ. Read all the chapters in this book on the Feast of Tabernacles.

- **Tabernacles as a Picture of Restoration:** Use passages like Zechariah 14:16-19, Ezekiel 37, and Romans 11:25-27 to examine the Messianic kingdom and restoration of Israel.

- **Future Fulfillment in the New Heavens and New Earth:** Explore Revelation 21:1-5 and Isaiah 65:17-25 to discuss the ultimate Tabernacles fulfillment in eternity.

- **The Tabernacle/Temple Connection:** Study Exodus 25-31 and 40 to appreciate parallels between the wilderness Tabernacle and elements of the Feast.

- **Pilgrimage and Worship in the Bible:** Use verses from Psalms 120-134 plus accounts in Ezra and Nehemiah to understand the centrality of pilgrimage for worship.

- **Importance of the Nations:** Study Zechariah 14:16-19 and Isaiah 56:6-8 to unpack the inclusion of the nations in worshipping Yahweh.

Conclusion

As we celebrate Sukkot, we're reminded of Jesus' desire to dwell among us, mirroring the Israelites' dependence on God's provision. Building temporary shelters signifies life's transience, and emphasizes finding eternal joy in Jesus. Sukkot is a celebration of His presence, fostering spiritual reflection, unity, and gratitude for His blessings. Let's embrace Jesus' abundant life and share His love with others. Sukkot encourages us to celebrate God's faithfulness, understand our Jewish roots, and see how Jesus fulfills these traditions. Building a sukkah and partaking in themed activities deepens our faith and highlights God's constant presence and protection.

Feast of Tabernacles Recipes

During the Feast of Tabernacles, or Sukkot, snacks, and meals often include ingredients that are seasonal and symbolic of the harvest, reflecting the agricultural nature of the festival. Here are some typical snacks served during Sukkot:

- **Stuffed Dates or Figs:** These sweet treats, often filled with nuts or cream cheese, symbolize the land's abundance.
- **Pumpkin and Squash Seeds:** Roasted and seasoned, these seeds are a popular, easy-to-make snack that reflects the fall harvest.
- **Fruit Platters:** Seasonal fruits, such as apples, pomegranates, grapes, and citrus fruits, are common, symbolizing fertility and the land's bounty.
- **Olives and Olive Oil Dips:** Olives are significant in Jewish tradition and can be served alongside bread for dipping in olive oil.
- **Cheese and Crackers:** A simple, crowd-pleasing snack that can be paired with figs or grapes to continue the theme of abundance.
- **Nuts and Dried Fruits:** Reflecting the harvest and winter storage ease, mixed nuts and dried fruits are a traditional and practical choice.
- **Honey Cakes or Cookies:** Small sweets made with honey highlight the theme of a sweet new year, which is also emphasized during the High Holy Days leading up to Sukkot.
- **Vegetable Trays with Hummus or Tahini Dip:** Fresh vegetables paired with dips made from sesame seeds or chickpeas offer a light, healthy snacking option.
- **Sukkot Soup Cups:** Miniature servings of soup, such as pumpkin or squash soup, can be a warm and comforting snack, especially for cooler

evenings in the sukkah.

Here are some delicious recipes that are perfect for Sukkot.

Stuffed Acorn Squash

Ingredients
2 acorn squashes, halved and seeded
1 cup quinoa or bulgur wheat
2 cups vegetable broth
1 small onion, chopped
½ cup dried cranberries
½ cup chopped walnuts
¼ cup chopped fresh parsley
2 tbs olive oil
Salt and pepper to taste

Instructions

- Preheat oven to 375°F (190°C).

- Place acorn squash halves with the cut side down on a baking sheet and bake for 25–30 minutes or until tender.

- Cook quinoa or bulgur in vegetable broth as per package instructions.

- Sauté onion in olive oil until translucent. Mix in cranberries, walnuts, parsley, and cooked quinoa/bulgur—season with salt and pepper.

- Fill the roasted acorn squash halves with the quinoa mixture and bake for 10 minutes.

Chicken with Apples and Honey

Ingredients
4 bone-in chicken breasts
2 apples, sliced
¼ cup honey
2 tbs Dijon mustard
1 tbs apple cider vinegar
1 tsp thyme

Instructions

- Preheat oven to 350°F (175°C).

- Season chicken breasts with salt, pepper, and thyme.

- Heat olive oil in a skillet and brown the chicken on both sides. Transfer to a baking dish.

- Add apples, honey, mustard, and vinegar to the same skillet. Cook until the apples are slightly softened. Pour the apple mixture over the chicken in the baking dish.

- Bake for 30–35 minutes or until the chicken is cooked through.

Israeli Couscous Salad

Ingredients
2 cups Israeli couscous
1 cucumber, diced
1 red bell pepper, diced
½ cup Kalamata olives, sliced
½ cup feta cheese, crumbled
¼ cup fresh mint, chopped
¼ cup olive oil
2 tbs lemon juice
Salt and pepper to taste

Instructions

- Cook Israeli couscous as per package instructions, then let it cool.

- Combine cooled couscous with cucumber, bell pepper, olives, feta, and mint in a large bowl.

- Whisk together olive oil and lemon juice, pour over the salad, and toss to combine. Season with salt and pepper.

Feast of Tabernacles Questions

Illuminating Reflections

These questions aim to help you reflect on the Feast of Tabernacles in a way that encourages deeper spiritual understanding and practical application in daily living.

1. How does the Feast of Tabernacles deepen your understanding of God's provision and protection in your life?

2. In what ways can reflecting on the temporary nature of the sukkah remind you of your dependence on God?

3. How does the historical context of Sukkot, commemorating the Israelites' wilderness journey, influence your view of God's guidance in difficult times?

4. Reflect on the prophetic significance of Sukkot (Zechariah 14:16–19). How does it shape your perspective on God's sovereignty and the future gathering of nations?

5. How can you cultivate a spirit of joy and thanksgiving daily, as emphasized during Sukkot?

6. Consider ways to express gratitude for your life's physical and spiritual harvests.

7. If you were to build a sukkah, what elements of God's creation would you include and why?

8. How might spending time in a sukkah enhance your meditation on God's Word and His presence?

9. Reflect on the symbolism of the Four Species. How can they represent different aspects of your life and devotion to God?

10. How can integrating elements of nature in your spiritual practice deepen your connection with God's creation?

11. In light of John 7:37–39, how do you see Jesus as the source of Living Water? How can this impact your spiritual life?

12. Discuss or journal how Jesus provides shelter and safety in your life, akin to the symbolism of Sukkot.

13. How can you practice hospitality and fellowship during this season to reflect the communal aspect of Sukkot?

14. Identify specific acts of service or charity you can engage in to share the joy and blessings of Sukkot with others.

15. What specific actions can you take to apply the principles of Sukkot, such as reliance on God and joy in His provision, in your daily routine?

16. How can studying passages related to Sukkot, like Leviticus 23:33–43, enhance your understanding of biblical festivals and their relevance today?

As we close this season of joyful celebration and spiritual reflection, may the enduring truths behind Sukkot take root in our hearts and bear fruit in our lives. Let us carry the spirit of thanksgiving, dependence on God, and hospitality from these temporary dwellings into our everyday walk of faith. And through a deeper understanding of the prophetic significance of the Feast, may our perspective be lifted to the glorious future gathering when people of all nations will worship the Lord together.

EXTRA HOLIDAYS
Hanukkah and Purim

Unlike sacred observances like Passover and the Day of Atonement, outlined in Leviticus 23, Hanukkah and Purim are considered minor Jewish festivals or holidays rather than biblically mandated "holy days." These feasts emerged from post-Torah historical events chronicled in extra-Pentateuchal books of the Hebrew Scriptures and later Jewish writings.

The Torah, comprised of the first five books of the Bible, anchors major observances to the foundational stories of the Exodus and wilderness wanderings. In contrast, Hanukkah commemorates the temple's rededication after the Maccabean revolt against Greek-Syrian oppressors in the 2nd century BCE. Its account appears in I and II Maccabees. Purim celebrates Esther and Mordecai's intervention to rescue Jews within the Persian empire, as recorded in the book bearing Esther's name.

Despite their extra-biblical origins, Hanukkah and Purim hold profound cultural and spiritual importance in Jewish life and tradition. Marked by feasting and rejoicing, they embody core themes of Jewish hope, resilience, and deliverance in the face of existential threat. Hanukkah evokes the miracle of preserved identity; Purim, the mystery of divine providence. Though not technically Sabbaths or appointed times like Passover, Hanukkah, and Purim, are nevertheless enthusiastically observed by Jews worldwide as seminal expressions of identity. Their rich histories and customs underscore God's faithfulness towards His covenant people.

Hanukkah

Feast of the Maccabees

HANUKKAH
FEAST OF THE MACCABEES

DATE OBSERVED:
Hanukkah lasts for eight days and nights, starting on the 25th of Kislev and ending on the 2nd or 3rd of Tevet, depending on the year (late November to late December).

BIBLE REFERENCE:
John 10:22

COMMEMORATES:
Hanukkah commemorates two interrelated events: the successful Maccabean Revolt against the Seleucid Empire in the second century BCE, and the miracle of the Temple menorah's oil.

OTHER NAMES:
Festival of Lights, Feast of Dedication, and Feast of the Maccabees

BRIEF INTRODUCTION:
Hanukkah is an eight-day Jewish holiday commemorating the Second Temple's rededication in Jerusalem. It's marked by lighting the menorah, symbolizing the miracle of oil burning for eight days, and includes joyous family gatherings, dreidel games, and traditional foods like latkes and sufganiyot. Celebrating themes of resilience and the triumph of light, Hanukkah is a cherished Jewish cultural and religious event.

Hanukkah Overview

Brief Introduction: Hanukkah is an eight-day Jewish holiday commemorating the Second Temple's rededication in Jerusalem. It's marked by lighting the menorah, symbolizing the miracle of one day's supply of oil burning for eight days, and includes joyous family gatherings, dreidel games, and traditional foods like latkes and sufganiyot. Celebrating themes of resilience and the triumph of light, Hanukkah is a cherished Jewish cultural and religious event.

Commemorates: Hanukkah commemorates two interrelated events: the successful Maccabean Revolt against the Seleucid Empire in the second century BC, and the miracle of the Temple menorah's oil.

Other Names: Festival of Lights, Chanukah. (Hanukkah can be spelled in various ways, including Chanukah, Hanukah, Chanuka, Chanukkah, and Hanuka.) These variations reflect differences in transliterating the Hebrew words into English (Feast of Dedication, and Feast of the Maccabees).

Bible References: John 10:22

Date Observed: Hanukkah lasts for eight days and nights, starting on the 25th of Kislev and ending on the second or third of Tevet, depending on the year (late November to late December).

The Intertestamental Period

In the Bible, the blank page between the Old Testament and the New Testament symbolizes a significant era of four hundred years, known as the intertestamental period or the Second Temple era. This time frame, often called the "four hundred silent years," saw no new prophetic revelations. Despite this, it was a period marked by God's ongoing presence. These four hundred years were characterized by substantial political, religious, and social changes in Israel (many that were predicted by the prophet Daniel).

This is a fascinating period rarely taught in any churches, full of political intrigue and Jewish persecution. Control of the land and the Jewish people passed from one governmental force to another throughout these years, including Persia, Greece (Alexander the Great), Egypt (the Ptolemies), Syria (the Seleucids), and the Maccabees (and the Hasmoneans).

The influence of Greek culture (Hellenization) significantly impacted Jewish society and religion. It introduced new philosophical ideas, languages, and cultural practices.

This period of transformation in Jewish religious life, marked by the emergence of groups like the Pharisees, Sadducees, and Essenes, also set the stage for historical events such as the story of Hanukkah.

The Story of Hanukkah

Hanukkah means "dedication" in Hebrew. You won't find it in the Jewish Bible (or the Old Testament) because it happened after the events recorded in the Jewish Bible.

This unique eight-day festival celebrates the momentous rededication of the Lord's Temple, a significant event that took place around a hundred and sixty years before the arrival of the Messiah. It marks a pivotal moment when God intervened to protect His people and maintain the essence of biblical Judaism. This preservation was vital; it ensured the fulfillment of the prophetic Scriptures concerning the Messiah's birth. It was essential for the lineage of the Jewish people to continue, mainly through the tribe of Judah and the descent from King David, to pave the way for the Messiah's birth by prophecy.

The Temple, constructed during Ezra's guidance, was initially consecrated around four hundred and fifty years before the coming of the Messiah. However, over the centuries, it faced desecration by adversaries against God. The rededication of this sacred space following its profanation led to establishing the festival known today as Hanukkah.

The Hellenistic Rule and the Jewish Resistance

In the second century BCE, Judea was controlled by the Hellenistic Greek empire led by Antiochus IV Epiphanes. He aimed to enforce a uniform Greek culture and religious practice, leading to a significant clash with the monotheistic Jewish community.

Antiochus imposed harsh measures against Jewish religious customs and defiled their holiest place, the Second Temple in Jerusalem. By setting up an altar to Zeus within it, he deeply infringed upon Jewish spiritual values.

The Maccabean Revolt

The Hasmonean family, led by Mattathias and his son Judah Maccabee, instigated a rebellion against the Seleucid Empire. Despite being outnumbered and less equipped, the Maccabees' determination and guerrilla tactics led them to an unexpected military and spiritual victory.

After their victory, the Maccabees focused on purifying and rededicating the defiled Temple. This involved the removal of Hellenistic symbols and spiritual cleansing, restoring the Temple's role as the heart of Jewish worship.

The Miracle of the Oil

A pivotal moment in the rededication was the lighting of the Temple's menorah, for which there was only enough consecrated oil for one day. Miraculously, this oil burned for eight days, which was the length of time needed to prepare more oil, symbolizing Divine affirmation of Jewish worship and tradition.

The Establishment of Hanukkah

Hanukkah was established to commemorate the miracle of the oil and the victory over Hellenistic oppression. The eight-day festival involves lighting a special nine-branched candelabrum, the Hanukkah menorah, with an additional candle lit each night, reflecting on themes of religious freedom and the triumph of light over darkness.

The story of Hanukkah is a significant chapter in Jewish history, underscoring the struggle for religious freedom, the preservation of cultural identity, and the resilience of faith against a dominant empire. It holds deep meaning, especially for adult audiences, in exploring religious and cultural perseverance.

Jewish Traditions of Hanukkah

Hanukkah is a time of joy and reflection, marked by several traditions and customs with deep historical and spiritual significance.

The Miracle of the Oil

The story of Hanukkah traces back to the 2nd century BCE, when the Maccabees, a Jewish militia, reclaimed the Holy Temple in Jerusalem from the Seleucid Empire. They lit the menorah's candles at rededication, having only one day's worth of oil. In a miracle, the oil burned for eight days until fresh oil was obtained. This event is the core Hanukkah miracle.

Hanukkah's light theme transcends physical meaning. It signifies a profound spiritual journey linked to ancient Israel and Jesus's teachings, rooted in wisdom, knowledge, and life.

Recall God piloting Israel's wilderness trek with a pillar of fire—not just illumination but divine wisdom made manifest. The menorah used on Hanukkah, fashioned from one gold piece, symbolizes the singular, unified wisdom emanating from the one Source—God. As articulated wonderfully by Isaiah.

> *The sun shall be no more thy light by day;*
> *neither for brightness shall the moon give light unto thee;*
> *but the LORD shall be unto thee an everlasting light,*
> *and thy God thy glory.*
> Isaiah 60:19

The Menorah

The menorah, central to Hanukkah's celebration, embodies more than historical remembrance. It represents the light of knowledge, understanding, and reason—key elements that make life meaningful and fulfilling. Its construction from one solid piece of gold further underscores that all wisdom emanates from one Divine Source.

Light as a Multifaceted Symbol

Jewish literature has richly employed the metaphor of light, applying it to various entities such as Israel, Jerusalem, the patriarchs, the Messiah, God, eminent rabbis, and the Law.

Lighting the Menorah

Hanukkah's most iconic tradition is the menorah's lighting, a nine-branched candelabrum. Each night of Hanukkah, a candle is lit by the Shamash (the "helper" candle which is the center candle), from left to right, until all of the other eight candles are lit on the final night.

In homes, the menorah is typically placed in a window or a place where it can be seen from outside, symbolizing the public display of the miracle.

Blessings and Prayers

Here's an overview of the blessings said before lighting the candles:

1. **First Blessing**: Blessing Over the Candles: This blessing praises God for commanding the lighting of the Hanukkah candles. The transliteration is "Baruch atah Adonai, Eloheinu Melech haolam, asher kid'shanu b'mitzvotav v'tzivanu l'hadlik ner shel Hanukkah." This translates to "Blessed are You, Lord our God, King of the universe, who has sanctified us with His commandments and commanded us to light the Hanukkah candles."

2. **Second Blessing**: Blessing on the Miracles of Hanukkah: This blessing thanks God for the miracles performed for the Jews' ancestors during Hanukkah. The transliteration is "Baruch atah Adonai, Eloheinu Melech haolam, she'asah nissim la'avotenu bayamim haheim bazman hazeh." In English, it's "Blessed are You, Lord our God, King of the universe, who performed miracles for our ancestors in those days at this time."

3. **Third Blessing**: Shehecheyanu: This blessing (recited only on the first night) expresses gratitude to God for enabling the family to reach this season. The transliteration is "Baruch atah Adonai, Eloheinu Melech haolam, shehecheyanu, v'kiyemanu, v'higi'anu lazman hazeh." In English, this is "Blessed are You, Lord our God, King of the universe, who has granted us life, sustained us and enabled us to reach this occasion."

Hanukkah Foods

Traditional Hanukkah foods are fried in olive oil, symbolizing the oil from the Hanukkah story. Popular dishes include latkes (potato pancakes) and sufganiyot (jelly-filled doughnuts). These delicious treats are enjoyed with family and friends throughout the festival.

The Dreidel Game

Playing with a dreidel (a four-sided spinning top) is a popular Hanukkah game. Each side of the dreidel bears a Hebrew letter, forming an acronym for Nes Gadol Haya Sham ("A great miracle happened there"). The game is often played for a pot of gelt (chocolate coins wrapped in gold-colored paper), symbolizing the coins that Jewish children have historically received as gifts during Hanukkah.

Gift-Giving

While not originally part of Hanukkah, giving gifts has become common, especially in the United States. This tradition is often seen as a way to enhance the joy and celebration of the festival, particularly for children.

Music and Songs

Hanukkah is celebrated with memorable songs and hymns. Ma'oz Tzur (Rock of Ages) is a traditional hymn sung after lighting the candles. Other popular songs, both traditional and modern, are also sung, adding to the festive atmosphere.

Reflection and Remembrance

Beyond the festivities, Hanukkah is a time for Jews to reflect on themes of freedom, resilience, and the miracle of survival against the odds. It is a reminder of their struggle for religious freedom and the enduring strength of the Jewish spirit.

Hanukkah is a joyful celebration, rich in traditions that carry deep historical and spiritual significance. From lighting the menorah and enjoying olive oil-based foods to playing dreidel and singing, each custom commemorates a miraculous event in Jewish history. It's a time for Jews globally to unite with family, celebrating the persistent light and resilience of their people.

How Hanukkah Reveals Messiah

Christ The Light of the World

HANUKKAH	JESUS
A key Hanukkah symbol is the menorah, representing God's light breaking into the world's darkness.	The Light of the World. Through his life, death, and resurrection, the darkness of sin was defeated.
Commemorates the miracle of oil meant for one night, lasting eight full nights.	His miracles, including healings and resurrection, offer hope and new life to believers.
Hanukkah celebrates the cleansing and rededication of the temple in Jerusalem.	Christ's body became the new, ultimate temple, allowing access to connect with God's presence.
The hero of Hanukkah, Mattathias was from the tribe of Judah.	Jesus, the Messiah is from the line of Judah.
Celebrates physical and spiritual freedom.	Jesus is the ultimate victory over sin and death, offering spiritual liberation to humanity.
Reminder of God's faithfulness and the power of dedication to Him.	Embodies hope for redemption and eternal life, encouraging believers to maintain faith in God.
Signifies God's enduring presence and guidance through times of darkness.	Offers guidance and light to all who follow Him.

As we explore the connections between Hanukkah and Christ, we uncover how the festival's themes of light conquering darkness, Divine intervention, and the rededication of the Temple illuminate the Messiah's role in God's redemptive plan.

The following comparisons between Hanukkah and Jesus Christ not only enhance our understanding of biblical prophecies and celebrations but also enrich our faith by highlighting the profound ways in which Jesus embodies and fulfills these ancient traditions.

- **Jesus as the Light of the World:** Just as the menorah is central to Hanukkah, representing God's enduring presence and light, Jesus declares, *"I am the Light of the world"* (John 8:12). His life, teachings, and resurrection illuminate the path to spiritual enlightenment and salvation, echoing the menorah's symbolism of Divine Light overcoming darkness.

- **Miracle Worker:** The miracle of Hanukkah, where oil sufficient for only one night burned for eight, symbolizes God's provision and the triumph of faith. Similarly, Jesus performed miracles that affirmed His divine identity and the inbreaking of God's kingdom, showcasing His authority over nature and Spirit.

- **Fulfillment of Jewish Festivals:** Hanukkah underscores Jewish identity and God's faithfulness. In a broader sense, Jesus fulfills the spiritual essence of Jewish festivals, including Hanukkah, embodying God's ultimate promise of redemption, and establishing a New Covenant that offers spiritual freedom to all humanity.

- **Inaugurator of the New Temple:** The rededication of the Jerusalem Temple is a pivotal aspect of Hanukkah. Jesus introduced a new paradigm by proclaiming Himself the true Temple (John 2:19–21), signifying that all people have direct access to God's presence through Him, thus transcending the need for a physical temple.

- **Messiah from Judah:** The Maccabean Revolt, celebrated during Hanukkah, was led by a family from the tribe of Judah, symbolizing resistance and faithfulness. Jesus, born into the tribe of Judah, is recognized as the prophesied Messiah, fulfilling the hope for a spiritual leader who would establish God's kingdom on earth.

The Hanukkah story's miracle of the oil, where a day's worth of oil burned for eight days, can be seen as a metaphor for the eternal life promised by Jesus. This poignant picture symbolizes the spiritual light Christ kindles within believers—a light that persists forever. Jesus proclaimed Himself *"the light of the world"* (John 8:12), the eternal flame whose brilliance will never fade or fail.

Through His death and resurrection, Jesus atoned for sin, conquered the grave, and opened the way for humanity to dwell eternally with God. Just as the menorah kept miraculously giving light during Hanukkah, Christ's light perpetually shines within the hearts of those who place their faith in Him. His Spirit guarantees the radiance of spiritual life both now and in eternity.

Dr. John Garr explains in *God's Lamp, Man's Light: Mysteries of the Menorah*, that in the ancient sanctuary, oil served two primary purposes: anointing and light production. Like the lamp oil, the anointing oil was specially formulated and consecrated. It featured the blending of pure oil with aromatic spices. This oil signaled God's approval of men and their efforts when applied. The delightful fragrance of the anointing oil served as a model for the pleasant state manifesting when believers dwell together in unity.

Light and anointing go hand in hand. Without the anointing of the Holy Spirit that brings the pure oil of divine revelation into the lives of God's lamp, there can be no illumination. Even Jesus himself, the very Light of the world, was anointed with the Spirit in fulfillment of Isaiah's prophecy. When he began his ministry, he went forth "in the power of the Spirit." The Spirit's oil provides the sweetness of anointing and the light of insight and understanding.

To usher in God's kingdom on earth, believers need to be blessed with the oil of joy in the Ruach HaKodesh (the Holy Spirit). This sacred anointing allows their lamps to shine brightly with the light of the Shekhinah, showcasing God's Eternal Presence to the world. And, they must do so in the same way ancient Israel accomplished the task, with "beaten olive oil."

There are no shortcuts to obtaining the clear, consecrated oil that illuminates the menorah. One can be anointed with the oil of joy that produces spiritual light through consecration and dedication to God. Becoming God's lamp and man's light is no simple task! [1]

Thus, the celebration of Hanukkah transitions from a historical commemoration to a profound spiritual journey guided by Jesus, the genuine Light of the World. It becomes an opportunity to reflect on our spiritual path, embracing the wisdom, knowledge, and life He offers. As we live as children of light, embodying divine wisdom, we remember a pivotal event in Jewish history and engage in a deeper exploration of God's presence and guidance in our lives, illuminated by Christ's eternal light.

---

1. Garr, John D. *God's Lamp, Man's Light: Mysteries of the Menorah*. Golden Key Press, 2001.

Celebrating Hanukkah
Embracing and Spreading the Light

Lighting the menorah is the central ritual of Hanukkah, and is a powerful symbol of faith, resilience, and God's providence. Each night of Hanukkah, a candle is lit to commemorate the miracle of the oil that burned for eight days. This act can serve as a reminder of Christ, the Light of the World, and the call to be a light in the darkness. Lighting the Hanukkah menorah (also known as a Hanukkiah) is a central part of the Hanukkah celebration. Here are specific instructions for lighting it:

- **Number of Candles:** The Hanukkah menorah has nine branches—eight for each night of Hanukkah, and the Shamash, which is the center helper or attendant candle, used to light the others. Some people choose to use oil lamps instead of candles for the Hanukkah menorah, echoing the original miracle of Hanukkah, which involved the miraculous burning of one night's oil for eight nights. In this tradition, each night small cups filled with oil are placed in the menorah, and wicks are inserted into the oil. The shamash is used to light the wicks from left to right, following the same procedure as with candles.

- **Placement of Candles:** Place the candles in the menorah from right to left, which is how Hebrew is read. Each night, you add one candle to mark the new night of Hanukkah.

- **Order of Lighting:** On the first night, place one candle at the far right of the menorah. Add a new candle to the left of the previous night's candles each subsequent night.

- **Lighting the Shamash:** The Shamash candle is usually set apart, either higher or lower, and most often in the center of the menorah. First light the Shamash.

- **Using the Shamash to Light Others:** Use the Shamash to light the other candles. Light the newest candle first (which is the one furthest to the left after you've added it for the new night), then proceed to light the others moving from left to right (contrary to the placement order). After using the Shamash to light the other candles, it should remain lit alongside them.

- **After Lighting:** After lighting the candles, it's traditional to sing Hanukkah songs. The most common is Ma'oz Tzur (Rock of Ages).

- **Placement of the Menorah:** If possible, place the menorah in a window or near a doorway where it can be seen from outside, symbolizing publicizing the miracle of Hanukkah.

- **Duration of Lighting:** Hanukkah candles should ideally be left to burn out naturally, with enough fuel (wax or oil) to last for at least thirty minutes after nightfall.

- **For Each Night of Hanukkah:** Place new candles in the menorah, starting from the right and moving to the left. However, when lighting them, you start with the newest candle on the left, moving toward the right. There's no need to relight candles from previous nights; you simply add and light new candles each evening.

Remember, safety is essential. Keep the menorah on a stable surface, away from anything flammable, and **never** leave lit candles unattended.

Traditional Foods: Celebrating with Joy

Hanukkah is also known for its traditional foods, especially those fried in olive oil, like latkes (potato pancakes) and sufganiyot (jelly-filled doughnuts), symbolizing the miracle of the oil (recipes provided in a later chapter). We can partake in preparing and sharing these foods to engage in the joyous spirit of the festival and remember God's provision.

Suggestions for Celebrating

- **Reflect on Religious Freedom:** The valiant struggle of the Maccabees for religious freedom echoes through the pursuits of believers aiming to express their faith freely. This serves as a poignant reminder of the importance of cherishing and championing religious liberty around the globe.

- **Dedication and Consecration:** Hanukkah's theme of rededication invites us to consider our lives as temples of the Holy Spirit. This period can be used for introspection and recommitment to living a life that honors God.

- **Recognizing God's Intervention:** The story of the oil is a reminder of God's continual presence and miraculous intervention. We can reflect on how God has been present and provided for them in their journeys.

- **Being a Light in the World:** Just as the Hanukkah candles are displayed, we are called to be visible examples of Christ's love and truth.

This festival can inspire acts of kindness, charity, and expressions of faith.

Conclusion

Observing Hanukkah is not about adopting another religion's practices, but rather it is about recognizing and honoring our shared heritage. and acknowledging the themes common to both faiths. It allows us to explore the Jewish roots of Christianity, reflect on the universal themes of faith and deliverance, and celebrate the enduring light of God's presence in the world. Through Hanukkah, we can find inspiration and a deeper understanding of their faith while also fostering respect and appreciation for the rich traditions of Judaism.

Hanukkah Recipes
Frying Up Festive Flavors

Hanukkah is famously celebrated with delicious, traditional foods like latkes and sufganiyot (jelly-filled doughnuts). Both recipes are listed below.

Latkes

Ingredients
2 pounds of russet potatoes (approximately 4–5 medium potatoes)
1 medium onion
1 large egg
½ cup all-purpose flour (or matzo meal for a Passover variation)
2 tsp salt (adjust to taste)
½ tsp black pepper (adjust to taste)
Olive oil for frying
Optional: sour cream and applesauce for serving

Instructions

- Peel the potatoes and grate them using the large holes of a grater or a mandoline (food chopper). Grate the onion in the same way.

- Place the grated potatoes and onion in a clean kitchen towel or cheesecloth and squeeze out as much liquid as possible. This step is crucial for crispy latkes.

- Mix the batter: In a large bowl, beat the eggs. Add the flour (or matzo meal), salt, and pepper, and combine.

- Add the grated potatoes and onion to the egg mixture. Stir the mixture until the potatoes are evenly coated.

- **Heat the oil:** Heat a generous amount of oil over medium-high heat in a large skillet. The oil should be about ¼ inch deep. It's ready when a small amount of the batter sizzles upon contact.

- **Fry the Latkes:** Spoon a heaping tablespoon of the potato mixture into the oil for each latke. Flatten the mixture slightly with the back of the spoon to form pancakes.

Sufganiyot

If homemade is not your thing, visit your local bakery the week before Hanukkah to ask if they plan on having Hanukkah doughnuts.

Ingredients for the Dough
2 ¼ teaspoons active dry yeast (1 standard packet)
½ cup warm water (not hot)
¼ cup plus one tsp sugar
2 ½ cups all-purpose flour
2 large eggs
2 tablespoons unsalted butter, room temperature
½ tsp freshly grated nutmeg
2 tsp salt
4 cups olive oil for frying

Ingredients for the Filling
1 cup raspberry or strawberry jelly
Topping: Powdered sugar

Instructions

- **Yeast Mixture:** In a small bowl, dissolve the yeast and one teaspoon of sugar in warm water. Let it sit until it's frothy, about 5–10 minutes.

- **Dough Preparation:** Combine the flour, remaining sugar, eggs, butter, nutmeg, and salt in a large mixing bowl. Add the yeast mixture and mix until a soft dough forms.

- Knead the dough on a floured surface until it's smooth and elastic, about 5–7 minutes. If the dough is too sticky, add a little more flour.

- **First Rise:** Place the dough in a lightly oiled bowl, cover it with a clean cloth, and let it rise in a warm place until it doubles, about 1–1½ hours.

- **Shaping the Doughnuts:** Once the dough has risen, punch it down gently and roll it out on a floured surface to about ½ inch thickness. Use a round cutter (or a glass) to cut out doughnut shapes. Let the cut doughnuts and doughnut holes rise for another 30 minutes.

- **Fry the Doughnuts:** Heat the vegetable oil in a deep fryer or large pot to 350°F (175°C).
Carefully place the doughnuts in the hot oil and fry until golden brown on each side, about 1–2 minutes per side. Remove the doughnuts with a slotted spoon and drain them on a paper towel.

- **Fill the Doughnuts:** Fill a pastry bag with jelly. Insert the tip into the side of each doughnut and gently squeeze in the jelly until filled. Dust the doughnuts with powdered sugar before serving.

Enjoy your homemade sufganiyot, a sweet and delightful treat perfect for celebrating Hanukkah!

Hanukkah Questions
Illuminating Reflections

The events surrounding Hanukkah foreshadowed the struggle for religious freedom that paved the way for Jesus' ministry. As we explore some key questions around Hanukkah, the connections to Jesus' life and teachings become clear.

1. **Historical Context:** How did the political and religious turmoil of the intertestamental period set the stage for the events of Hanukkah?

2. **Divine Guidance in the Wilderness:** How does the menorah's light during Hanukkah parallel the Divine guidance represented by the pillar of fire that led Israel into the wilderness?

3. **Menorah's Symbolism:** How does the construction of the menorah from a single piece of gold reflect the concept of unified Divine wisdom in religious teachings?

4. **Hanukkah and the Maccabees:** How did the actions of the Maccabees during their revolt against Hellenistic rule reflect the struggle for religious freedom and identity?

5. **Jesus and Hanukkah:** Considering that Jesus observed Hanukkah (John 10:22), what significance might this festival have held for Him and His teachings?

6. **Light of the World:** How does celebrating Hanukkah, emphasizing light, parallel Jesus' declaration of being the Light of the World in the New Testament?

7. **Hanukkah Oil and the Holy Spirit:** How can the miraculous sustaining of the Hanukkah menorah's oil be seen as a metaphor for the enduring presence and guidance of the Holy Spirit in the lives of believers, as described in the teachings of Jesus?

8. **Resistance and Triumph:** How can the Maccabees' struggle and victory, commemorated during Hanukkah, foreshadow Jesus' spiritual victory over sin and death?

9. **Healing the Blind Man:** How does the story of Jesus healing the blind man in the Gospel of John symbolize the transition from spiritual blindness to enlightenment, and how does this relate to the themes of Hanukkah?

10. **Jesus' Teachings and Hanukkah's Themes:** How do the themes of resilience, faith, and divine intervention in the Hanukkah story align with the core messages of Jesus' teachings?

11. **Rededication and Renewal:** The rededication of the Temple celebrated during Hanukkah could symbolize spiritual renewal. How does this concept relate to the teachings of Jesus about personal transformation and rebirth?

12. Intertestamental Reflections: What can the intertestamental period, during which Hanukkah occurred, tell us about the religious and cultural environment in which Jesus was born?

13. **Hanukkah's Symbolism:** How might we find spiritual meaning in Hanukkah's symbolism, especially about Jesus' life and mission?

14. **Christ's Light and Hanukkah's Candles:** How might the lighting of the Hanukkah candles reflect how Jesus' presence brings light into the world's darkness?

The themes of Hanukkah - divine deliverance, spiritual enlightenment, the miracle of light piercing darkness - find their ultimate fulfillment in the person of Jesus. As the promised Messiah, Jesus built on Hanukkah's rich foundation to declare the coming of God's Kingdom in a new and everlasting way. Just as the oil miraculously burned for 8 days, the light of Christ eternally shines.

Purim

Celebration of Joy

PURIM
FEAST OF LOTS

OTHER NAMES:
Feast of Lots, the Festival of Esther, Mordecai's Day.

BIBLE REFERENCE:
Book of Esther. The establishment of Purim is at Esther 9:20-32.

DATE OBSERVED:
Purim is celebrated on the 14th day of the Jewish month of Adar. It usually falls in February or March.

COMMEMORATES:
Purim commemorates the salvation of the Jewish people from a plot to exterminate them, as narrated in the Book of Esther. This event took place in ancient Persia under the reign of King Ahasuerus (Xerxes I).

BRIEF INTRODUCTION:
Purim is a joyous Jewish festival celebrating the deliverance of the Jews in ancient Persia, as told in the Book of Esther. It features the reading of the book of Esther, festive meals, costumes, gift exchanges, and charity.

Purim Overview

Brief Introduction: Purim is a joyous festival celebrating the deliverance of the Jews in ancient Persia, as told in the book of Esther. It features the reading of the book of Esther, festive meals, costumes, gift exchanges, and charity. The holiday commemorates Queen Esther and Mordecai's defeat of Haman's plot against the Jews, symbolizing survival, bravery, and a reversal of fortune.

Commemorates: Purim commemorates the salvation of the Jewish people from a plot to exterminate them as narrated in the book of Esther. This event took place in ancient Persia under the reign of King Ahasuerus (Xerxes I). "Pur" is a term directly associated with the festival of Purim, deriving from the ancient Persian word for "lot." The festival's name, Purim, is actually the plural form of pur, thus meaning lots.

Other Names: Feast of Lots, the Festival of Esther, Mordecai's Day.

Bible References: Book of Esther. The establishment of Purim is at Esther 9:20–32.

Date Observed: Purim is celebrated on the fourteenth day of the Jewish month of Adar. It usually falls in February or March. To determine the exact date of Purim in a specific year, one would need to consult a Jewish calendar or a conversion to the Gregorian calendar for that year.

The Story of Purim

In the rich and vibrant fabric of biblical history, the story of Purim emerges as a profound testament to bravery, faith, and divine orchestration. Set against the backdrop of the Persian Empire as chronicled in the book of Esther, this narrative weaves a tale of intrigue, courage, and the triumph of good over evil.

The story of Purim begins with the Persian King Ahasuerus, ruler of a vast realm, who decided to display his immense wealth and power through a lavish six-month celebration.

During this extravagant festivity, King Ahasuerus, in a moment of revelry and drunkenness, demanded that his queen, Vashti, display her beauty before his guests. Vashti's refusal to be paraded as an object of entertainment led to her immediate dismissal and the king's search for a new queen.

This quest for a new queen reached its climax three years later with the choice of Esther, a young Jewish woman of exceptional beauty. Born Hadassah, her Hebrew name signified "mytrle", a symbol of righteousness. In the courts of Persia, she was known as Esther, which translates to "star" in Persian, a name under which she veiled her Jewish heritage. This dual aspect of her identity became pivotal in the dramatic events that followed, underscoring the profound impact of her concealed roots and her destined role.

Around this time, Mordecai, Esther's adoptive father and a man of unwavering integrity, uncovered a plot by two eunuchs, Bigthan and Teresh, to assassinate the king. Through Esther, he relayed this information, saving Ahasuerus and silently laying the groundwork for future events.

Haman's Decree

Haman, the king's chief adviser, convinced Ahasuerus to issue a decree that all should bow before him. Mordecai, standing firm in his Jewish faith not to bow before anyone but the LORD, refused. Enraged, Haman plotted not only against Mordecai but against all Jews in the empire, casting lots to determine the date of their destruction—a dark declaration against the sovereignty of God.

As word of Haman's decree spread, the Jewish community increasingly mourned. Clad in sackcloth, Mordecai implored Esther to use her position to intercede with the king. Despite the risk of approaching Ahasuerus unbidden—a crime punishable by death—Esther resolved to act, urging her people to join her in fasting.

Esther's Banquets

Esther's strategy began with a private banquet for the king and Haman. Holding back her plea, she invited them to a second banquet. Meanwhile, Haman, in his hubris, prepared a gallows for Mordecai. However, a twist of divine fate intervened. That night, the king, who had insomnia, read the chronicles of his kingdom and learned of Mordecai's unrewarded act of loyalty.

Haman's Humiliation and Mordecai's Honor

In an ironic twist, the king ordered Haman to honor Mordecai—the man he sought to kill—by parading him through the streets in royal garments. This act was a prelude to Haman's downfall.

Esther Reveals Her Jewish Identity

During the second banquet, Esther disclosed her Jewish identity and Haman's genocidal plot against her people to the king. In his anger, King Ahasuerus ordered Haman to be hanged on the gallows intended for Mordecai.

The Triumph of the Jewish People

The king granted the Jews the right to defend themselves, leading to their victory over their enemies. This deliverance marked the establishment of Purim, celebrating Jewish survival against overwhelming odds.

The Enduring Legacy of Purim

The book of Esther concludes with the establishment of Purim as a permanent festival. Queen Esther and Mordecai decreed its observance as a time for feasting, joy, and giving gifts. Purim serves as a lasting testament to God's providence and the triumph of His people over adversity.

And Mordecai recorded these things and sent letters to all the Jews who were in all the provinces of King Ahasuerus, both near and far, obliging them to keep the fourteenth day of the month Adar and also the fifteenth day of the same, year by year, as the days on which the Jews got relief from their enemies, and as the month that had been turned for them from sorrow into gladness and from mourning into a holiday; that they should make them days of feasting and joy, days for sending gifts of food to one another and gifts to people experiencing poverty. Esther 9:20–22.

In the story of Purim, the threads of individual lives weave together a narrative of faith, courage, and Divine oversight. It is a reminder that the light of providence and hope shines undimmed even in the shadows of danger and uncertainty.

Jewish Traditions of Purim

A Celebration of Liberation

In the rich mosaic of festivals, Purim stands out as a vibrant celebration steeped in tradition and joyous commemoration. This festival, marking the Jewish people's deliverance as recounted in the book of Esther, is a time for rejoicing, reflection, and community spirit.

The celebration of Purim in ancient times centered around public readings of the Book of Esther, which tells the dramatic story of how the Jewish people in the Persian Empire were saved from destruction.

On Purim day, Jewish communities would gather in synagogues or public spaces to hear the Megillat Esther, the scroll of Esther, read aloud by an honored community member. The reading was often accompanied by a captivated audience, who would vocally express disdain for the villain Haman and cheer for the heroes Mordecai and Esther. Groggers, noisemakers, were spun at every mention of Haman's name to "blot out" his evil reputation.

The festivities also involved sharing gifts of food and drink, known as mishloach manot, and giving charity to the poor. Families would feast together on traditional hamantaschen pastries and participate in carnivals for the children.

Many Jews would put on costumes, masks, and pageants to dramatize the defeat of Haman. The costumes and masking allowed a flavor of immorality and gender-bending that inverted societal norms as part of the carnival atmosphere.

The day was marked by vibrant public celebrations in the streets expressing the Jewish community's relief and joy at their ancestors being saved from annihilation while living under Persian rule. These dramatic public observances recalled God's salvation, sustaining communal memory and identity.

Purim Traditions

- **The Reading of the Megillah:** Central to Purim's observance is reading the Megillah, or the book of Esther. This is a time-honored tradition where the story of Esther, Mordecai, Haman, and King Ahasuerus is recounted in synagogues. The congregants listen intently, often with spirited reactions—booing at the mention of Haman and cheering for Esther and Mordecai, bringing the ancient story to life in a communal experience.

- **The Custom of Masquerade:** Purim is synonymous with costumes and masquerade, symbolizing the hidden aspects of the story. This tradition reflects Esther's concealed identity and Divine intervention, bringing joy and mystery to the celebration.

- **Festive Meal:** Special baked goods like hamantaschen are served, typically along with wine. More liberal meals with meat were historically allowed.

- **Reciting Blessings and Prayers:** Special prayers, including the "Al HaNissim" (On the Miracles) addition, are recited in the Amidah and the blessing after meals to acknowledge the miracles of Purim.

- **Performing Purim Plays (Purimspiels):** Communities often put on humorous plays that retell the story of the Megillah, incorporating local humor and satire.

- **Gifts of Food:** Mishloach Manot involves sending food baskets to loved ones, fostering community bonds and fulfilling the Purim mitzvah, ensuring that all can partake in the feast.

- **Gifts to the Poor:** Matanot La'evyonim emphasizes giving charity to the less fortunate, highlighting community responsibility and compassion during times of celebration.

- **The Purim Feast:** The Seudah, or Purim feast, is a joyous occasion marked by feasting, music, and dancing, commemorating the deliverance and celebration of Purim.

- **Carnivals & Street Festivals:** Purim has a carnival atmosphere for the community, with rides, games, food booths and entertainment in cities with large Jewish populations.

How Purim Reveals Messiah

CHTIST OUR DELIVERER

PURIM	JESUS
Celebrates the deliverance of the Jewish people from Haman's plot to destroy them.	The ultimate deliverance of humanity from sin and death.
Recounting God's providence and the courage of Esther and Mordecai.	Invites all to find rest in Him, Matthew 11:28–30.
Story comes from the Book of Esther.	Story comes from the the Gospels.
A time for wearing costumes and masks, symbolizing the hidden aspects of the story.	Jesus often spoke in parables, revealing spiritual truths in hidden ways.
Esther showed bravery, approaching the king unsummoned, risking death to save her people.	Jesus faced death courageously, enduring crucifixion for the redemption of mankind.
Esther was chosen to be queen, placed in a position of influence for a divine purpose.	Jesus sacrificed His life to intercede for all humanity, offering salvation.
Purim is celebrated annually, commemorating their deliverance.	Resurrection is celebrated, symbolizing the ultimate victory over death and sin.

Purim embodies a profound narrative of deliverance and salvation, and Jesus stands as the ultimate symbol of deliverance and salvation. Esther, a Jewish queen concealed in a foreign court, emerges as a figure of intercession, much like Christ. Just as Esther risked her life to intercede on behalf of her people, Christ stepped into the breach to intercede for humanity. Esther's courage and willingness to sacrifice herself for her people mirror Christ's ultimate sacrifice on the cross.

Purim is a Story of Salvation

- **Esther's Courage: Esther** showed unparalleled bravery by risking her life to save her people, stepping forward with the famous resolve, "If I perish, I perish."

- **Jesus' Courage: Jesus** faced His destiny with absolute courage, accepting His path to crucifixion with "Not my will, but yours be done," embracing His role in God's salvation plan despite knowing the cost.

- **Esther's Sacrifice: Esther's** bold move to intercede with the King led to the Jewish people's survival, her actions driven by selfless love and a deep sense of duty.

- **Jesus' Sacrifice: Jesus** offered the ultimate sacrifice on the cross, dying for humanity's sins, His resurrection marking the promise of eternal life for believers, showcasing the depth of divine love and redemption.

- **Esther's Divine Mission: Esther** was positioned "for such a time as this," her rise to queenhood part of a divine orchestration for her people's deliverance.

- **Jesus's Divine Mission: Jesus**, fulfilling ancient prophecies, brought spiritual salvation to the world, His life, and mission underscoring His eternal reign as King.

- **Inspiration:** Both Esther and Jesus inspire us to face challenges with courage, always trusting God's grand plan.

- **Mordecai's Righteousness:** Mordecai's unwavering faith and refusal to bow to Haman mirrors Christ's resistance to sin and evil. His rise to prominence foreshadows Christ's divine exaltation.

- **Evil Haman:** Embodiment of Evil: Haman's schemes against the Jews epitomize sin. His defeat echoes Christ's victory over sin and death, symbolizing the triumph of good over evil.

- **Divine Providence in Decision-Making:** The use of lots (pur) in the Purim story to determine the Jews' doom, later overturned, showcases God's sovereign control over fate. This reflects God's salvation plan, where even evil intentions are turned to good, highlighting divine intervention.

The celebration of Purim, while not directly mentioning the Savior, showcases a critical truth found in the story of Esther. This story beautifully illustrates a promise God made long ago that is as steadfast as it is divine.

In the heart of the Book of Esther, we see a reflection of a profound, unbreakable promise God made to Abraham, which is crucial for us to understand. This promise, found in the Abrahamic Covenant (Genesis 12:3), boldly declares: "I will bless those who bless you, and whoever curses you, I will curse." This isn't just a fleeting statement; it's a divine guarantee that has echoed throughout history.

This principle from the Abrahamic Covenant isn't just about blessings and curses. It's a testament to the enduring survival of the Jewish people, especially during the most challenging times. The Jewish people will persevere, no matter the adversity they face. This is not merely a hope; it's a biblical guarantee—a promise that God's protection and favor rest upon His chosen people through all ages.

Purim's narrative of salvation and the turning of tides prefigures Christ's redemptive sacrifice. Esther and Mordecai's story echoes the Gospel, offering a preview of God's overarching plan of salvation, making Purim a Jewish celebration of survival and a symbol of the ultimate salvation through Christ.

Celebrating Purim

A Joyous Festival

Purim, a joyous festival, commemorates the Jewish people's deliverance from a plot to destroy them, as recounted in the book of Esther. Observing Purim can be a meaningful way to celebrate themes of deliverance, courage, and God's providential care.

Here's how a believers can observe Purim, incorporating elements such as a costume party, and a play or puppet show.

Understanding Purim's Story and Themes

The story of Esther is a powerful narrative about courage, faith, and Divine intervention. We can observe Purim by reading the book of Esther, perhaps as part of a Bible study, to understand the historical and spiritual context of the festival. It's a time to reflect on God's unseen hand and the importance of standing up for righteousness.

Costume Party

Purim often involves dressing up in costumes. This tradition reflects the theme of hiddenness in the Esther story—God's name is never directly mentioned in the book, yet His presence is felt throughout. Attendees can dress up as characters from the book of Esther or other biblical figures, celebrating the many ways God works behind the scenes in our stories.

Staging a Play or Puppet Show

A play or puppet show is a creative and engaging way to bring Esther's story to life. This can be an exciting activity for both adults and children. It offers an opportunity to delve into the story's dramatic narrative, highlighting the themes of bravery, faith, and deliverance. The play can be followed by discussing how Esther's themes relate to Christian beliefs and personal faith experiences.

Purim Groggers

Children shake the groggers (noisemakers) during the Esther story while they cheer Queen Esther and boo the evil Haman. There are dozen of ways to make noisemakers (check Pinterest for ideas).

I made them last year with Altoid tins for preschoolers, so instead of beans or rice, I used crunchy chickpeas (just in case they got eaten). I created Purim stickers to fit the tins. Visit JesusintheBiblicalHolidays.com to download.

Esther Bible Study on Redemption

An integral component of observing Purim as a Christian community involves delving into the book of Esther through a focused Bible study. This can be a profound time of learning and reflection, especially around the theme of redemption. The story of Esther is not just a historical account; it is ripe with symbolic meanings of redemption and God's saving grace, elements that resonate deeply with Christian theology.

Organizing a Bible study session allows participants to explore how Esther's bravery and God's providential guidance led to the redemption of the Jewish people. It's an opportunity to draw parallels between this story and the broader Christian understanding of redemption through Christ.

Participants can discuss how the themes of risk, intervention, and deliverance in Esther's story reflect the redemptive work of Jesus. This Bible study can be a time to reflect on personal experiences of redemption and to recognize the ways in which God's redemptive plan is continually unfolding in individual lives and throughout history. Delving into the study of Purim not only broadens comprehension of this significant event but also enriches faith by linking its fundamental principles to this impactful biblical story.

Exchanging Gifts

In the tradition of Purim, Jews send gifts of food to friends (Mishloach Manot). We can adopt this practice by exchanging small gift baskets with each other. This act fosters community spirit and friendship, embodying the message of mutual support and kindness that is central to the Purim celebration.

Festive Meal

Hosting a festive meal is another significant aspect of Purim. This can be a potluck dinner where everyone contributes a dish. During the meal, share stories of personal deliverance and God's faithfulness. This gathering can be a beautiful time of fellowship and gratitude, reminiscent of the joyous banquet in the book of Esther.

Prayer and Reflection

Purim can also be a time for prayer and reflection, recognizing God's protection and guidance. It can serve as a reminder to pray for those who face persecution and injustice, just as Esther and the Jewish people did.

Conclusion

Celebrating Purim offers us a unique opportunity to connect with a significant festival, to learn more about the Bible, and to celebrate the universal themes of deliverance and Divine providence. Through costume parties, plays, gift exchanges, and communal meals, we can experience the joy of Purim while acknowledging and learning from the rich traditions of the Jewish faith.

Purim Recipes

Traditional Purim Treats

Hamantaschen cookies, traditionally baked during Purim, are more than just treats; they embody the story of the festival with their distinctive triangular shape, said to resemble the hat of the villain Haman from the Purim narrative.

Our Haman Cookie Disaster

Before I share the Hamantaschen recipe, though, I have a funny story. One year as I prepared for a Messianic Purim celebration, I decided to make a large batch of these symbolic cookies. Our three youngest kids eagerly joined in, perched on chairs around the kitchen counter, ready to assist.

I usually lay out all the ingredients so the children can hand them to me as needed. In the midst of our baking, I retrieved a plastic container filled with various spices and seasonings from the cabinet and set it on the counter. The phone rang. I was engrossed in the conversation, and I didn't notice my eighteen-month-old, Michael (now 28), making his own contribution to the recipe. He gleefully added an entire large bottle of imitation bacon bits into the Hamantaschen batter—an unexpected twist for a Jewish cookie!

The sight of bacon bits in the dough left me speechless, especially since I had just used the last of my eggs and butter. With the Purim party looming that evening, I hurriedly tried to remove the red bits from the batter. It seemed successful until the cookies were baked and the remaining bits surfaced on each one!

Surprisingly, the cookies still tasted great. Given that the bacon wasn't real, I decided to take them to the party. This incident gave birth to a new family joke—we now fondly refer to them as the "Pagan Bacon Haman Cookies." It's moments like these that remind me of the unpredictable yet joyous nature of life with children—truly, you can't make this stuff up!

Hamantaschen Cookie Recipe

Ingredients
⅔ cup butter, softened
½ cup sugar
1 egg
¼ cup orange juice (no pulp)
1 cup white flour
1 cup whole wheat flour
1 tsp baking powder
Fillings: poppy seed filling (traditional), fruit preserves, or chocolate spread

Instructions

- Cream the butter and sugar together. Beat in the egg and orange juice. In a separate bowl, mix the flours and baking powder. Blend with the wet ingredients to form a dough.

- Chill the dough for a few hours.

- Roll out the dough to a ¼ inch thickness. Cut into circles using a cookie cutter or glass.

- Place a spoon full of your chosen filling in the center of each circle.

- Fold the edges to form a triangle, pinching the corners to seal. Leave the center open, exposing some of the filling.

- Bake at 350°F (175°C) for 20–25 minutes or until lightly golden.

Cheese-Filled Triangles

Cheese-Filled Triangles, also known as Cheese Sambusak, are a delightful treat for Purim. They're savory, cheesy, and perfect for a festive celebration. Here's a simple recipe to make these delicious pastries:

Ingredients for the Dough
2 cups all-purpose flour
½ tsp salt
½ cup unsalted butter, chilled and cubed
½ cup sour cream
1 large egg, beaten (for egg wash)

Ingredients for the Filling
1 cup ricotta cheese
1 cup feta cheese, crumbled
1 egg
1 tbs fresh parsley, chopped
Salt and pepper to taste

Instructions

- **Prepare the Dough:** In a large bowl, mix the flour and salt. Add the cubed butter and use your fingers or a pastry cutter to mix until the mixture resembles coarse crumbs. Stir in the sour cream and mix until the dough begins to come together.

- Turn out onto a floured surface and knead briefly until smooth. Wrap in plastic wrap and chill in the refrigerator for at least 1 hour.

- **Make the Filling** In a bowl, combine the ricotta and feta cheeses, egg, chopped parsley, and season with salt and pepper. Mix well.
reheat your oven to 350°F (175°C) and line a baking sheet with parchment paper.

- **Assemble the Triangles:** Roll out the chilled dough on a floured surface to about ⅛ inch thickness. Cut the dough into squares or circles (about 3 inches across). Place a small spoonful of the cheese filling in the center of each piece. Fold the dough over to form a triangle and press the edges firmly to seal. You can use a fork to crimp the edges for a decorative touch.

- **Make the Triangles:** Place the filled triangles on the prepared baking sheet. Brush the tops of the triangles with the beaten egg (egg wash) for a golden finish.

- Bake for 20–25 minutes, or until golden and puffed.

- Let the Cheese-Filled Triangles cool slightly before serving. These can be served warm or at room temperature.

Purim Questions

Illuminating Reflections

The story of Esther conveys profound lessons that have reverberated through centuries of interpretation. On the surface lies a gripping epic full of courage, danger and dramatic reversal. Further study opens up intriguing theological dimensions. Consider the following thought-provoking questions Esther's account inspires:

1. **Exploring Queen Vashti's Defiance**: What can Vashti's refusal to be paraded before King Ahasuerus' guests tell us about dignity and resistance against objectification? (Esther 1:19).

2. **Esther's Dual Identity**: How does Esther's hidden Jewish identity impact the story's unfolding and what does it teach about the importance of embracing one's roots?

3. **Mordecai's Integrity**: In what ways does Mordecai's refusal to bow to Haman reflect the theme of standing firm in one's faith and convictions? How does this compare to other biblical examples of steadfastness? (Esther 3:2-6)

4. **The Role of Fasting**: Esther asked her people to fast with her before she approached the king. How does this act of fasting enhance the significance of her bravery and faith? (Esther 4:16)

5. **The Significance of Haman's Decree**: What does Haman's plot to destroy the Jews and the subsequent reversal of his plans reveal about the themes of divine justice and retribution in the Bible? (Esther 3:8-15; 7:10)

6. **Divine Intervention and Human Action**: How does the story of Purim illustrate the balance between divine providence and human agency in achieving deliverance? (Esther 9:20-32)

7. **The Symbolism of Haman's Gallows**: What can be inferred from the fact that Haman was executed on the gallows he built for Mordecai? How does this reflect the biblical theme of "reaping what you sow"?

(Esther 7:10)

8. **Purim's Parallels with Jesus**: In what ways does the story of Purim foreshadow salvation and redemption through Christ?

9. **The Meaning of Purim for Today**: How can the lessons of courage, faith, and providence in the Purim story be applied in contemporary life, especially in facing adversity and injustice?

10. **Esther as a Model of Intercession**: How does Esther's role as an intercessor compare to the role of intercessors in other religious or historical contexts? How might this be seen as a type of Christ's intercession?

The story of Esther poses a wealth of timeless questions to enrich our understanding. As we contemplate them, may we become part of Esther's legacy of faith, boldness and divine purpose unfolding in everyday lives.

Treasure Unveiled
Spread the Light of Christ

Thank you for joining this quest for the greatest treasure. As our journey through *Jesus in the Biblical Holidays* concludes, we stand at the cusp of profound revelation, where ancient rituals meet timeless truths.

These festivals are vibrant calls to experience Jesus's ongoing presence in our lives, inviting us to see Him not just as a figure from the past but as our constant guide, enlightening and advising us. Let these festivals kindle in our hearts the enduring light of Christ, shining brightly for all to see.

Keep this book close as a yearly companion through each holiday season. It serves as a beacon, directing us back to Jesus and enriching our celebration and understanding of each feast. With every annual reading, may you find new depths of Jesus's love and intentions for us.

As we wrap up this voyage, let's carry Jesus's light into every facet of our lives, a beacon of hope, love, and mercy, navigating us through trials and celebrations. With the book's close, keep your heart receptive, eager to spread and revel in Christ's eternal light.

Website

Visit JesusintheBiblicalHolidays.com to continue the journey. On the website you'll find additional resources like blog posts and articles with more details not in this book. There's also a free email newsletter with inspiration sent to your inbox. Most importantly, you can interact with other learners - ask questions, share experiences, and grow together in understanding Jesus in light of the biblical feasts.

May you always walk in His splendid light, blessed by the true wealth found in Jesus, the essence of the biblical holidays.

Jesus int he Holidays

ONLINE BIBLE JOURNAL CLASS

If "Jesus in the Biblical Holidays" has enriched your understanding and awakened a desire for deeper exploration, consider embarking on the next step of your journey with the ***Jesus in the Biblical Holidays Bible Journal Online Class* at BibleJournalClasses.com**

This distinctive course offers an extended exploration, blending in-depth study of these significant holidays with the creative expression of Bible journaling. Engage with lessons, videos, and downloads at your own pace, enriching both your spiritual walk and creative expression.

Discover the Rich Tapestry of Biblical Celebrations: Seven Holidays from Leviticus 23**: Dive into the meaning behind Passover, Unleavened Bread, First Fruits, Pentecost, Trumpets, Day of Atonement, and Tabernacles, along with the added depth of Hanukkah and Purim.

Your Journey, Your Way

- **Flexible Learning Options:** Choose individual classes that intrigue you or the comprehensive Nine Class Bundle for a holistic experience.

- **Customizable Resources:** Opt for classes with or without optional printable and digital thematic Bible Journal kits, tailoring your learning materials to your preference.

- **Reminder Emails:** Receive timely reminders before each holiday to ensure you're prepared to fully engage with the material.

- **At Your Own Pace:** Enjoy the convenience of accessing lessons, videos, and downloads whenever you choose, fitting your study into your life seamlessly.

- **Community Support:** Ask questions and interact within the Bible Holiday Facebook Group, joining a community of like-minded learners.

Special Offer: Coupon Code

In appreciation of your journey thus far and to encourage your continued exploration, we are delighted to offer a special discount for the Bible Journal Online Class. Use the coupon code JESUSBOOK for a discount on your enrollment. This course is more than a study; it's a vibrant opportunity to create, reflect, and celebrate the intersection of faith and art, deepening your connection to these timeless celebrations.

12 Bible Eras Class

See the Bible as One Unified Story

Join Robin Sampson in an enlightening online journey through the Bible, enhanced by the beauty of art. This course, meticulously crafted over 30 years of teaching, simplifies the Bible's complexity by guiding you through its twelve historical eras. Discover the Bible as one unified story, revealing Jesus in every book, through Robin's expert instruction and engaging art-based activities. When you put the pieces together it is like a beautiful symphony.

Each month, Robin delves into one of the Bible Eras with concise lessons designed for busy schedules—requiring just 20-30 minutes five days a week.

12 Bible Era Classes

1. **Creation Era Bible Journal Class:** Journey through Genesis' first eleven chapters, exploring creation, the first murder, Noah's Ark, the first covenant, the Tower of Babel, and more. Discover God's character and promises.

2. Patriarch Era Bible Journal Class: Dive into Genesis 12-50, focusing on Abraham, Isaac, Jacob, and Joseph. Uncover God's relationship with humanity and His unfolding plan.

3. **Exodus Era Bible Journal Class:** Learn from Exodus about the life of Moses, liberation from sin and servitude, guided by the God who led Israel to freedom and promised a heavenly homeland.

4. **Conquest Era Bible Journal Class:** Follow Joshua's faithful life as a model for overcoming today's challenges with courage and devotion to God.

5. **Judges Era Bible Journal Class:** Examine the cycle of prosperity, abandonment, and redemption in Judges and Ruth, emphasizing the Bible's central message of salvation through Jesus.

6. **Kingdom Era Bible Journal Class:** Covering 1 Samuel through 2 Kings, this class traces the rise and fall of Israel's kings, highlighting the consequences of faithfulness and unfaithfulness to God.

7. **Exile Era Bible Journal Class:** Explore Jeremiah, Ezekiel, and Daniel to uncover key Messianic prophecies and their fulfillment in Christ, offering transformative insights.

8. **Return Era Bible Journal Class:** Through Ezra and Nehemiah, witness the power of faith in rebuilding the temple and setting the stage for the Messiah, showcasing God's mercy despite human imperfection.

9. **Silence Era Bible Journal Class:** Delve into the 400-year gap between the testaments, a time of divine preparation for Jesus' arrival, including

the miracle of Hanukkah.

10. **Gospel Era Bible Journal Class:** Focus on Christ's life, from birth to Resurrection, portrayed from a Hebrew perspective, highlighting His role as teacher, healer, and Savior.

11. **Church Era Bible Journal Class:** Explore the early church's evolution from a small movement to a dominant faith, emphasizing the church as a community of service and love beyond just a physical building.

12. **Missions Era Bible Journal Class:** Follow Paul's journeys and impact, understanding his significant role in spreading Christianity and the importance of being active in God's mission.

This course is more than just learning; it's a community experience led by Robin in a Facebook Group. You'll explore the Bible's key figures, events, and places, finishing with a rich collection of art journal entries, new friendships, and a deeper scriptural understanding.

Embark with Robin on an artistic and spiritual journey that redefines your interaction with the Bible. Through the 12 Bible Eras, discover Jesus's presence from Genesis to Revelation and the narrative of God's pursuit of humanity.

Set off on a quest to unveil the Bible's grand narrative, showcasing Jesus's enduring presence and the Bible's unity as God's love story with us. Join us to explore this extraordinary story and deepen your connection with the divine narrative.

See BibleJournalClasses.com for more.

A Hebraic Prespective Bible Women

31 Stories of Faith, Courage, & Feminine Wisdom

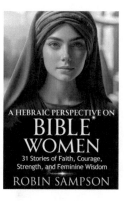

Discover the radiant power of biblical heroines in *Illuminating Bible Women: Reflections on Feminine Energy, Strength, and Faith.* This transformative book sheds light on these women's dynamic energy and enduring spirit in Scripture, revealing how their stories of courage, grace, and wisdom empower us to live out God's purposes today.

From Deborah's fiery leadership that commanded nations, to Ruth's loyal heart that sparked new beginnings from sorrow, and from Esther's formidable presence that saved her people, to Lydia's entrepreneurial spirit that spread faith far and wide, and Hannah's steadfast prayer that awaited God's promises—each story is a beacon of inspiration.

Illuminating Bible Women delves deep into the essence of feminine strength, showcasing how qualities like nurturing, reconciliation, strategic influence, and persistent prayer have not only shaped history but continue to light our way in stewarding family, community, vocations, and culture for God's glory.

Join us on a journey through the ages as we connect with our spiritual foremothers, igniting our passion and guiding us to embrace our identity, heal injustices, and boldly step into God's divine destiny for each of His daughters. Embrace the spark within and let *Illuminating Bible Women* guide you to a life of vibrant purpose and Divine fulfillment.

Visit BibleJournalClasses.com for a free chapter.

Bibography

Download a ed PDF version of this Biblography from JesusintheBiblicalHolidays.com.

- Akins, Alicia J. *Invitations to Abundance: How the Feasts of the Bible Nourish Us Today.* Harvest House Publishers, 2022.

- Bradford, Tom. *Exodus: Toward Freedom and Redemption, Study Guide.* Seed of Abraham Ministries. 2012.

- Booker, Richard. *Celebrating Jesus in the Biblical Feasts Expanded Edition: Discovering Their Significance to You as a Christian.* Destiny Image, 2016.

- ——. *Discovering the Miracle of the Scarlet Thread in Every Book of the Bible: A Simple Plan for Understanding the Bible.* Destiny Image, 2009.

- ——. *Jesus in the Feasts of Israel: Restoring the Spiritual Realities of the Feasts to the Church.* Bridge Publishing, 1998.

- ——. *Shabbat Shalom.* Sounds of the Trumpet, 2013.

- Buksbazen, Victor. *The Gospel in the Feasts of Israel.* Friends of Israel, 2004 (Original 1954).

- Davis, Erin. *7 Feasts: Finding Christ in the Sacred Celebrations of the Old Testament.* Moody Publishers, 2020.

- Bivin, David; Blizzard Jr., Roy. *Understanding the Difficult Words of Jesus: New Insights From a Hebrew Perspective.* Destiny Image Incorporated, 1994.

- Freeman, James M., and Chadwick, Harold J. *Manners & Customs of the Bible.* Bridge-Logos Publishers, 1998.

- Friedman, David. *They Loved the Torah: What Yeshua's First Followers Really Thought About the Law.* Messianic Jewish Communications,

2001.

- Garr, John D. *God's Lamp, Man's Light: Mysteries of the Menorah.* Golden Key Press, 2001.

- Garr, John D. *Christian Fruit, Jewish Root: Theology of Hebraic Restoration.* Golden Key Press, 2015.

- Garr, John D. Living Emblems: Ancient Symbols of Faith. Golden Key Press, 2007.

- Garr, John D. Our Lost Legacy: Christianity's Hebrew Heritage. Golden Key Press, 2006.

- Glaser, Mitch, and Glaser, Zhava. The Fall Feasts Of Israel. Moody Publishers, 1987.

- Kasdan, Barney. God's Appointed Customs: A Messianic Jewish Guide to the Biblical Lifecycle and Lifestyle. Messianic Jewish Publishers, 1996.

- Kasdan, Barney. God's Appointed Times: A Practical Guide for Understanding and Celebrating the Biblical Holidays. 2nd ed., Messianic Jewish Publishers, 2007.

- Keller, W. Phillip. A Shepherd Looks at Psalm 23. Zondervan, 2019.

- Keller, W. Phillip. What Is the Father like? A Devotional Look at How God Cares for His Children. Bethany House, 1996.

- Knowles, Andrew. The Bible Guide. 1st Augsburg books ed., Augsburg, 2001.

- Kushner, Aviya. The Grammar of God: A Journey into the Words and Worlds of the Bible. Random House Publishing Group, 2015.

- Leslie, Michael A. The Feast Days of the Lord: In Light of the New Testament. WestBow Press, 2017.

- Linafelt, Tod, ed. Eerdmans Dictionary of the Bible. Edited by David Noel Freedman et al., W.B. Eerdmans, 2000.

- Lipson, Irene. The Greatest Commandment: How the Sh'ma Leads to More Love in Your Life. Messianic Jewish Publishers, 2007.

- Lumbroso, Patrick Gabriel. *Under the Vine: Messianic Thought through the Hebrew Calendar.* Lederer Books, A division of Messianic Jewish Publishers, 2013.

- Levitt, Zola. *The Seven Feasts of Israel.* Zola Levitt Ministries, 2012.

- Mangum, Douglas, editor. *Lexham Context Commentary: Old Testament.* (5 Volumes). Lexham Press, 2020.

- Missler, Chuck. *The Feasts of Israel.* Koinonia House, 2014.

- Norten, Michael. *Unlocking the Secrets of the Feasts.* Thomas Nelson, 2012.

- Rubin, Barry. *Dedicate and Celebrate!: A Messianic Jewish Guide to Hanukkah.* Messianic Jewish Publishers, 1999.

- Rudolph, David J. *The Voice of the Lord: Messianic Jewish Daily Devotional.* Messianic Jewish Publishers, 1998.

- Sacks, Stuart. *Hebrews through a Hebrew's Eyes: Hope in the Midst of a Hopeless World.* Messianic Jewish Publishers, 1995.

- Shannon, Jill. *Prophetic Calendar: The Feasts of Israel.* Destiny Image, 2009.

- Sampson, Robin. *A Family Guide to the Biblical Holidays: With Activities for All Ages.* Heart of Wisdom Publishing, 2001 (original 1999).

- Sobel, Rabbi Jason. *Mysteries of the Messiah Bible Study Guide: Unveiling Divine Connections from Genesis to Today.* HarperChristian Resources, 2021.

- Stern, David H. *Complete Jewish Bible: An English Version of the Tanakh (Old Testament) and B'rit Hadashah (New Testament).* Messianic Jewish Communication, 2011.

- Stein C.M., Renee W. *Everything Old is New Again: A Jewish Midwife's Look into Pregnancy and the Feasts of Israel.* Whatever is Lovely Publications, 2011.

- Wiersbe, Warren W. *Be Worshipful: Glorifying God for Who He Is.* 1st ed., Cook Communications Ministries, 2004.

- Wiersbe, Warren W. *Be God's Guest: Feasts of Leviticus 23.* Back to the Bible, 1982.

- Wiersbe, Warren W. *Be Holy (Leviticus): Becoming "Set Apart" for God.* Victor Books, 1996.

- Wilber, David. *A Christian Guide to the Biblical Feasts.* Freedom Hill Community, 2018.

- Wilson, Marvin R. *Exploring Our Hebraic Heritage: A Christian Theology of Roots and Renewal.* William B. Eerdmans Publishing Company, 2014.

- Wilson, Marvin R. Our Father Abraham: Jewish Roots of the Christian Faith. William B. Eerdmans Publishing Company; Center for Judaic-Christian Studies, 1989.

- Wright, Paul H., et al. *Rose Guide to the Feasts, Festivals and Fasts of the Bible*. Rose Publishing, 2022.

Made in the USA
Thornton, CO
01/03/25 11:33:23

76809196-c24b-4836-94de-8b46db6082a7R01